Applications of
ECONOMETRICS

David G. Mayes

Applications of
ECONOMETRICS

Applications of
ECONOMETRICS.

David G. Mayes

National Institute of Economic and Social Research
and University of Exeter, England

Prentice/Hall International

ENGLEWOOD CLIFFS, NEW JERSEY   LONDON   NEW DELHI
SINGAPORE   SYDNEY   TOKYO   TORONTO   WELLINGTON

British Library Cataloguing in Publication Data

Mayes, David G.
   Applications of econometrics.
   1. Econometrics
   1. Title
   330'.028   HB139
   ISBN 0-13-039180-8

PRENTICE-HALL INTERNATIONAL, INC., *London*
PRENTICE-HALL OF AUSTRALIA PTY., LTD., *Sydney*
PRENTICE-HALL CANADA, INC., *Toronto*
PRENTICE-HALL OF INDIA PRIVATE LIMITED, *New Delhi*
PRENTICE-HALL OF JAPAN, INC., *Tokyo*
PRENTICE-HALL OF SOUTHEAST ASIA PTE., LTD., *Singapore*
PRENTICE-HALL, INC., *Englewood Cliffs, New Jersey*
WHITEHALL BOOKS LIMITED, *Wellington, New Zealand*

Printed in the United States of America

10 9 8 7 6 5 4 3 2 1

CONTENTS

PREFACE

The idea for this book arose out of work for courses of lectures at the University of Exeter in applications of econometrics and quantitative economics. It reflects my belief that to encourage economics students to take an interest in econometrics it is necessary to show how it can be used in practice to explain economic behaviour. I have therefore taken a series of eight topics across the whole range of economics from the analysis of family budgets to macroeconomic policy and forecasting models. These reflect increasing econometric difficulty to fit in with a course in econometrics or economic statistics for general students of economics. The reader does not require any special knowledge of mathematics, although all economists require some sympathy with the formal presentation of ideas and analysis. The topics are all self-contained with their own set of references and suggested reading and can be read in any order to complement their study in courses of economics.

After an introductory chapter setting out the framework of econometric modelling and the approach used in subsequent chapters, chapter 2 discusses the specification of models of consumers' expenditure. In particular, this chapter considers the appropriate means of deciding between competing explanations, illustrated by an examination of whether the effects of inflation should be incorporated directly or whether they should be explained in terms of the value of consumers' holdings of liquid assets. The explanation of consumers' expenditure raises several important methodological issues, including the appropriate treatment of dynamic behaviour, the specfication of lag structures, the relation between long-run and short-run properties of models and the testing of the validity of restrictions on models.

Since chapter 2 relates to aggregate time-series models, the modelling of non-linear production functions is introduced in chapter 3 as a micro-economic topic. In addition to the treatment of non-linearity the chapter also raises the problem of simultaneity between equations in models. The problems relating to lag structures in time-series models are then followed up in chapter 4 with a discussion of investment behaviour where dynamic structure is crucially important. This discussion is taken further in chapter 5 with the specifications of the demand for money, particularly with regard to the stability of the functions over time. The chapter also introduces multiple equation models with a discussion of the monetarist approach to the explanation of economic behaviour. This includes an evaluation of the 'reduced form' St. Louis types of model.

The approach in chapter 5 is not simultaneous and simultaneity is introduced progressively in the next four chapters. In the first of these four, chapter 6 presents two equation models of wages and prices and deals specifically with the effects on estimates of the joint effects of autocorrelation and simultaneity. In the treatment of the Phillips curve and its breakdown, there is a discussion of the role of price expectations, incomes policies and the strength of trades unions in the bargaining process.

By way of contrast chapter 7 shows how large models of trade flows mainly ignore the problems of simultaneity and impose simplicity in many cases largely because of the sheer mass of data to be considered. The use of these models and the disadvantages of simplicity are considered in the framework of estimating the effects of the formation of the EEC and EFTA. Chapter 8 looks at the opposite extreme by tackling the subject of demand analysis where economic theory suggests strong constraints both within and between equations in the modelling of behaviour. The study of individual topics in economics is completed in chapter 9 by an examination of a model of the whole economy which is actually used in the practical forecasting of the future. The emphasis of this chapter is on showing how macroeconomic forecasting is done in practice, how errors can be assessed and how models can be used to simulate the effects of economic policy and external shocks to behaviour.

It has always been my view that not only is econometrics an inherently practical subject, but that it can only be studied effectively if the student undertakes practical analysis of his own. Judgement and a methodical approach are essential ingredients for successful econometric work and these require experience to achieve. As a small contribution towards this practical work the final chapter of the book describes a number of the computer packages which are widely available for econometric analysis. Fortunately, these days it is easy to compute estimates of even quite complex models with a small expenditure of time and money.

I owe substantial debt to many friends, colleagues and students who have helped me, sometimes unwittingly, in the writing of this book and I take this opportunity of thanking them publicly. I am especially grateful for the editorial help provided by the publisher and the reviewers whom they appointed—particularly Bruce Curry and David Higham who were kind enough to set aside their cloak of anonymity after the book was completed. Not only did they influence the structure of the book, but their attention to detail saved me from several irritating unwanted errors. Any remaining blunders must unfortunately be my responsibility. Brian Henry and David Savage made helpful comments on the first draft of a number of chapters which proved valuable in rewriting. Early versions were typed by Vi Palfrey at the University of Exeter and Melba Coleman at the University of Otago but by far the bulk of work and the painstaking and excruciatingly dull job of producing the camera-ready copy was undertaken by Myrna Monsurate. My thanks to them.

Finally I should record my gratitude to my family for putting up with my use of my spare time in writing this book when it really should have been devoted to them.

D.G.M.

Applications of
ECONOMETRICS

Chapter 1
INTRODUCTION

Economics is a subject which is very much alive. New
ideas are appearing all the time and older theories are being
developed and reappraised.   Much of the basis for these
changes lies not in abstract theorizing but in the reasoned
consideration of empirical evidence from actual observed economic behaviour. It is the econometrician's happy task to
undertake this empirical analysis and to develop the whole
area of quantitative economic methodology. In this book we
shall show how econometrics contributes to the understanding
and development of the main areas of economic interest: consumption, production, investment, the determination of wages
and prices, unemployment, inflation, the analysis of family
budgets, etc. We shall not make any attempt to derive or
prove the propositions of econometric method; there are many
textbooks available which accomplish that task with skill and
clarity and the reader is referred to them specifically when
each issue arises. It is the purpose of this book to show how
much econometrics has to offer when used in the analysis of
economic problems.

The structure of econometric analysis is inherently
simple although the actual computation involved in any particular case may be extremely complex. With the use of modern
computers and computer program packages the constraint of
computational complexity has become largely a matter of a financial cost in computer time rather than a feat of endurance
and mathematical skill.

The process of econometric analysis can be characterized by a four stage procedure.   In the first place it is
necessary to draw up a formal model of the behaviour to be
examined. In general this will take the form of a system of
one or more equations or inequalities where one variable is
thought to be determined by a set of further variables, some
of which may themselves be determined within the model. The
second step is to proceed to the estimation of the parameters
of these equations and it is this step which usually excites
most interest among econometricians. Obviously there are some
intermediate steps between the initial specification of what
is thought to be the ideal theoretical model and its empirical
estimation in practice, not least because of drawbacks in the
existence or obtaining of data.   Having obtained the estimates
of the parameters of the model the third step is to evaluate
whether they conform with the hypotheses about the nature of
economic behaviour which were set down at the outset of the

analysis. Clearly if these hypotheses are rejected by statistical inference we must think again and go back to the first
step of formalizing the model and see if we can provide an
improved specification.   Under some circumstances the successful testing of hypotheses about the parameters of the model
may complete the required analysis, but usually we would like
to make further use of the estimated model either for drawing
conclusions about the most suitable sorts of economic policies
to employ or to predict or forecast what we would expect to
happen on other occasions if people and institutions behaved
in the same way that we have just observed. This constitutes
the fourth and final stage of our structure of econometric
analysis. Clearly if the forecasts or policy prescriptions do
not appear plausible we would return to the stage of estimation
or even specification.

This is only a very introductory survey of the structure
of econometric analysis, so let us now deal with the four
stages - specification, estimation, hypothesis testing and
forecasting - in rather more detail so we can appreciate
their main facets when we consider each of the economic problems in the ensuing chapters.   More importantly we must be
in a position to appraise the difficulties posed by the analysis and the drawbacks of the chosen methods and results.
While the investigator may be willing to leave the analysis

to the econometrician it is essential that he, and all
other economists for that matter, be able to consider criti-
cally the results and conclusions made.

1.1   The specification of models

It is easy to produce a caricature of the process of
specification of models by suggesting that the economist can
produce a clear formalization of the nature of the relations
between variables which he wishes to examine and hence proceed with the appropriate estimation technique to produce
estimates of the parameters of the model and conclude by an
appraisal of their meaning and implication. In practice behaviour is nothing like so simple. While it is possible to
produce generalizations there is considerable doubt over the
form of any model which can only be resolved by an appeal to
the data which are available. Hence specification is not independent of the results of estimation and hypothesis testing.
It is often not independent of forecasting either, since a
model which performs well over the period used for estimation
but gives poor forecasts leads one to question the validity
of the original specification in case the original performance
was purely the result of some particular sampling variation.
(One would also, of course, examine the assumptions of the
forecasts closely in case it was they and not the specification which were at fault.)

In general, therefore, specification begins by setting
up the nature of the problem to be examined. Let us take the
determination of imports as an example. We are here concerned with the volume of goods and services imported into a
country during a particular time period. The determinants of
this variable will depend upon the wishes of those purchasing
the products and the wishes of those selling. Thus a simplis-
tic approach would suggest the setting up of a demand equation
(or equations) and similarly a supply equation or set of
equations. The demand side of such a model would commonly suggest that purchases, M, are a function of the purchasers'
current ability to buy, income, Y, the price of the product,
P_M, and the price of substitutes, P_D - see for example Evans
(1969) or Houthakker and Magee (1969).   Thus we have

$$M = f \ (Y, \ P_M, \ P_D).$$ (1)

The economist has more to offer than this in the specification, however, even if he believes that this simple form
is correct.   First, it is possible to specify the variables
more closely - by defining the sorts of imports we are considering, total imports of goods and services, imports of
French apples, etc., establishing the relevant prices, the
domestic wholesale price index, the retail price of apples in
the UK etc., and choosing the appropriate form of income,
GDP, etc. Second, it is possible to say more about the form

of f, and these remarks can be of more than one type. We expect imports to rise with income, but we do not expect all income to be spent on imports. Similarly we expect imports to be greater the lower their price and the higher the price of substitutes. Evans and Houthakker and Magee go further than this by constraining the effect of changes in own price to be equal to the effect of changes in the inverse of the price of substitutes

$$M = f\ (Y,\ P_M/P_D).\tag{2}$$

These constraints on f may be expressed even more closely by assuming a linear relation

$$M = f_0 + f_1\ Y + f_2\ (P_M/P_D),\tag{3}$$

where the f_i are parameters, as in Evans. Alternatively one could make the assumption of constant elasticity,

where $(\frac{\partial M}{\partial Y})\ (\frac{Y}{M})$ and $[\frac{\partial M}{\partial (P_M/P_D)}]\big/[\frac{(P_M/P_D)}{M}]$ are constants.

(2) can then be expressed as

$$M = f_0\ Y^{f_1}\ (P_M/P_D)^{f_2}\tag{4}$$

which is linear in a logarithmic transformation

$$\log M = f_0^* + f_1\ \log Y + f_2\ \log\ (P_M/P_D)\tag{5}$$

where $f_0^* = \log f_0$, as estimated by Houthakker and Magee.

There is always a limit to how far this procedure can go. It may be that the investigator is not really convinced that (4) rather than (3) is the correct specification, or that the constraint imposed on equation (1) to obtain equation (2) may not be valid. At this point it is, therefore, necessary to proceed to estimation and see whether particular functional forms or constraints are rejected by the data. However, it is important to check that the specification has been considered as carefully as possible, because as is explained on pp. 15-16, if variables are wrongly included in the model or excluded from it, inferences drawn about the effects of other variables which are correctly included, may be incorrect.

There are, however, two further characteristics of specification that we should consider before turning our attention to estimation. The first is that under normal circumstances the economist cannot specify a relation exactly, unless it is true by definition. Thus although we can define the balance of trade, B, as being

$$B \equiv X - M \qquad (6)$$

where X is exports, all the import equations contain an extra unspecified element, let us call it u, which we cannot explain.

For example, writing equation (5) in full

$$\log M = f_0^* + f_1 \log Y + f_2 \log (P_M/P_D) + u.$$ (7)

Equations of the form of (7) are behavioural rather than det-
erministic and contain the unknown 'stochastic' element u.
The term u is straightforwardly defined as the residual which
is left after we have specified all the elements we can in
the equation. It is therefore unknown and is not related to
any of the other variables in the equation. Frequently stronger
assumptions are made, namely that each individual u is independently drawn from the same distribution which has a zero
mean and unknown variance σ_u^2. (Thus $E [u_i] = 0$, $E [u_i u_j] = 0$,
if $i \neq j$ and σ_u^2, if $i = j$.) This may seem a harsh set of
assumptions, however, it is purely that the unknown factor
is random but occurs under the same framework on each occasion.
(The reader should look at Mayes and Mayes (1976) pp. 86–89,
for example, for a full discussion of this.)

The second further point concerns the nature of the
variables in the model. The general argument so far has been
that the variables on the right-hand side of the equation
determine that on the left. However, in multi-equation models
life is often not so simple and some of the variables on the
right-hand side are themselves determined within the model.
We must therefore distinguish between variables which are

determined by the model, endogenous variables, and variables
which are predetermined or exogenous.

Not all models which have more than one equation are
simultaneous in the sense that a group of equations determine
some or all of the endogenous variables jointly. The model may
be separable in that there are no endogenous variables on the
right-hand side of any equation, or it may be recursive in
that each equation can be solved in turn because they have an
ordering in time and the solved value can enter the next
equation as a 'predetermined' variable. A simple example of
this would be if the exporter decides how much he will sell
next period on the basis of the prices prevailing *this* period
while the actual price next period is determined in such a way
that the market clears. Thus imports are determined first and
then prices are determined - the model is not simultaneous.
It is simultaneity equations which presents serious problems
for estimation of multi-equation systems.

1.2   Estimation

As we have said already estimation forms the centre of
the econometricians' interest and in making this introduction
we are not attempting to cover the range of problems which
exist, merely to place before the reader the context of the
discussion in the rest of the chapters of the book. The method

of estimation is highly dependent upon the nature of the
specification of the model and in practice characteristics of
estimation tend to be taken into account in forming the final
specification.

The whole process of this second stage of econometric
analysis is intended to produce estimates of the parameters
of the model which are thought the best, subject to any constraints the specification might impose on their values. If
it were not for the existence of the unknown residual (as set
out in equation (7)) this would be an easy task and there
would be a single exact solution to the equation. The presence
of the residual means that a decision has to be made over the
most appropriate way to proceed. As we have seen it is
usually assumed that for any set of values of the exogenous
variables, u is distributed with zero mean and constant
variance. Thus, for example, if we take the very simplest example of an import function for a product which has no domestically produced substitute and is a necessary input to the
productive process, say

$$M = f_0 + f_1 Y + u, \tag{8}$$

where Y is industrial production, we have that if $E[u] = 0$
then $E[M] = f_0 + f_1 Y$ for that value of Y i.e. $E[M|Y] =$
$f_0 + f_1 Y$. For each value of Y which we observe the possible

values of M are distributed round $E\ [M|Y]$ in the form of the
distribution of u. For example, in Fig. 1.1 we have shown the
position for three such values of Y, i.e. Y_1, Y_2 and Y_3. The
points actually observed in any particular case will be distributed round the true line, as in Fig. 1.2 for example. We
cannot therefore determine f_0 and f_1 exactly; we can only
estimate them. There are many methods of estimation and we
would choose an estimator which had desirable properties.

Clearly we want to calculate the estimates which will
be closest to the true values.   However, we cannot know how
accurate any particular estimate is because we would have to
know the correct answer in order to do so. Thus we would want
to use the estimator which, in our opinion, gives the greatest
probability of an accurate answer. The properties of estimators which we would want to take into account are well
known and are set out in, for example, Mayes and Mayes pp.
41-43 and Maddala pp. 36-38. Three of these properties are
worth considering here: first, unbiasedness - the expected
value of the estimator is equal to the value of the parameter
to be estimated; second, minimum variance - no other estimator
has a smaller variance; and third consistency - as the size
of the sample increases the bias in the estimator falls and
its variance decreases, both becoming zero as the sample size
approaches infinity. Clearly the first two properties may be

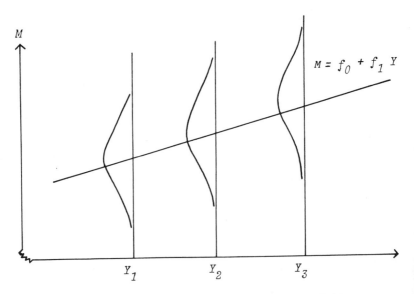

Figure 1.1   The distribution of two variables

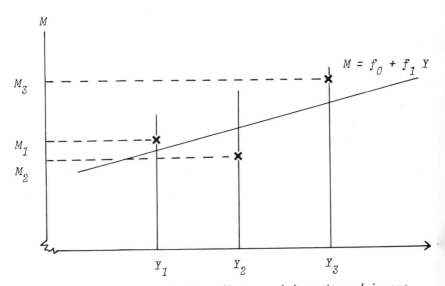

Figure 1.2   Scatter diagram of imports and income

offset against each other; a biased estimator may have a
smaller variance than an unbiased estimator and may or may
not be preferable according to the relative importance of the
bias and the variance.

Given the assumptions we have mentioned (and assuming
the variables have been observed accurately – a heroic assumption with many economic data, the minimum variance linear unbiased estimates of f_0 and f_1 in equation (8) can be obtained
by the method of least squares. For any given sample of size
N they are the estimates $\hat{f}_0$ and $\hat{f}_1$ calculated such that
$\sum_{i=1}^{N} \hat{u}_i^2$ is a minimum where $\hat{u}_i = M_i - (\hat{f}_0 + \hat{f}_1 Y_i)$. The general
derivation of these in both scalar and matrix terms together
with the proof of the properties of the estimators is given
in most economic statistics and econometrics textbooks – see
for example Johnston (1972) Ch. 5, Intriligator (1978) Ch. 4.
Least squares is by far the most widely used technique in the
estimation of economic relations.

Ordinary Least Squares does not by any means apply to
all cases, however, and before leaving the topic of estimation
we should consider the nature of its inadequacies, as these
affect the whole subject of estimation. The main difficulty
stems from the precise nature of the assumptions made about
the characteristics of the residuals in the equation, namely,

that they are independent, with zero mean and the same
variance. In practice it is easy to think of occasions where
the residuals are not independent but related. This is most
commonly true in analysing time series where the residuals are
related between consecutive time periods or with some other
fixed lag. This form of 'autocorrelation' can occur for example if the dependent variable does not adjust fully to its
desired level in each time period. The assumption of constant
variance or 'homoscedasticity' is also unrealistic in many instances. A simple example occurs when a variable has a large
range of magnitudes - when an importer is importing on a very
small scale the fluctuations in his behaviour round the underlying relation may be small but when the scale of his business
expands, while the fluctuations may retain the same size
relative to imports, they will increase in absolute terms and
the residuals will be 'heteroscedastic'.

Another of the assumptions in the use of least squares is
that errors are distributed independently of the values of the
variables on the right-hand side of the equation. It is easy
to think of examples where large values of a variable imply
extraordinary occurences which are not reflected in changes in
the endogenous variable and hence that the errors are indeed
correlated with the explanatory variable. Furthermore it
was also assumed that the variables were observed without

error. Since many economic data are themselves estimated from
partial survey information of indicators of behaviour they
will be subject to error. This error may be systematic in
which case it will bias the estimates. If it is random, then,
if it is in the endogenous variable it will merely increase the
variance of the estimators, but if it is in the exogenous
variables the OLS estimators will be biased and inconsistent.
The very prevalence of this problem tends to mean that it is
widely disregarded by economists in practice.

In the next section on hypothesis testing we shall explain how we can decide if the assumptions behind the residuals have been violated. However, at this point it is important to note the difference between the residuals in the
specified relation, $u = M - (f_0 + f_1 Y)$, and the calculated
errors from the particular sample of data, $\hat{u} = M - (\hat{f}_0 + \hat{f}_1 Y)$.
While the $\hat{u}$ may have various sample characteristics which do
not accord with the OLS assumptions the reason for this may
be misspecification of the model. If for example we omit
relative price and estimate equation (8) instead of equation
(3) not only will our estimates of f_0 and f_1 be biased but
the $\hat{u}$ will reflect the omission of P_M/P_D. Let us say that we
have used a moving average for the income series to reflect
the trend, but that imports and their prices fluctuate on a
seasonal basis, then the errors, $\hat{u}$, will show the seasonal

pattern and will hence be autocorrelated in quite a complex
manner. Similarly if a linear form (3) is fitted when the logarithmic form (7) was the correct specification then the
errors will vary round a simple curve and will hence have
positive first order (between consecutive time periods) autocorrelation. It is therefore very important to consider the
pattern of the calculated errors as they may tell us not just
that we have used an inappropriate estimation method but that
we may have misspecified the model in the first place. (This
is discussed in some detail later on in Chapter 2 and Chapter
4.)

There are two other problems which we should note concerning the estimation of single equation models, before passing on
to hypothesis testing. The first is that the exogenous variables in the model should not themselves be perfectly linearly
related otherwise the OLS estimates cannot be calculated. This
problem is called 'multicollinearity' and occurs because, if
it is impossible to distinguish between the effects on the
endogenous variable of several of the exogenous variables,
there is an infinite number of solutions to the parameters
consistent with the data. The real difficulty in practice,
however, occurs when the collinearity is close but not perfect.
Under these circumstances the results will tend to be inaccurate because of great differences in orders of magnitude in

calculation; they will also tend to fluctuate widely in response to small changes in the data; lastly erroneous inferences may be derived (for a full discussion see Maddala pp. 183-194).

The second further problem is much more straight-forward, namely, if the equation to be estimated cannot be expressed in a form which is linear in parameters then OLS is not possible and an iterative method must be used. For example, while (4) could be transformed to (5) to allow OLS estimation (9) cannot

$$M = f_0 + f_1 Y + (P_M/P_D)^{f_2} + u. \tag{9}$$

Finally before leaving estimation we should consider the problem of simultaneous equations. OLS should not normally be applied to each simultaneous equation directly as the residuals are not independent of the other endogenous explanatory variables in the equation and biased estimates will hence result. Many methods such as Two Stage Least Squares, Instrumental Variables, Maximum-Likelihood, etc. (see for example Intriligator pp. 368-428) can be used to overcome this, but a further constraint must be met, namely that the model be 'identified'. This is in fact a very simple requirement — it must be possible to distinguish each equation in a system

and there must be as many distinct equations as there are
endogenous variables to explain. For example if the supply
and demand for imports both depended on price alone

$$M = f_0 + f_1 P_M + u_1 \qquad \text{(demand)} \qquad (10)$$

and

$$M = f_0' + f_1' P_M + u_2 \qquad \text{(supply)} \qquad (11)$$

we clearly cannot distinguish them and any estimated equation
of their common form would be a hybrid of the two. If $f_1 < 0$
and $f_1' > 0$ the resulting compromise estimate will lie between
the two and might even be zero.

There are three circumstances which can arise in
identification - an equation can be unidentified as we have
just seen, or if there are just enough differences or constraints to distinguish each equation from a commom form then
it is just identified, and finally if there are more differences than are necessary it is over-identified. In the first
case the model cannot be estimated without being re-specified
and in the third there is no unique solution to the system so
a decision must be made over the most suitable estimation
method. This last point is best explained by a further

example. Let the demand be

$$M = f_0 + f_1 Y + f_2 (P_M/P_D) + f_3 P_p + u \qquad (12)$$

and supply be

$$M = g_0 + g_1 OF + g_2 (P_M/P_D) + v \qquad (13)$$

where P_p is the price of pears in the UK, OF is production
of apples in foreign exporting countries, all other variables
being defined as before. Then equation (12) has one difference
from the common form (the variable OF is omitted) but equation
(13) has two differences (both Y and P_p are omitted) and hence
the second equation is over-identified. If each endogenous
variable is expressed in terms of only the three exogenous
variables Y, P_p and OF (and the constant)

$$M = h_0 + h_1 Y + h_2 OF + h_3 P_p + u^*$$

$$P_M/P_D = h_4 + h_5 Y + h_6 OF + h_7 P_p + v^* \qquad (14)$$

there will be eight parameters to determine only seven
coefficients in equation (12) and (13). This setting of

the endogenous variables in terms of the exogenous is
known as the 'reduced form' of the model - the original
equations (12) and (13) are the 'structure' of the model.

1.3   The testing of hypotheses

It is evident from the previous section that, although a
model may be specified fully and with care, it may nevertheless be the case that the model cannot be estimated
or if it can be the estimates obtained do not support the
specification. It is often immediately clear that the
economic theory embodied in the specification is not borne
out by the data - if, for example, the marginal propensity
to import is negative or the sign of the price ratio in
(7) is perverse. It may also be clear that the specification
is incorrect if, as was noted on pp. 15-16, the calculated
errors suggest the omission of a variable. However, on many
occasions no such obvious rejection is present and we have
to look to statistical inference to answer our queries.

As was noted on pp. 10-12 the estimators we have been
discussing have probability distributions, so if we make

assumptions about the form of the distribution of errors
it is possible to set up suitable test statistics to test
hypotheses about the parameters. In particular we are
likely to want to ask questions about the value of individual parameters - is there any effect of income on imports
(i.e. $H_0 : f_1 = 0$ in equation (3)), or is the price elasticity of demand greater than unity? ($H_0 : f_2 = -1$, $H_A:$
$f_2 < -1$ in equation (5); signs are reversed between the
conventional formulation of elasticities and the coefficients
of the equation. Elasticities in (5) are constant - see Black
and Bradley (1973).) In practice it is usually assumed that
the residuals in the model are normally distributed, $u_i \sim N(0,$
$\sigma_u^2)$. This enables us to form a t-statistic of the form
$(\hat{f}_j - f_j) / \hat{\sigma}_{\hat{f}_j}$ with $N - k$ degrees of freedom, where j is
the particular coefficient, $j = 1, \ldots, k$, and $\hat{\sigma}_{\hat{f}_j}$ is the
estimated standard error of $\hat{f}_j$ (as $\hat{f}$ is a linear function
of M and linear functions of normal variates are themselves
normally distributed). The actual standard error is unknown
as it depends on the unknown σ_u^2 -see Mayes and Mayes pp. 119-
121, Maddala pp. 79-81.

It is also possible to test hypotheses about whether the
regression as a whole tells us anything about M, by considering a test relating to the variation in M explained by the
regression and to that left unexplained

$$F_{(k-1,\ N-k)} = \frac{[\Sigma(M_i - \overline{M}) - \Sigma\hat{u}_i^2]/(k-1)}{\Sigma\hat{u}_i^2 / (N-k)}$$

$$= \frac{R^2 / (k-1)}{(1 - R^2) / (N-k)}$$

where $\Sigma(M_i - \overline{M})^2$ is the total variation in M, the residual variation, $\Sigma\hat{u}_i^2$, is clearly the unexplained variation, hence $\Sigma(M_i - \overline{M})^2 - \Sigma\hat{u}_i^2$ is the variation explained by the regression and

$$R^2 = \frac{\text{explained variation in } M}{\text{total variation in } M} = \frac{\Sigma(M_i - \overline{M})^2 - \Sigma\hat{u}_i^2}{\Sigma(M_i - \overline{M})^2},$$

$$0 \leqslant R^2 \leqslant 1.$$

We have also already mentioned testing for autocorrelation of the residuals, heteroscedasticity and multicollinearity and suitable tests can be derived for each of these. (The particular tests are explained in the chapters which follow.) The principle at issue here which the reader should bear clearly in mind in the ensuing applications, is that after obtaining a set of estimates the analysis is not complete. The estimates will only tell us about the nature of the economic relations we are investigating if the model is specified correctly and estimated suitably. We must therefore consider the nature of our estimates very closely to determine whether both these criteria are met before we go on to draw

any conclusions. This is often a complex task which leads to
re-specification and re-estimation on several occasions before
we are convinced that the difficulties have been overcome.
Even so it must always be remembered that our eventual conclusions are only statements in probability. We can never be
certain about our conclusions and it may be that the characteristics of our particular sample of data lead us to draw
the wrong inferences.

1.4   Forecasting and prediction

Under many circumstances when the final estimates have
been obtained and the conclusions drawn this represents the
end of the analysis. However, this is not always the case, and
it is arguable that it should never be the case, in that
unless it is possible to show that reasonable results can be
obtained from the model under circumstances other than those
used for estimation there is no real proof that the model has
any practical value. This is rather an overstatement, but it
is clear that forecasting ability (not necessarily of a
future event but merely outside the sample information) is an
important characteristic of a well specified and estimated
model. It is common practice to leave out some of the available data when estimating and then see if the model will
predict the remaining values accurately - for example we may
have import data, quarterly, over the period 1955-75, but

only use the years 1955-74 for estimation, seeing whether
we can predict the last four quarters.

The prior conditions for a successful forecast are that
the model be correctly specified and the assumptions about
behaviour apply to the circumstances to be forecast as well.
Thus forecasts of very different circumstances are unlikely
to be accurate however good the original specification. The
main drawback is usually the difficulty of predicting structural change. We can evaluate forecasts in the same way as
other estimates by considering confidence intervals or significance tests, especially if we are 'predicting' a known
result. However, a good forecast is not necessarily the one
with the smallest error (or root mean square error); in a
time series the path of a forecast is also important - a
cyclical forecast round a horizontal trend could be completely
out of phase with the true series and yet be correct on
average!

Forecasts can of course be made under more than one set
of circumstances. We can forecast the effect of hypothetical
policy changes, or different patterns of the determining
variables in order to provide a basis for policy making or to
plan for different eventualities. This is an important area
of economic work and will be developed in the applications

particularly in Chapter 9 with models of the whole economy.

1.5   The structure of the rest of the book

The rest of this book considers eight applications of
econometrics to economic problems drawn from the whole
range of experience, consumption, production functions,
investment, money, wages and prices, international trade,
demand analysis and models of the whole economy. The first
four topics concern what are largely single equation problems
and the second four extend the analysis into three rather
different types of simultaneous equations models. Chapter 2
deliberately takes one of the most well known areas of economics so that the reader is introduced to econometric analysis in a context with which he is familiar. This chapter
puts rather more weight on specification and shows with the
help of some recent work by Davidson *et al.* (1978) how difficulties posed by specification error can be resolved. Consumption is also an application which is well suited to introducing some of the main econometric problems of estimation
which we have mentioned in this chapter.

In Chapter 3 we move from macro- to micro-economics with
a consideration of production functions. This application
allows us to develop the ideas of estimation further and in
particular shows how econometric analysis can cope with

non-linearities in both variables and parameters of the
model. Chapter 4 moves on to investment behaviour because
this gives us the opportunity to consider in some detail how
variables behave over time and how lag structures should be
specified and estimated.

In Chapter 5 we return to a macro-economic topic which
has excited considerable interest in recent years, namely
money. The first part of this chapter deals with the demand
for money, developing single equation analysis further,
particularly in regard to constraints on parameters and the
use of autoregressive models to simplify the treatment of
lag structures. However, it also becomes clear that the
existence of other equations in the model cannot be ignored.
The second part of the chapter, therefore, considers a
multiple equation 'monetarist' model, which has a recursive
structure. The chapter concludes by consideration of the
'St Louis' type of reduced form monetarist model, thus
providing an introduction to the 'monetarist controversy'.

By Chapter 6 the reader will have developed sufficient
experience in applying econometrics that we can consider a
simultaneous equations problem. In order to keep the subject
manageable we look at a two-equation system of the determination of wages and prices. This area is of fundamental

importance in modern policy making where both unemployment
and inflation are running at levels which are unwelcome to
governments in most countries. We show how misspecification
and the existence of simultaneous equation bias can lead to
the drawing of false inferences about the nature of the
inflationary process and the effects of government policy
upon it.

The study of simultaneous equations is then expanded
to much larger systems in Chapter 7 with the examination of
international trade models. The chapter not only includes a
study of imports, exports and the matrix of world trade flows,
but also considers the effects of the formation of trading
areas such as the EEC on trade.

Having introduced simultaneity we move on to consider
one of the most highly developed areas of economic theory,
namely demand analysis, in Chapter 8. Consumer demand for
all the various products presents a whole system of equations
which are highly interrelated by constraints of additivity
(the sum of the parts must come to the whole), homogeneity
(absence of money illusion) and symmetry (relative price
changes have the same effect whichever of the two prices
change). The really interesting conclusion here is the discrepancy between the findings from the data (for several

countries) and the expectations from economic theory.

In the final application we move on to the economy as
a whole and consider how models which are useful for analysis,
forecasting and policy simulation can be developed. We concentrate on the National Institute model of the UK economy
as this provides a fairly small and comprehensible model which
is in current use. Other larger models in both the UK and
other countries are mentioned, but a detailed analysis of
this area would take several books in itself. The focus is on
macro-econometric forecasting in practice and the assessment
of its success.

Suggestions for further reading are made in each chapter
on the particular applications and Chapter 10 sets out the
details of some of the computer packages which are currently
available to enable further analyses of these problems.

References and Suggested Reading

BLACK, J. AND BRADLEY, J.R. (1973) *Essential Mathematics for
      Economists*, Chichester: Wiley.

EVANS, M.K. (1969) *Macroeconomic Activity*, New York:
      Harper and Row.

HOUTHAKKER, H.S. AND MAGEE, S.P. (1969) 'Income and price
      elasticities in world trade', *Review of Economics and*

Statistics (May).

INTRILIGATOR, M.D. (1978) *'Econometric Models, Techniques and Applications'*, New York: North Holland.

JOHNSTON, J. (1972) *'Econometric Methods'*, New York: McGraw-Hill.

MADDALA, G.S. (1977) *'Econometrics'*, New York: McGraw-Hill.

MAYES, A.C. AND MAYES, D.G. (1976) *'Introductory Economic Statistics'*, Chichester: Wiley.

Chapter 2

CONSUMPTION

The elementary theory of the consumption function is so
well known it is easy to forget what the nature of the original Keynesian rationale was. It was simply that a consumer's
expenditure in real terms is a function of his real personal
disposable income. Both the marginal propensity to consume
and the income elasticity of demand are positive but less
than unity (Keynes, 1936). Most current interest in the
consumption function concerns much more complex relations of
aggregate consumers' behaviour. It is therefore necessary to
consider not only the justification for these refined specifications but also the treatment of aggregation. These refine-
ments involve the shape of the function, the exclusion of
short run fluctuations in income, the inclusion of wealth
variables, distinctions between sources of income and
categories of expenditure and the development of lag structures. They illustrate very clearly the sorts of considerations
we have just explained in the first chapter and form the basis
of this chapter.

2.1   The development of the specification

Given the simple exposition of Keynesian theory we are
trying to model the relation

$$C = f \ (Y) \tag{1}$$

where C is a consumer's expenditure and Y is personal disposable income. The variables are expressed in real terms
thus excluding the possibility of 'money illusion'. If we
ignore the problems of aggregation for the time being the
first step, given the absence of any further detail, would
probably be the estimation of a simple linear function

$$C = \alpha + \beta \ Y + u \tag{2}$$

where the variables are now expressed in aggregate. Fitting
(2) to annual data for the UK over the period 1949-75 we
obtain the following estimates by ordinary least squares

$$C = 4141 + 0.78 \ Y.$$
$$(312) \ (0.01)$$

(The data are drawn from various issues of the *National
Income and Expenditure*, Blue Book and are measured in 1970
prices.) The marginal propensity to consume $\frac{dC}{dY}$ is thus 0.78
and the income elasticity of demand ranges from 0.79 at the
beginning of the estimation period to 0.91 at the end. (Frequently people quote only a single elasticity, that at the

mean, but the relation should be plausible over its entire

range.) In general this seems a highly satisfactory equation.

The hypotheses that either α or β are zero are decisively

rejected (t_α = 13.3 and t_β = 74.3). The overall fit of the

equation as indicated by R^2 is 99.6 per cent and the co-

efficients and elasticities have plausible signs and magnitudes.

In practice, however, (see Davis (1952) for example) the

forecasts achieved with estimates of equations of the form

of (2) all tended to be less than the actual consumption

levels observed. Most of these results were obtained using

inter-war data from the United States. This, therefore, im-

plies a misspecification. In our case the equation tends to

overestimate, giving £36,624 mn for 1976 instead of £35,406 mn

and £36,217 mn for 1977 instead of £35,133 mn (all in 1970

prices). These latter findings are rather more readily under-

standable - first the years 1976 and 1977 can scarcely be

said to have been typical as the result of rapid inflation,

and second the model is incomplete. There is a second identity

in the model, that total incomes are equal to total expendi-

tures

$$\text{GDP} = C + Z \qquad\qquad\qquad (3)$$

where Z represents all other expenditures (and the adjustment

to factor cost). Since personal disposable income is also a

component of GDP we can obtain a second equation relating
consumers' expenditure and personal disposable income. The
nature of this problem is clearer if we make the harsher
assumption that Y in equation (2) is actually GDP. It is
then possible to show (see Wallis (1972) p. 98 for example)
that the direction of the bias in the estimate of β from
using OLS and ignoring (3) is upwards. If Y is personal
disposable income the bias is still in the same direction but
the effects of the missing equations in the model are more
complex.

However, as we noted for the United States data this
bias could not be the only specification error since the
forecasts underestimated the actual values. Three well-known
solutions were suggested for this and we shall include them
not just because they are important in themselves, but
because they have also been used in various forms to attempt
to find the solution to our own specification problem. All
three hypotheses relate to the same problem, namely that
equation (2) suggests that consumption responds too freely
to changes in income. The three hypotheses developing the
specification explain why consumers' expenditure should be
more stable than income. A glance at Fig. 2.1 shows this
relative stability to be the case for the United Kingdom,
using quarterly data for the period 1958-75. The annual

*Figure 2.1   Changes in Consumers' Expenditure and Income over
the previous year*

(United Kingdom, 1958-1977, quarterly)

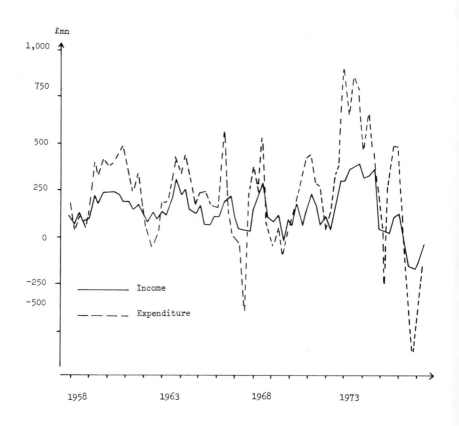

Source: Economic Trends

change in both variables $(C_t - C_{t-4}, Y_t - Y_{t-4})$ is plotted.
However the economic circumstances in the United States
between the wars and those in the United Kingdom in the mid-
1970's are very different. With the slump in the United
States personal disposable incomes fell heavily but consumers' expenditure did not fall commensurately. With rapid
inflation in the United Kingdom disposable incomes in money
terms rose rapidly, but consumers' expenditure, also in
money terms, did not keep pace and hence real consumption
actually declined compared with real incomes.

2.1.1   *The relative income hypothesis*

This model, normally associated with Duesenberry (1949),
relates very specifically to the problem of behaviour in the
United States. His specification entails a ratchet effect.
Consumers are influenced not only by their current incomes
but by the highest income in their experience. Thus if
incomes decline consumption does not fall to the same extent.
If we call this level of income, Y_{max}, $(Y_{max} = \text{Max } (Y_{t-1},$
$Y_{t-2}, \ldots, Y_0))$ we have the relation

$$C = \alpha + \beta Y_t + \gamma Y_{max} + u_t. \tag{4}$$

(Duesenberry's own exposition of this relates to individual
households and is set out in terms of relative income,

$$\frac{C_{it}}{Y_{it}} = \alpha + \beta \frac{\overline{Y}_{it}}{Y_{it}} + u_{it} \tag{5}$$

where $\overline{Y}_t$ is mean income and i refers to the individual household. (4) is obtained by multiplication and aggregation.) If
incomes are rising $Y_{max} = Y_{t-1}$ and (4) can be rewritten as

$$C_t = \alpha + \beta\, Y_t + \gamma Y_{t-1} + u_t \;. \tag{6}$$

For post-war data (on an annual or seasonally adjusted basis)
there is little practical difference between (4) and (6).

If we estimate equation (6) with the same data for the
United Kingdom that we used for equation (2), we obtain

$$C_t = \underset{(308)}{4153} + \underset{(0.11)}{0.93}\, Y_t - \underset{(0.12)}{0.16}\, Y_{t-1}.$$

This specification is not without its difficulties as Y_t
and Y_{t-1} are highly related ($r_{Y_t Y_{t-1}} = 0.996$). Not only is
the coefficient of Y_{t-1} insignificantly different from zero
at the 5 per cent level, but its sign is the opposite to that
suggested by Duesenberry. This illustrates both the difficulties encountered under multi-collinearity and those which
arise from transferring a specification to very different
circumstances (there are also estimation problems which are
considered later).

Duesenberry's original formulation has been developed further, with a shift in emphasis, by Brown (1952) who suggested that people only change their behaviour slowly and hence that the previous period's consumption affects current consumption as well as current disposable income. This therefore means that, whether we are considering upward or downward shifts in incomes, consumption changes only slowly towards a new equilibrium value. Brown therefore incorporated a lagged value of the dependent variable in the equation,

$$C_t = \alpha + \beta Y_t + \gamma C_{t-1} + u_t. \qquad (7)$$

Using (7) we can obtain the following estimates from our data:

$$C_t = 3505 + 0.65 Y_t + 0.16 C_{t-1}.$$
$$ (750)\ (0.13) \quad (0.18)$$

The short run marginal propensity to consume is 0.65 and in the long run (when $C_t = C_{t-1}$ in equilibrium) it is 0.77, both rather higher than was obtained with United States data. Again there are collinearity problems ($r_{Y_t C_{t-1}} = 0.997$) and the coefficient of C_{t-1} is not significantly different from zero at 5 per cent.

2.1.2 The permanent income hypothesis

It is possible to consider equation (7) in a different light. If we think that consumption only reacts slowly to income changes we could suggest that current consumption is a function not just of current disposable income but also of income in previous periods with the effect of the previous periods dying rapidly away towards zero – thus

$$C_t = \alpha + \sum_{i=0}^{M} \beta_i \, Y_{t-i} + u_t \qquad (8)$$

where M is the number of periods in the past before which there is no effect of past income on current consumption. A simple geometric lag function would achieve a version of this

$$C_t = \alpha + (1 - \beta) \sum_{i=0}^{\infty} \beta^i \, Y_{t-i} + u_t \qquad (9)$$

which we can transform (using the Koyck (1954) procedure) to equation (7) with a proviso about the nature of the disturbance term, u. Multiplying (9) by the factor in the geometric series in the previous time period

$$\beta C_{t-1} = \alpha\beta + (1 - \beta) \sum \beta^{i+1} \, Y_{t-i-1} + \beta u_{t-1}, \qquad (10)$$

subtracting (10) from (9)

$$C_t - \beta C_{t-1} = (1 - \beta) \, \alpha + (1 - \beta) \, Y_t + u_t - \beta u_{t-1} \qquad (11)$$

and adding βC_{t-1}

$$C_t = (1 - \beta)\, \alpha + (1 - \beta)\, Y_t + \beta C_{t-1} + (u_t - \beta u_{t-1})$$

$$(12)$$

which is clearly of the same form as (7) although we now have
a moving average process in the error term - which has consequences in estimation.

The reason for showing this relation is clear when we
consider the nature of the permanent income hypothesis, attributed to Friedman (1957), because it too is formulated in
terms of a geometric lag distribution on income. The basic
contention in the permanent income hypothesis is that consumption is proportional to what the consumer considers is
normal income not just to whatever happens to be his measured
income during the observation period. Thus

$$C_t^* = \alpha YP_t \qquad\qquad (13)$$

where YP_t is permanent income and income is divided into its
permanent and transitory (YT_t) components

$$Y_t \equiv YP_t + YT_t. \qquad\qquad (14)$$

We have expressed the left-hand side of (13) as C_t^* and not
C_t as Friedman considers that actual consumption expenditures

can also be divided into planned or permanent and transitory
components

$$C_t \equiv CP_t + CT_t \tag{15}$$

hence it is CP_t $(= C_t^*)$ on the left-hand side as (13) represents the 'permanent' relation. The two transitory components
are assumed to be independent of each other, of themselves
in different time periods and of the permanent components.
They also have zero means, thus

$\text{E } (YT_t) = \text{E } (CT_t) = 0 \text{ (for all } t)$

$\text{Cov } (YT_t, YT_s) = \text{Cov } (CT_t, CT_s) = 0 \text{ (for all } t \text{ and } s,$

$$t \neq s)$$

$\text{Cov } (YT_t, YP_s) = \text{Cov } (CT_t, CP_s) = \text{Cov } (CT_t, YT_s) = 0$

$$\text{(for all } t \text{ and } s \text{).}$$

$$\tag{16}$$

As in the case of the relative income hypothesis, (13)
enables us to reconcile the fact that the long-run average
propensity to consume, C/Y, appeared to be relatively constant
in the United States between the wars (and previously, see
Kuznets (1942))while the marginal propensity dC/dY was
lower. Again this can be achieved by showing that if the
permanent income model is correct the OLS estimator of β in
(2) is a downward biased estimator of α in (13). This can only

be shown in the limit in probability,

$$\text{plim } \hat{\beta}_{OLS} = \alpha \frac{\sigma^2_{YP}}{\sigma^2_{Y}} \qquad (17)$$

where σ^2_{YP} and σ^2_{Y} are the variances of YP and Y. Since from
(16) $\sigma^2_{Y} = \sigma^2_{YP} + \sigma^2_{YT}$ where σ^2_{YT} is the variance of YT and
$\sigma^2_{YT} > 0$, $\hat{\beta}_{OLS}$ is biased downwards.

Friedman suggests that YP can be estimated by a geometric
lag on actual income although he sets M, the earliest period
with a non-zero effect as 16 periods in the past. Also, since
there is no constant in (13) there will be none in the estimating equation. Without imposing Friedman's constraint on M
we obtain

$$C_t = \underset{(0.09)}{0.10} \; Y_t + \underset{(0.10)}{0.91} \; C_{t-1}$$

which again gives us a very different result for our UK data
from that obtained with the original United States data.

2.1.3   The life-cycle hypothesis

For completeness we shall also consider the Life-Cycle
Hypothesis of Modigliani, Brumberg and Ando (MBA) – (see
M & B (1954), M & A (1960) and A & M (1963)) because this
suggests a different lag distribution for Y and C in the
estimation of current consumption. Their initial hypothesis

is that consumption is related not just to income but to the
individual's holdings of wealth and expected future incomes
as well. Hence the individual decides on his consumption on a
lifetime basis and not just on a single period basis. Thus if
he consumes over the periods 1 to T his lifetime utility is a
function of consumption in each of those periods

$$U = U (C_1, C_2, \ldots, C_T).$$

The resulting consumption function is of the form (see M & B
(1954))

$$C_t = \alpha A_{t-1} + \beta Y_t + \gamma Y_t^e + u_t \tag{18}$$

where A is assets and Y^e is the present value of expected
income over the rest of the consumer's lifetime. Because of
the problems of aggregation A & M (1963) express Y_t^e in terms
of Y_t so that the estimated form is

$$C_t = \alpha^* A_{t-1} + \beta^* Y_t + u_t \tag{19}$$

(a more complex version is also estimated).

This can be further simplified to avoid measuring assets,
as is pointed out by Davidson et $al.$ (1978).

$$A_t = A_{t-1} + Y_t - C_t, \tag{20}$$

hence

$$C_t - C_{t-1} = \alpha^*(Y_{t-1} - C_{t-1}) + \beta^*(Y_t - Y_{t-1}) + u_t^* \tag{21}$$

and

$$C_t = \beta^* Y_t + (\alpha^* - \beta^*) Y_{t-1} + (1 - \alpha^*) C_{t-1} + u_t^* \tag{22}$$

when $u_t^* = u_t - u_{t-1}$, thus giving yet a third form for the lag distributions of C and Y.

2.2   Recent findings

All three of the developments we have considered in the previous section are of the general form

$$C_t = \alpha + \sum_i \beta_i Y_{t-i} + \sum_j \gamma_j C_{t-j} + u_t \tag{23}$$

where there are different constraints on the parameters, α, β_i and γ_j. They are all formulated to take account of the fact that on the basis of United States data, largely between the wars, the average propensity to consume remained fairly constant while the short-run marginal propensity had a lower value thus resulting in under-prediction when the simple Keynesian function (2) was used to explain consumers' expenditure. As we have seen from annual post-war United Kingdom data (using ordinary least squares like most of the original

estimates cited although this is not always the most appropriate technique) the same patterns and problems do not all
appear to be present. The estimated marginal propensity to
consume (0.78) was less than the average propensity to consume throughout the post-war period, but the average propensity fell steadily as is shown in Fig. 2.2 from around
unity immediately after the war to 0.86 by 1975/7. Although
the income elasticity of demand was rising it was also less
than unity, increasing from 0.79 to 0.91.

We shall now move on to consider how recent econometric
work has attempted to explain these findings. In particular
we shall look at the work of the London Graduate Business
School ((1976) and Ball et al. (1975)),Hendry (1974) and
Davidson et al. (1978), Townend (1976) and H.M. Treasury
(1976, 1977). This is not an exhaustive survey and it is not
intended to be so. The particular models are chosen because
they illustrate very clearly the econometric and economic
logic used in trying to solve the difficulties posed by the
aggregate consumption function. All these models refer to
quarterly data for the United Kingdom for a period of approximately twenty years up to the mid-1970's. The choice of the
United Kingdom rather than say the United States or Japan is
partly arbitrary as many countries present suitable evidence
and analysis, but it is also deliberate in that the special

circumstances of the United Kingdom in the 1970's lead us
to question some of the assumptions of the simple Keynesian
model in a way which was not previously necessary with the
United States data.

The particular issue highlighted by Townend and the
Treasury is the unprecedented rise in the savings ratio
(decline in the average propensity to consume). This is shown
clearly in Fig. 2.2. As existing models stood this change in
behaviour could not easily be explained and a search was made
for additional variables. Let us begin, however, by setting
out a common framework and clear set of definitions for the
various models. Not surprisingly there are discrepancies
between almost all the models, so the equations used are set
out in Table 2.1 with their attendant definitions.Some of
these equations look complicated but between them they illustrate seven developments of the explanation of consumers'
behaviour suggested at the beginning of this chapter, namely,

(i) in the case of all except the Treasury models consumers'
expenditure on durable goods and on non-durables and services are distinguished and in the more recent version of the
Treasury model, Treasury (1979), the same distinction is also
made; (ii) all except 1 and 7 distinguish between different
sources of current income as determinants of consumption;

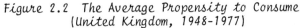

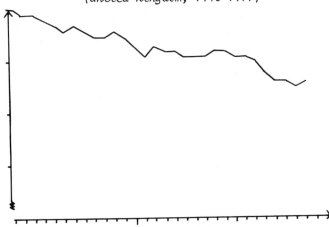

*Figure 2.2   The Average Propensity to Consume
(United Kingdom, 1948-1977)*

Source: *National Income and Expenditure.*

(iii)   equations 5 and 7 employ a different functional form;

(iv)   equations 1, 2, 4 and in a complex way, 7, include a lagged
value of the dependent variable; (v) equations 3, 5, 6 and 7 include lagged as well as current values of income; (vi) equations
4, 5 and 6 include liquid assets as a variable (Davidson *et al.*
also consider this hypothesis but include variables relating to
the rate of inflation and the rate of change of the rate of inflation); (vii) all equations except 1 include dummy variables
to take account of specific events.

There are other distinctions such as the choice between
using seasonally adjusted data and specifying the model to incorporate the seasonal fluctuation which can also be made. We shall
deal with each of these points in the discussion which follows,
although some will be taken together as they overlap.

Table 2.1 Models of the consumption function in the UK 1974-1978

1. Hendry (1974)

$$CN_t = a_1 + a_2 Y_t + a_3 CN_{t-1} + \sum_{i=1}^{3} a_{i+3} Q_{it} + \sum_{i=1}^{4} a_{i+6} Q_{it} + u_{1t}$$

2. Ball et al. (1975)

$$\overline{CNS}_t = b_1 + b_2 \overline{YS}_t + b_3 \overline{CNS}_{t-1} + \sum_{i=0}^{1} b_{i+4} D1_{t-i} + u_{2t}$$

3. Treasury (1976)

$$\overline{C}_t = c_1 + \sum_{i=0}^{9} c_{i+2} \overline{YWD}_{t-i} + \sum_{i=0}^{2} c_{i+12} \overline{YGD}_{t-i} + \sum_{i=0}^{10} c_{i+15} \overline{YOD}_{t-i} + R_t + D2_t + u_{3t}$$

4. Townend (1976)

$$CNS^*_t = d_1 + d_2 YS_t + d_3 CNS^*_{t-1} + d_4 NLA_{t-\frac{1}{2}} + \sum_{i=0}^{1} d_{i+5} D1_{t-i} + d_7 D3_t + \sum_{i=1}^{3} d_{i+7} Q_{it} + e_{4t}$$

$$(e_{4t} = d_{11} e_{4t-1} + u_{4t})$$

5. LGBS (1976)

$$(\overline{YS}_t - \overline{CNS^*})/\overline{YS}_t = f_1 + \sum_{i=1}^{3} f_{i+1} (\overline{Y}_{t-i-1} - \overline{Y}_{t-i})/(\overline{Y}_{t-i}) + \sum_{i=0}^{2} f_{i+5} (\overline{YO/YW})_{t-i}$$

$$+ f_8 (LA/YD)_{t-1} + \sum_{i=0}^{1} f_{i+9} D1_{t-i} + f_{11} D3_t + u_{5t}$$

6. Treasury (1977)

$$\overline{C}_t = g_1 + \sum_{i=0}^{9} g_{i+2} \overline{YWD}_{t-i} + \sum_{i=0}^{2} g_{i+12} \overline{YGD}_{t-i} + \sum_{i=0}^{9} g_{i+15} \overline{YOD}_{t-i} + \sum_{i=0}^{11} g_{i+25} GLA_{t-i}$$

$$+ R^{**}_t + g_{37} BA_t + D2_t + u_{6t}$$

7. Davidson et al. (1978)

$$CNL4_t = h_1 YL4_t + h_2 (YL4_t - YL4_{t-1}) + h_3 (C/Y) L_{t-4} + h_4 PL4_t + h_5 (PL4_t - PL4_{t-1})$$

$$+ h_6 [(D1_t - D1_{t-1}) + (D3_t - D3_{t-1})] + u_{7t}$$

Definitions of variables in Table 2.1

BA	Bank advances in constant prices.
C	Consumers' expenditure in constant prices.
CN	Consumers' expenditure on non-durable goods and services in constant prices.
$D1$	Dummy variable to take account of expected and actual tax changes in 1968.
$D2$	Variable to take account of changes in HP regulations.
$D3$	Dummy variable to take account of the effect of the introduction of VAT in 1973.
GLA	Gross liquid assets of the personal sector (deflated).
LA	Liquid assets of the personal sector.
NLA	Net liquid assets of the personal sector.
Q	Dummy variables for each quarter.
R	Imputed rent from owner-occupied dwellings in constant prices.
Y	Real personal disposable income.
YG	Government grants to persons in real terms.
YO	Other personal income in real terms.
YW	Real income from wages and salaries.
D	At the end of a variable name denotes net of tax.
L	At the end of a variable name denotes the natural logarithm.
S	At the end of a variable name denotes that current grants to persons by the government have been deducted.
$*$	At the end of a variable name denotes that current grants to persons by the government, G, have been deducted using the following weights $0.6G_t + 0.3G_{t-1} + 0.1G_{t-2}$.
$**$	At the end of a variable name denotes deflation by council rents.
—	Over a variable denotes seasonally adjusted.
4	At the end of a variable, X, denotes the fourth difference, $X4_t = X_t - X_{t-4}$.
t	Is the time subscript.
u	Is an error term — usually $E[u] = 0$; $E[u_i, u_j] = 0$ $i \neq j$, $= \sigma_u^2 \; i = j$. (e_4 is also an error term.)

The a_i, b_i, ..., d_i, f_i, ..., h_i are the parameters of the models.

2.2.1 *The choice of the dependent variable*

Elementary demand analysis suggests (as is developed in Chapter 6) that the relation between disposable income and consumers' expenditure varies from product to product. While aggregation of expenditures on some products before estimation of the determinants of consumers' behaviour has a negligible effect on the estimates, a fundamental distinction in the nature of consumption can be seen between durable and non-durable goods. 'Consumption' normally implies that the item purchased is consumed - used up - during the measurement interval. However, economic accounting conventions classify all personal expenditures as consumption with the exception of the purchase of dwellings. Thus many household items such as washing machines, radios and cars are treated as consumption although they are not normally used up in the measurement interval. More criteria therefore come to bear in the determination of this form of consumption - stocks, the rate of interest, the availability of credit, etc. This provides a much more complex framework than for the consumption of non-durables - see for example Evans (1969) for an introduction to the subject - and the attempt to mix both relations in the same equation is clearly shown to result in a worsening of the estimates of aggregate consumption.

2.2.2   The specification of the income variable

Only Hendry uses the original specification of personal disposable income; all the other models distinguish current grants to persons by the government from the rest of disposable income. The rationale is very simple and is set out clearly in Treasury (1977) p. 11.2; the bulk of these grants goes to people who are in immediate need – old age pensioners, the unemployed, etc. – who are likely to spend the whole sum on consumption relatively quickly. Thus, especially in models where there is a substantial lag structure, this source of income and hence expenditure should either be accounted for specifically or deducted from both sides of the equation before estimation. In each case where this technique is used the coefficients of the lags in the re-spending of current grants are imposed on the basis of other evidence and not estimated directly from the sample of data used to determine the rest of the equation.

The Treasury model and the LGBS (1976) model also distinguish wage and salary income from other incomes – largely dividends, interest, profits and earnings from self-employment – again on the grounds of differing effects. This argument (also used in the National Institute Model described in Chapter 9) is not quite so clearly defined but appears to bear fruit in practice. A final distinction is also made

by the Treasury in the case of imputed rent income from
owner-occupation. Clearly this should also be removed from
the analysis as the income so derived is not freely disposable; it can only be 'spent' on imputed rents for owner-
occupation.

2.2.3   The form of the function

The previous two points are relatively trivial and refer
to the definition of the problem rather than the characteristics of its solution. The choice of the functional form does
not. We argued at the outset (p. 30) that the only *a priori*
constraints on the form of equation (1) were on the marginal
propensity to consume and the income elasticity of demand.
The choice of form can best be considered by returning to a
consideration of the data itself. Both consumers' expenditure
and income have a strong seasonal pattern, which must be
taken into account. Furthermore, this pattern increases with
time.

If the fluctuations in each season are the same in every
year then we can take account of this by adding seasonal
constraints to the equation (see for example Mayes and Mayes
(1976) pp. 149-150 for a description of this technique) as
in equation 1. But the seasonal pattern is increasing over
time, not constant. In his 1974 paper Hendry accommodates this

by adding a further set of seasonal constants which incorporate a time trend. However, Davidson *et al.* point out that
this procedure would yield meaningless results if extrapolated
much beyond the sample period and that a transformation of
CN_t into logarithms gives a stable seasonal pattern throughout
the period. Davidson *et al.* develop this further by showing
that if the model is expressed in fourth differences, i.e.
year on year changes, $C_t - C_{t-4}$ and $Y_t - Y_{t-4}$, then the
problem of seasonality is removed if the original equation
were

$$C_t = \alpha + \beta\, Y_t + \gamma_1 Q_{1t} + \gamma_2 Q_{2t} + \gamma_3 Q_{3t} + u_t$$

where Q_{it} denotes a seasonal constant which is unity in
quarter i and zero otherwise, then

$$Q_{1t} = Q_{1t-4}, \; Q_{2t} = Q_{2t-4}, \text{ etc.,}$$

and hence taking fourth differences removes the seasonal constants from the equation. (There are, however, effects on the
structure of the error term.) Furthermore, taking *logarithms*
of the fourth differences also largely eliminates the tendency
for the fluctuations to increase over time and expresses the
model in terms of proportionate changes in behaviour.

2.2.4   The lag structure of the model

In the previous section, we have seen that the relative
income hypothesis, the permanent income hypothesis and the
life-cycle hypothesis all involve the use of lag structures
on either consumption or income or both. In some circumstances
the form of the structure was clear, but most of the particular structures used were merely convenient approximations to
enable estimation. The lag structures used in equations 1, 2
and 4 on Table 2.1 are consistent with versions of the
permanent income hypothesis and to a lesser extent with the
life-cycle hypothesis - they certainly do not represent any
important new development of theory (leaving aside the
liquid asset question until the next subsection, 2.2.5). All
of them give estimates of the marginal and average propen-
sities to consume which are very much in line with our
original simple annual estimates (for example the MPC from
equation (2) is 0.74 and the APC = 0.84 at the sample mean).
The LGBS model introduces a slightly more complex structure
but the Treasury model has a completely different philosophy.
In this case lags of increasing length are fitted until
further periods appear to have no effect on the relation.
There is no particular theoretical justification behind this,
and the nature of the lag distributions is different in the
1977 estimates (equation 6) from those made in 1976 (equation
3). In general it is a much more satisfactory state of affairs

to have a restricted lag structure of, say, the form of
equation 7, where the meaning of each variable is clear in
economic terms。

Let us take the first two variables in 7 as an example –
the fourth difference and logarithmic specification has already been justified in terms of a constant proportionate
reaction and the comparison of like periods (the current
period with this time last year). As we noted on p。 51
this not only avoids problems of seasonality by differencing
but it also avoids any problem of heteroscedasticity in the
errors, which might have occurred as a result of the increasing fluctuations in the untransformed data, by the use of the
logarithmic form. The first term, therefore, $YL4_t$ gives the
direct relation between income and consumption which we set
out at the outset p. 30 $(C = \beta Y)$. The second term shows how
this relation is modified in the light of short-run changes
$(YL4_t - YL4_{t-1})$.

The third term $(C/Y)L_{t-4}$ illustrates a very important
point in the use of lags to represent the dynamic properties
of the model and the inclusion of long-run effects. Davidson
et al. pp. 672–676 and 677–679 show that 7 including only
the first two terms (and $D1_t - D1_{t-1}$) represents the best

simple description of the data (sample period is 1958 (ii)
to 1970 (iv)). In linear terms

$$CN4_t = \underset{(10.1)}{78.5} + \underset{(0.04)}{0.34}Y4_t - \underset{(0.04)}{0.14}(Y4_t - Y4_{t-1})$$

$$+ \underset{(22)}{61}(D1_t - D1_{t-1})$$

$$R^2 = 0.70 \quad SEE = 40.5 \quad DW = 1.7$$

$$x_1^2(20) = 94.0 \quad x_2^2(16) = 20$$

where SEE is the standard error of estimate of the regression
– our estimate of σ_u – DW, the Durbin–Watson statistic, is
a test of first order autocorrelation; $x_1^2(20)$ is a test of
parameter stability over the forecast period; and $x_2^2(16)$ is
a test of the absence of other higher orders of the autocorrelation. (The SEE is explained in Mayes and Mayes pp. 141–
146 and the Durbin–Watson statistic on pp. 183–186: The forecast test $x_1^2(n_1)$ is a test of the accuracy of one period
ahead forecasts, $\hat{CN4}_t$, for each of n_1 periods, using the estimated values of the parameters and the actual values of the
variables on the right-hand side of the equation.

$$x_1^2(n_1) = \overset{n_1}{\underset{t}{\Sigma}}(\hat{CN4}_t/\hat{\sigma}_u)^2 \text{ is approximately distributed as}$$
$\chi^2(n_1)$. The autoregression test is also approximately $\chi^2(n_2)$
where n_2 is the maximum order of autoregression considered
and is derived in Pierce (1971).) While R^2 may seem low, a
standard error of 40.5 is only a fraction of 1 per cent of the

mean value of *CN* during the sample and hence the explanation
is extremely close. There is no evidence of autocorrelation
at the first or higher orders at the 1 per cent level, but
the forecast statistic leads us to reject the hypothesis
of stable parameters at the 5 per cent level. Thus while the
equation works well for the estimation period it does not
for the forecast period. It is at this point that the third
term (C/Y) L_{t-4} is introduced.

Following Ball·and Drake (1964) and Evans (1969)
Davidson *et al.* suggest that the underlying relation $C = \beta Y$
only applies to some steady state growth path and that if
the rate of growth varies the average propensity to consume
will vary. On the basis of our data this will only make sense
if the average propensity to consume is a declining function
of the rate of growth. Hence we can take account of these
shifts by including the average propensity to consume in the
equation (with a one-period lag as this is the adjustment
period) and expect to obtain a negative coefficient,

$$CNL4_t = \underset{(0.04)}{0.49YL4_t} - \underset{(0.05)}{0.17}(YL4_t - YL4_{t-1}) - \underset{(0.01)}{0.06}(C/Y)L_{t-4}$$

$$+ \underset{(0.004)}{0.01}(D1_t - D1_{t-1})$$

$$R^2 = 0.71 \quad \text{SEE } 0.0067 \quad \text{DW} = 1.6 \quad x_1^2 (20) = 80.7$$

$$x_2^2 (12) = 23$$

All the parameters are closely determined, but it is clear
from x_1^2 that the model is not complete if it is to explain
the period 1971-5. The constant is omitted because deviations
from the growth relation are now explained by C/Y and will
only be constant if C/Y is constant.

2.2.5   *The inclusion of liquid assets and other variables*
        to account for the change of behaviour in the 1970's.

As we have seen in the previous section equation 7
without the two inflation variables gives what appears to be
a very good explanation of the behaviour of consumption over
the period up to 1970. The LGBS, the Treasury and Townend
all include liquid assets as the main variable to explain
changes in consumption in the further period. This does not
represent any particularly new departure because as we
noticed in the life-cycle hypothesis, equation (19), the
lagged value of assets should be included in the equation.
The assumptions in this case are first that liquid assets are
the section of an individual's assets which are readily con-
vertible into consumption, and second that they form the
most easily measurable part of an individual's wealth.

The form of the hypothesis is that inflation erodes the
real value of people's wealth, hence consumption is reduced
in an effort to maintain wealth and hence future consumption

in the life-cycle. If we take Townend's results in particular
he gives as the equation used by the Bank of England in their
forecasting before the attempt to explain behaviour in the
1970's:

$$\overline{CN}_t = \begin{array}{c} 580.7 \\ (123.1) \end{array} + \begin{array}{c} 0.15345(\overline{YS}) \\ (0.03) \end{array} + \overline{YG}* + \begin{array}{c} 0.72031 \ \overline{CNS}*_{t-1} \\ (0.06) \end{array}$$

$$+ \ d_6 D1_t + d_7 D1_{t-1} + d_8 D3_t + e_t,$$

$$(e_t = - \begin{array}{c} 0.32637 \\ (0.15) \end{array} e_{t-1})$$

$$SEE = 37.3 \quad R^2 = 0.991$$

(the errors, e, follow a first order autoregressive process,
$\overline{R}^2 = 1 - \dfrac{N-1}{N-K} (1 - R^2)$ and is R^2 adjusted for the number
of degrees of freedom, see Maddala pp. 120-122) and the
accuracy of the forecasts from this are shown in part A of
Table 2.2. Forecasts are shown on two bases: first forecasts
for a single period ahead using actual values of all variables
on the right hand side of the equation, and second a forecast
for the whole period using actual values of the exogenous
variables only and the calculated values of the lagged
endogenous variable. Thus when liquid assets are not included
the model consistently overforecasts the actual values.

Table 2.2   Forecasts of consumers' expenditure on non-durables UK:

(£mn 1970 prices, seasonally adjusted)

	1974 (i)	(ii)	(iii)	(iv)	1975 (i)	(ii)	(iii)[a]
A. Without liquid assets							
Actual	6,836	6,778	6,824	6,850	6,922	6,748	6,604
Single period forecasts	6,877	6,873	6,877	6,881	6,932	6,913	6,775
Error	-41	-95	-53	-31	-10	-165	-171
Full period forecast	6,877	6,872	6,900	6,933	6,994	6,967	6,939
Error	-41	-94	-76	-83	-72	-219	-335
B. With liquid assets							
Single period forecasts	6,837	6,827	6,834	6,835	6,884	6,843	6,707
Error	-1	-49	-10	15	38	-95	-103
Full period forecast	6,837	6,816	6,826	6,853	6,886	6,821	6,752
Error	-1	-38	-2	-3	36	-73	-148

a) provisional

Source: Townend (1976), Tables A and B

When equation 4 itself is estimated Townend obtains

$$CNS^*_t = \begin{array}{c} 687.5 \\ (105.5) \end{array} + \begin{array}{c} 0.18878YS_t \\ (0.02) \end{array} + \begin{array}{c} 0.58051CNS^*_{t-1} \\ (0.05) \end{array}$$

$$+ \begin{array}{c} 0.01979NLA_{t-\frac{1}{2}} \\ (0.004) \end{array} + d_5 D1_t + d_6 D1_{t-1} + d_7 D3_t$$

$$+ \sum_{i=1}^{3} d_{i+7} Q_{it} + e_t$$

$$e_t = \begin{array}{c} - 0.63893 \\ (0.14) \end{array} e_{t-1}$$

SEE = 25.9 $\overline{R}^2$ = 0.995

where not only is the coefficient for the liquid assets
variable positive and different from zero at the 1 per cent
level but the standard error of estimate is reduced and $\overline{R}^2$
increased (these two effects are not identical as the sample
period is different). Furthermore as we can see from Table 2.2
the forecasts are greatly improved, although the model still
overforecasts on average some individual forecasts are less
than the actual observed values.

The reason for the introduction of liquid **assets** into
these equations was not so much out of belief in the life-
cycle hypothesis, but to explain the effects of inflation
on consumers' expenditure. Deaton (1977) therefore proposed
that this be tackled directly by developing a simple
explanation of how consumers' behaviour under inflation will

result in increased saving. The important feature of this model is that the consumer is acting under uncertain circumstances (certainly true of the United Kingdom in the period 1972-7) and is unable to predict what the rate of inflation is going to be. In particular when the consumer tries to purchase any item the only price which he knows accurately is the price of that item; all other prices are recalled with varying accuracy depending upon the time interval since they were last observed. Under conditions of rapid inflation the item to be purchased will appear to have risen in price compared with the out-of-date prices recalled for other items. The consumer will therefore tend to substitute against the item and thus reduce the size of the purchase. However, this will apply to most products and hence aggregate consumption will fall. Deaton does not assume misinformation with respect to personal disposable income, so his results could be expected to be offset by an income effect from inflation in salaries and wages. However, it is likely in practice that consumption behaviour does not respond rapidly to changes in money income in the same way that we have argued that it does not respond immediately to real changes.

There are two factors involved in the reduction of consumption under inflation - first, at any given rate of inflation consumers will fail to adjust spending patterns

immediately, the higher the inflation the greater the failure
to adjust, but secondly consumers also fail to react to
changes in the rate of inflation because these are largely
unanticipated. Thus if inflation rises consumption will fall
back even further, and if it falls consumers will not adjust
to the lower rate immediately. Therefore, we need to include
both the rate of inflation and the rate of change of the rate
of inflation in our estimation. Deaton finds that these
effects are present even before 1971 and this finding is
confirmed by Davidson *et al.* in equation 7 of Table 2.1.

$$CNL4_t = \underset{(0.04)}{0.47 YL4_t} - \underset{(0.05)}{0.21} (YL4_t - YL4_{t-1}) - \underset{(0.02)}{0.10} (C/Y)L_{t-4}$$

$$- \underset{(0.07)}{0.13 PL4_t} - \underset{(0.15)}{0.28} (PL4_t - PL4_{t-1})$$

$$+ \underset{(0.003)}{0.01} \quad [(D1_t - D1_{t-1}) + (D3_t - D3_{t-1})]$$

$$R^2 = 0.77 \quad SEE = 0.0061 \quad DW = 1.8 \quad x_1^2 (20) = 21.8$$

$$x_2^2 (12) = 19.$$

Not only do the two new variables contribute significantly
to the explanation but they have little effect on the coefficients of the other variables, implying that our basic
hypothesis in real terms was well specified. The equation now
shows the ability to forecast - i.e. we accept the null
hypothesis of stable parameters over the forecast period of

1971–1975, so we do not need to estimate using data for the period of really rapid inflation to be able to explain its effects – a really substantial achievement.

If the estimation period is lengthened to include the whole data period 1958 (i) to 1975 (iv) then the parameters of the model are largely unaltered (as we would expect from the value of x_1^2 in the previous equation) but the whole equation is better determined.

$$CNL4_t = \underset{(0.03)}{0.48\,YL4_t} - \underset{(0.04)}{0.23}\,(YL4_t - YL4_{t-1}) - \underset{(0.01)}{0.09}\,(C/Y)L_{t-4}$$

$$- \underset{(0.02)}{0.12\,PL4_t} - \underset{(0.10)}{0.31}\,(PL4_t - PL4_{t-1})$$

$$+ \underset{(0.002)}{0.006}\quad[(D1_t - D1_{t-1}) + (D3_t - D3_{t-1})]$$

$$R^2 = 0.85 \quad SEE = 0.0062 \quad DW = 2.0 \quad x_2^2\,(12) = 23$$

To get a measure of comparison of the two suggestions for coping with the effects of inflation on consumption, Davidson *et al.* try incorporating liquid assets into their framework and find that changes in them are correlated with the rate of growth – average propensity to consume term $(C/Y)L_{t-4}$. The equation also has a poor forecasting ability and they feel that liquid assets should not be included. Part of the decision over which of the two methods to employ depends upon

which is a proxy for which. If it is inflation (and changes
in it) which causes changes in both consumers' expenditure
and personal holdings of liquid assets, then liquid assets
will affect consumers' expenditure through their simultaneous
determination, whether or not they are also a separate determinant. The relation observed by Townend could therefore be
one of association rather than causation. If on the other
hand we do not accept even the temporary existence of money
illusion or poor information caused by inflation, we would
argue that the correct decision variables (like liquid
assets) should be included in the equation and not proxies
for them in the form of inflation variables.

Subsequently Hendry and von Ungern-Sternberg (1979)
suggested that the reason Davidson *et al.* preferred the two
inflation terms to liquid assets was because they misspecified
the form of the effect of liquid assets. If real income is
specified after an allowance for a proportion of the change in
the value of liquid assets and the cumulative effect of the
change in the liquid assets/income ratio is included then the
liquid assets specification is preferred. However, further work
by the London Business School (LGBS 1980) suggests that both a
liquid assets/income ratio term *and* an inflation term should
be included, while the 1979 Treasury model includes an inflation term and the change in the rate of growth in unemploy-

ment. It is clear from the variety of specification that Hendry and von Ungern-Sternberg (p. 3) are correct to conclude that we are 'undoubtedly far from ... the final resolution of the complex subject.'

2.2.6   The use of dummy variables

There are three main uses of dummy variables in econometrics (see Mayes and Mayes pp. 145-150): first to take account of structural changes in parameters, second to take account of special events which would otherwise distort the rest of the estimates and third to represent categorical variables. It is the second form which is used here where variables are constructed which have the value unity in the time period when the special event takes place and zero else-where. The coefficient of this variable then gives the addi-tive effect of the special event - in this case the effects of anticipations and reactions to the 1968 budget, $D1$., the introduction of VAT, $D3$, and changes in HP regulations, $D2$.

2.3   Conclusions

This first application to consumption illustrates several of the major features of econometric analysis. In particular we have seen how specification starts with a simple idea and a general form, but that this idea is refined in the light of a closer look at the evidence and examination of the

estimates of the model. In this case we saw that the simple
Keynesian function under-predicted consumption in the
United States betwen the wars and how a lower short-run
marginal propensity to consume was reconciled with a near
constant average propensity. Following this we also examined
how the over-prediction of consumers' expenditure in the
United Kingdom in more recent years led to respecification
to take account of inflation.

At the outset we examined the data closely and saw
how the seasonal pattern could present problems of heteroscedasticity and autocorrelation in the errors if the model
were not specified appropriately. We also showed how all the
statistical characteristics of equations had to be taken
into account in evaluating the specification - sign and size
of coefficients, significance tests of the effect of individual variables and groups of variables, the size of the
standard error of estimate, the absence of autocorrelation
in the residuals, the stability of parameters in forecasting
and when small changes are made to the specification or data.
We also noted the importance of a clear economic meaning and
justification for the specification so that models can
forecast under considerable changes in circumstances.

This chapter is only an analysis of some of the contribution of econometrics to the understanding of the consumption function in economics. It is not an exhaustive survey and by no means completes what can be usefully said on the subject. In the list of suggested reading which follows we have included the original sources and a number of helpful further commentaries.

References and Suggested Reading*

ANDO, A AND MODIGLIANI, F (1963) 'The Life-cycle Hypothesis of Saving: Aggregate Implications and Tests', *American Economic Review*, vol. 53 No. 1.

BALL, R.J. AND DRAKE, B.S. (1964) 'The Importance of Credit Control on Consumer Durable Spending in the UK, 1957-61', *Review of Economic Studies*, vol. 30.

BALL, R.J., BOATWRIGHT, B.D., BURNS, T., LOBBAN, P.W.M. and MILLER, G.W. (1975) 'The London Business School Quarterly Econometric Model of the UK Economy' Ch. 1 in Renton (1975).

BROWN, T.M. (1952) 'Habit Persistence and Lags in Consumer Behaviour', *Econometrica*, vol. 20, No. 3.

CENTRAL STATISTICAL OFFICE, *National Income and Expenditure* (Blue Book), HMSO, annually.

*DAVIDSON, J.H., HENDRY, D.F., SRBA, F. AND YEO, S. (1978)
    'Econometric Modelling of the Aggregate Time-Series
    Relationship Between Consumers' Expenditure and Income
    in the United Kingdom', *Economic Journal*, vol. 88.

DAVIS, T.E. (1952) 'The Consumption Function as a Tool for
    Prediction', *Review of Economics and Statistics*,
    vol. 34.

*DEATON, A.S. (1977) 'Involuntary Saving Through Unanticipated
    Inflation', *American Economic Review*, vol. 67.

DUESENBERRY, J. (1949) *'Income, Saving and Theory of Consumer
    Behaviour'*, Cambridge: Harvard University Press.

*EVANS, M.K. (1969) *'Macroeconomic Activity'* New York: Harper
    and Row.

*FRIEDMAN, M. (1957) *'A Theory of the Consumption Function'*,
    Princeton: National Bureau of Economic Research.

HENDRY, D.F. (1974) 'Stochastic Specification in an Aggregate
    Demand Model of the United Kingdom', *Econometrica*, vol. 42.

HENDRY, D.F. AND VON UNGERN-STERNBERG, T. (1979) 'Liquidity
    and Inflation Effects on Consumers' Expenditure', mimeo
    (April).

JOHNSTON, J. (1972) *'Econometric Methods'* New York: McGraw-
    Hill (2nd. edition).

KEYNES, J.M. (1936) *'The General Theory of Employment, Interest
    and Money'*, London: Macmillan.

KOYCK, L.M. (1954) *'Distributed Lags and Investment Analysis'*, Amsterdam: North Holland.

KUZNETS,S. (1942) *'Uses of National Income in Peace and War'*, National Bureau of Economic Research, Occasional Paper, No. 6.

LONDON GRADUATE BUSINESS SCHOOL, ECONOMETRIC FORECASTING UNIT (1976) 'Relationships in the Basic Model' (amended as at April 1976), Appendix to Discussion Paper No. 34 ((1980) as at February 1980).

MADDALA, G.S. (1977) *'Econometrics'*, McGraw-Hill.

MAYES, A.C. AND MAYES, D.G. (1976) *'Introductory Economic Statistics'*, Wiley.

MODIGLIANI, F. AND ANDO, A. (1960) 'Tests of the Life-cycle Hypothesis of Savings', *Bulletin of the Oxford Institute of Statistics*, vol. 19.

MODIGLIANI, F. AND BRUMBERG, R. (1954) 'Utility Analysis and the Consumption Function' in K.K. Kurihara (ed.) *Post-Keynesian Economics*, New Brunswick: Rutgers University Press.

PIERCE, D.A. (1971) 'Distribution of Residual Autocorrelation in the Regression Model with Autoregressive-Moving Average Errors', *Journal of the Royal Statistical Society*, 13, vol. 33.

RENTON, G.A. (1975) ed. *'Modelling the Economy'*, London: Heinemann.

*TOWNEND, J.C. (1976) 'The Personal Saving Ratio', *Bank of England Quarterly Bulletin*, vol. 16.

H.M. TREASURY (1976) 'Macroeconomic Model Technical Manual 1976', London: H.M. Treasury.

H.M. TREASURY (1977) 'Macroeconomic Model Technical Manual 1977', London: H.M. Treasury.

H.M. TREASURY (1979) 'Macroeconomic Model Technical Manual 1979', London: H.M. Treasury.

WALLIS, K.F. (1972) *'Introductory Econometrics'*, London: Gray-Mills.

Chapter 3

THE PRODUCTION FUNCTION

The production function is a rather more difficult relation to handle than the consumption function which we considered in the previous chapter. The first reason for this difficulty is that although the relation itself is technological it is embedded in economic behaviour and hence specification has to be established with great care. The second complication from the econometrician's point of view lies in the fact that the relation is not expected to be linear, hence providing complications in estimation. Furthermore it is by no means clear that the postulated determinants of production are themselves independent of the production decision and hence the production function may have to be treated as only one of a number of relations which determine productive activity.

The purpose of the production function is to determine the relation between the inputs to a productive enterprise and its output. This relation, although most easily thought of as a micro-economic problem concerned with individual firms, is also often tackled for the industrial sector of

economies as a whole. The more aggregate the function the
less its determinants are related to any particular technology. Taking the simple technological case to begin with,
the output of a particular firm (industry) can be thought
of as requiring certain inputs of raw materials, of products
from other industries, imported products and labour for any
given technology. If we label these inputs as Z_j, $(j = 1,$
..., $N)$ where N is the total number of possible inputs then
output in industry i can be observed to use a particular set
of inputs. This is not a production 'function' as such,
merely a set of observations in any particular period t which
can be related as an identity if the variables are measured
in values

$$Q_t = Z_{1t} + Z_{2t} + \cdots Z_{Nt} \qquad (1)$$

where Q is output and all value added including profits as
well as labour incomes are included in the Z_j. It becomes a
production 'function' when the form of the technology tells
us what output we can expect given any set of inputs.

The input-output framework of Leontief (1951), developed
for the United Kingdom by Stone and Brown (1963), gives the
simplest form for such a function, namely, inputs bear a fixed
proportion to output.

Thus

$$Z_j/Q = A_j \qquad\qquad\qquad (2)$$

where A_j is a constant input-output 'coefficient' for all t.
Any other level of output Q^* would require inputs of
$Z_j^* = A_j Q^*$. The interest of such a rigid system is that the
input requirements of any given level of outputs for the
economy as a whole can be determined. The produced inputs of
any industry i will be the outputs of other industries, k
(or even industry i itself) and these outputs will themselves
require inputs and so on backwards through the system in an
infinite sequence. Input-output analysis determines the eventual requirements of the whole sequence which is convergent
providing the sum of produced inputs is less than the value
of output for each industry.[1]

The traditional 'neo-classical' treatment of the
production function which is the subject of this chapter is
not based on this purely technological idea. It sets aside
the question of material inputs and concentrates on the two
major 'economic' factors in production, labour and capital.
Denoting labour by L and capital by K the relation is thus

[1]
  See Leontief (1951) for example.

$$Q = f\ (L,\ K),\qquad\qquad\qquad\qquad\qquad (3)$$

This function is usually assumed to be such that there are positive but diminishing returns to each input (factor) as amounts of that factor are increased [2,3]

$$\frac{\partial Q}{\partial L} > 0,\ \frac{\partial^2 Q}{\partial L^2} < 0,\ \frac{\partial Q}{\partial K} < 0 \text{ and } \frac{\partial^2 Q}{\partial K^2} < 0.\qquad (4)$$

This ensures the non-linearity of the function that we mentioned at the outset. A linear function

$$Q = a_0 + a_1 L + a_2 K \qquad\qquad\qquad (5)$$

as we used for the simple consumption function in Chapter 2 would have constant returns to each factor ($\partial Q/\partial L = a_1$, $\partial Q/\partial K = a_2$ and $\partial^2 Q/\partial L^2 = \partial^2 Q/\partial K^2 = 0$). It is rather difficult to draw a suitable non-linear relation directly as it involves projecting the three dimensions of Q, K and L onto a two-dimensional piece of paper. The function is therefore drawn

---

[2] In the fixed coefficient model, as in the input-output model, there is the limiting case of equality to zero of all four differentials.

[3] There is also the cross-factor condition that

$$\frac{\partial^2 Q}{\partial L^2}\ \frac{\partial^2 Q}{\partial K^2}\ -(\frac{\partial^2 Q}{\partial L \partial K})^2 > 0.$$

using the labour and capital axes alone with levels of output

being shown by 'contours' (normally referred to as isoquants).

The general nature of this is shown in Fig. 3.1 in a form

familiar in introductory micro-economics, where the curves

(isoquants) $Q_1 \, Q_1'$, $Q_2 \, Q_2'$, $Q_3 \, Q_3'$ represent levels of out-

put where $Q_1 < Q_2 < Q_3$.

The isoquants have been drawn consistent with conditions

(4) but otherwise their shape and (lack of) similarity are

arbitrary.   Much of the rest of this chapter will be concer-

ned with the particular shape of these curves. Any shape is

possible, consistent with (4), between the limits of a

straight-line such as AA' in Fig. 3.2 and a right-angle, BB'.[4]

This presents us with a much more complicated econometric

problem than we posed in Chapter 2, although at the end of

that chapter some of the consumption functions were also in

effect non-linear.

The other major econometric problem which faces us here

is that a firm is not normally faced by given quantities of

labour and capital which it transforms into output.

---

[4] The slope of AA' and the origin of BB' are of course
arbitrarily chosen.

Figure 3.1   The relation between labour, capital and output

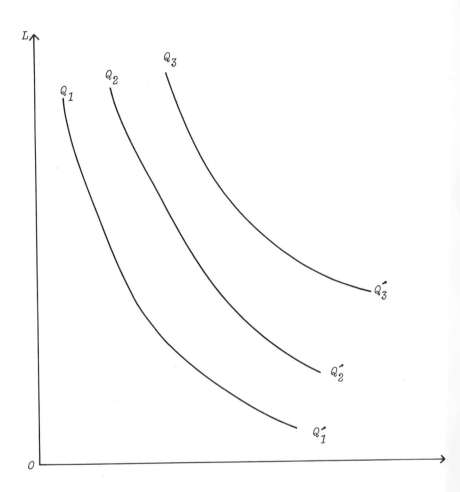

Figure 3.2   Limits to the production function

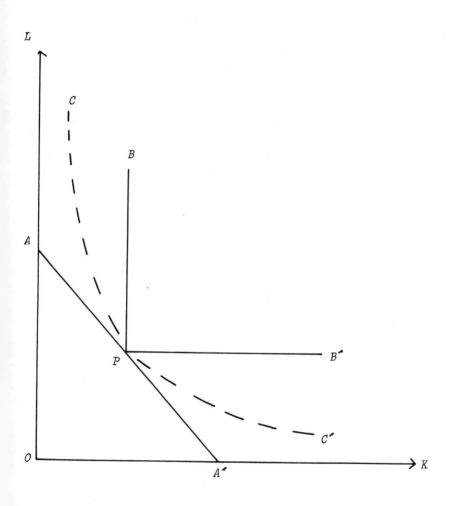

It also chooses the capital and labour which it will employ
although the degree of choice may be severely restricted in
the short-run. Thus not only is Q an endogenous variable but
L and K are also. This presents an example of a simultaneous
equation problem which we explained in Chapter 1 pp.17-20.
However, we shall not consider the direct estimation of
simultaneous equations until Chapter 6 and will deliberately
restrict ourselves here to cases where a single equation method
is appropriate.

In the rest of this chapter we begin by examining the
form of the production function which has been used most
widely, the Cobb-Douglas function. In this context we also
examine the problem of returns to scale as the level of
operation of the enterprise increases.   In section 3.2 we
move on to consider the problem of simultaneity which was outlined in the previous paragraph. A second important feature
of the form of the production function is the substitutability
of labour and capital. The third section therefore deals with
the elasticity of substitution and in this context introduces
a second widely used form, the CES production function. The
chapter is completed by a section on further developments where
the elasticity of substitution is allowed to vary.

Inevitably in keeping the treatment brief, important issues have been neglected. Foremost among these is the discussion of technical change, which could easily merit a chapter to itself. The reader could look at Kennedy and Thirlwall (1972) and Harcourt and Laing (1971) for a helpful discussion of this.

3.1 The Cobb-Douglas production function

The first production function to come into widespread use which embodies the qualities we have just discussed in the previous section is that suggested by Cobb and Douglas (1928)

$$Q = a_0 L^{a_1} K^{a_2}. \tag{6}$$

As it stands this presents no particular problems for estimation using the ordinary least squares methods we have already encountered. If we take logarithms of (6) we obtain

$$\log Q = \log a_0 + a_1 \log L + a_2 \log K \tag{7}$$

which is linear in the transformed variables, $\log Q$, $\log L$ and $\log K$. It is frequently possible to find a linearizing transformation of non-linear functions in this sort of way. In other cases the linearization may have to be approximate such as the use of a Taylor series expansion.[5] The aspect to watch

---

[5]
Explained on pp.102-104.

however is that (6) and (7) are expressed without an error term. In practice the Cobb-Douglas production function is thought to have a multiplicative error

$$Q = a_0 L^{a_1} K^{a_2} e^u \tag{8}$$

which becomes additive in the logarithmic transformation

$$\log Q = \log a_0 + a_1 \log L + a_2 \log K + u \tag{9}$$

and hence permits straightforward estimation. In general it is very important to realise that the error is not an after-thought to be tacked on as convenient but an integral part of the specification of the model.

Having expressed the function in the form of (9) we must immediately qualify this by admitting that this was not the form that Douglas himself used for estimation. His initial results using (9), see Table 3.1, showed that $a_1 + a_2$ seemed to be approximately unity, and he therefore concluded that $a_2 = (1 - a_1)$ and hence reformed the equation as

$$\log (Q/K) = a_0 + a_1 \log (L/K) + u. \tag{10}$$

This has the advantage that Douglas could circumvent the problems of collinearity between K and L which were inherent in his time series data.[6] Imposing the restriction on the coefficients in (10) has a noticeable effect on the value of a_1 (= k) shown in Table 3.1 for the time series, even though in the unconstrained estimation the condition $a_2 = (1 - a_1)$ was nearly met already. The less collinear a pair of variables, the less the omission of one of them from an equation affects the estimate of the other, there being no effect when the variables are independent.

3.1.1 The problem of measurement

The occurrence of a data difficulty is a timely reminder that, although we mentioned at the beginning of the chapter that production functions are used both at different levels of aggregation and for cross-section, time series and pooled data, we have not traced out what the consequences of this are for the measurement of variables. Our initial formulation, equation (3), expressed all the variables in quantitative terms. As soon as the data are aggregated we may have to use constant price measures to retain common units. Thus output will normally be measured as value-added and labour input as number of employees or number of hours worked.[7] Capital

---

[6] This problem of collinearity is widespread in the study of time series production functions in many countries. Mohmed-Ahmed (1979), for example, even gets negative capital co-efficients in his study of the Sudan as the result of severe collinearity.

[7] Leslie and Wise (1980) include both hours *and* men in an attempt to overcome this problem.

inputs are more difficult to deal with as it is arguable that
it is not the capital stock which is the input but the
capital utilized - the services derived from the capital.

One straightforward problem of capital utilization is the
working of shifts. The same set of machinery may be used
virtually three times as intensively in a firm working full
shifts compared with another operating only an eight-hour day.
Similarly the treatment of either labour or capital as homogeneous factors is obviously incorrect in many circumstances.
It makes no allowance for the age or 'vintage' of capital nor
the effects of labour hoarding. As soon as a firm deliberately
operates below its normal capacity it will distort the estimates of the parameters of the production function. It is
therefore clear that there are substantial practical problems
from the data in the way of estimating the production function
even if it is possible to determine the appropriate functional
form.

3.1.2 Returns to scale

In the time series case we are likely to be observing
the function at a series of increasing levels of scale of
operation and will not be observing movements along any
isoquant. If expansion were to be along a path AA' such as that
shown in Fig. 3.3 through levels Q_1, Q_2, Q_3 and Q_4 in

Table 3.1 Estimates of Cobb-Douglas production functions for manufacturing industry in various countries[a]

	N	Model 1 $P = bL^k C^j$				(b)		Model 2 $P = bL^k C^{1-k}$	
		k	σ_k	j	σ_j	$k+j$	b	k	σ_k
1. Time series									
(a) U.S. 1899–1922	24	0.81	0.15	0.23	0.06	1.04	0.84	0.75	0.04
(b) Victoria (Australia) 1907–29	22	0.84	0.34	0.23	0.17	1.07	0.71	0.71	0.07
(c) New South Wales 1901–27	26	0.78	0.12	0.20	0.08	0.98	1.14	0.86	0.05
(d) New Zealand 1915–6, 1918–35	18	0.42	0.11	0.49	0.03	0.91	2.03	0.51	0.03
2. Cross-sections									
(a) U.S. 1919	556	0.76	0.02	0.25	0.02	1.01	244.21	0.75	0.02
(b) Australia 1936–7	87	0.49	0.04	0.49	0.04	0.98	21.57	0.50	0.04
(c) South Africa 1937–8	17	0.66	0.08	0.32	0.08	0.98	54.48	–	–
(d) Canada 1937	164	0.43	0.04	0.58	0.04	1.01	15.42	0.42	0.04
(e) New Zealand 1938–9	61	0.46	–	0.51	–	0.97	0.73	–	–

(a) These results are all reproduced from Douglas (1948), but this is not the original source – these are quoted in the article.

(b) Douglas defines the variables as follows P = production, L, labour and C, capital, and σ_k and σ_j are the standard errors of k and j.

consecutive time periods, L and K will be highly collinear.

The Cobb-Douglas production function estimated in Table
3.1 has the property of constant returns to scale which
entails that along any straight-line expansion path from the
origin, output increases in strict proportion to inputs so
that isoquants are equally spaced for any given equal steps
in Q and hence all isoquants are of the same shape –
'homothetic'.   It is worth noting at this stage that $a_1 + a_2$
is the 'scale factor' in the production function.   If the
scale of production is increased by some proportion, k, so

$$Q^* = a_0 \ (kL)^{a_1}(kK)^{a_2} \tag{11}$$

where Q^* is the new level of output

$$Q^* = k^{a_1 + a_2}Q, \tag{12}$$

then there are constant returns to scale if $a_1 + a_2 = 1$ and
decreasing (increasing) returns to scale as $a_1 + a_2 < (>) \ 1$.
Obviously we shall want to see if Douglas' finding of constant
returns to scale is a universal experience and in particular
we shall look (pp.101-102) at the work of Griliches and Ringstad
(1971) who suggest a contrary result.   However, in the
meantime we can show the sorts of results which can be obtained
for the Cobb-Douglas function in other contexts by examining
cross-section results for 11 different industries in Nigeria

Figure 3.3   Expansion path of aggregate production

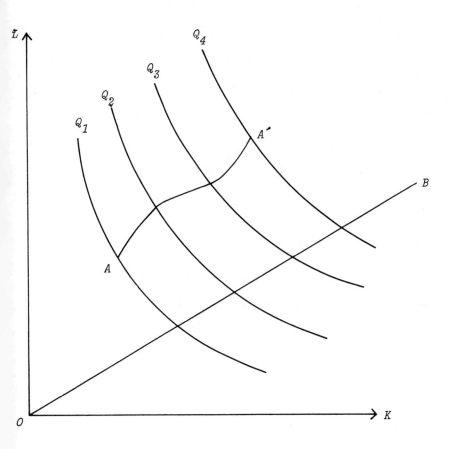

(Table 3.2) as calculated by Iyaniwura (1974). Although the individual estimates of a_1 and a_2 in (9) vary widely the resulting values of $a_1 + a_2$ are all in the range of 0.8929-1.3817. Thus the Cobb-Douglas function appears to be applicable to individual firms in one time period as well as to aggregate time series. However, the poor determination of some of Iyaniwura's results should be borne in mind.

As they stand Douglas' results are extremely impressive. It is possible to apply his model to a wide range of data as is shown in Table 3.1. The equations are well determined and the constant returns to scale assumption seems well founded. However, there is considerable evidence to show that this approach has a number of drawbacks which would lead us not only to reconsider Douglas' results but to look for other forms of production function. Some of these drawbacks will be considered in turn in the three sections which follow.

3.2 Simultaneity

Our analysis of production functions has been deliberately simple up to this point to avoid obscuring the basic framework of the relation. Such simplification inevitably omits important features and provisos which must not be ignored. In the first place the existence of a definable production function which can be estimated implies the existence of some

Table 3.2   Cross-section estimates of Cobb-Douglas Production Functions for Nigerian industry 1969

Industry	No. of firms	Elasticity with respect to capital (1)	labour (2)	R^2	Scale factor (3)=(1)+(2)
Bakery products	26	0.3904 (0.1218)	0.7259 (0.2195)	0.77	1.1163
Beverages	10	0.7063 (0.4897)	0.4768 (0.7291)	0.55	1.1831
Textiles	28	0.5980 (0.2916)	0.4838 (0.2675)	0.86	1.0818
Tannery and leather furnishing	13	-0.0325 (0.4052)	1.1056 (0.4022)	0.66	1.0731
Sawmills	29	0.8099 (0.2462)	0.3166 (0.2733)	0.68	1.1265
Furniture and fixtures	25	0.8492 (0.1396)	0.0437 (0.1993)	0.62	0.8929
Printing and publishing	30	0.4282 (0.1933)	0.9535 (0.2064)	0.79	1.3817
Chemical industry	17	0.5332 (0.1774)	0.7273 (0.2659)	0.63	1.2605
Rubber industry	15	-0.1659 (0.2839)	1.3698 (0.2993)	0.62	1.2039
Plastics industry	11	0.2767 (0.1972)	0.6913 (0.2572)	0.81	0.9680
Metal industry	28	0.5739 (0.1022)	0.3648 (0.1396)	0.83	0.9387

Source: Iyaniwura (1974)

market conditions and objectives of firms, which have only
been implicit in the initial analysis. In particular it implies
a form of production which is in some sense 'efficient'. Quite
clearly although there may be some maximum level of output
obtainable with a particular combination of labour and capital
it is certainly possible to obtain less than the maximum with
the same inputs by inefficient operation. Elementary economic
analysis would usually begin by assuming that the market is
competitive and that firms are profit maximizing. While these
are not the only possible assumptions, this last condition
means that the price of the factors becomes important in the
determination of the production point.

Under profit maximization the value of output less
inputs is maximized

$$Y = QP - (LW + KR) \tag{13}$$

where Y is the profit (income to the firm), W is the wage
rate and hence LW is the total labour cost, R is the cost of
each unit of capital and hence KR is the total capital cost.
For any given set of P, R and W we can find the maximum profit
by differentiating Y with respect to L and to K and then
solving the two equations derived by setting the differentials

equal to zero.[8] Thus

$$\frac{\partial Y}{\partial L} = P \frac{\partial Q}{\partial L} - W \qquad (14)$$

and

$$\frac{\partial Y}{\partial K} = P \frac{\partial Q}{\partial K} - R. \qquad (15)$$

Setting (14) and (15) equal to zero and rearranging

$$\frac{\partial Q}{\partial L} = \frac{W}{P} \qquad (16)$$

and

$$\frac{\partial Q}{\partial K} = \frac{R}{P}. \qquad (17)$$

The production function itself, (6), enables us to solve (16) and (17),

$$\frac{\partial Q}{\partial L} = a_0 \, a_1 \, L^{a_1 - 1} K^{a_2} = a_1 Q/L \qquad (18)$$

and

$$\frac{\partial Q}{\partial K} = a_0 \, a_2 \, L^{a_1} K^{a_2 - 1} = a_2 Q/K. \qquad (19)$$

---

[8] If this were not a perfectly competitive world the firm would be able to affect P, W and R and hence we would have non-zero derivatives with respect to these variables

$$\frac{\partial Y}{\partial L} = \frac{\partial Q}{\partial L} \, P + Q \, \frac{\partial Q}{\partial L} \frac{\partial P}{\partial Q} - W - \frac{\partial W}{\partial L} \, L,$$

and similarly for $\partial Y/\partial K$.

Thus from (16)

$$a_1 Q/L = W/P$$

and hence

$$a_1 = \frac{LW}{QP} \tag{20}$$

and

$$L = a_1 \, QP/W. \tag{21}$$

Similarly from (17)

$$a_2 \, Q/K = R/P$$

and hence

$$a_2 = \frac{KR}{QP} \tag{22}$$

and

$$K = a_2 \, QP/R. \tag{23}$$

We thus have the simultaneous equation problem which we mentioned at the outset, that the two determinants of output, capital and labour, are themselves endogenous to the system. However, the problem is even more complicated because the model is still not identified[9] even, if P, W and R are the same

---

[9] In the sense of 'identification' outlined on pp. 17-20.

for each firm since there are then no exogenous *variables* just
three constants. This problem is easy to understand: each
firm is faced by the same problem and since it has the same
objectives it comes to the same conclusion, hence we would
observe only one production point (plus the variations due
to residual error) and this would be consistent with any
production function which passed through that point.[10]

In practice it is necessary to introduce some restrictions on the model to be able to estimate a production function.
The simplest possibility is to introduce a time dimension as
we observed with the original Douglas (1948) results where
the aggregate functions had only one observation for each
time period. Zellner *et al.* (1966) have shown that this method
of identification can be extended to the case of a cross-
section of firms during a number of time periods and the
ordinary least squares estimators of (9) will be both unbiased
and consistent. However, a procedure for estimating a cross-
section alone was suggested much earlier by Klein (1953) for
railway data. Since the industry was regulated, revenue (QP)

---

[10]
    This problem was first set out fully by Marshak and Andrews
(1944) and is thus not a modern discovery. Douglas (1948) was
himself aware of the 'marginal productivity' conditions (16)
and (17) and used them in his analysis.

was demand determined, hence the problem for each individual
railway company was to choose the optimal levels of inputs
given output and prices. The coefficients (a_1 and a_2 in (9))
are then estimated from (20) and (22) as the geometric
averages of the ratio of the cost of the factor to total
revenue. They are geometric because the equation is transformed into logarithms. (20) thus becomes

$$\log \hat{a}_1 = \frac{1}{N} \sum_i \ (\textbf{log } WL_i - \log QP_i) \qquad\qquad (24)$$

where ^ denotes the estimate, and the i subscript refers to
each of the N(= 81) railways companies.[11]

It is thus possible to estimate this simultaneous
equation model using single equation techniques and we shall
persevere in this chapter with cases where such single
equations are used, leaving the introduction of full
simultaneity to Chapter 6.

Klein's methodology is not ordinary least squares but a
direct estimate of the mean value of the parameters in the

---

[11] This also emphasizes the difficulty in accepting Douglas'
constant returns to scale finding since if in aggregate $QP = WL + KR$ then this entails that $a_1 + a_2$ is unity from (24).

sample. It is important to realise that it is not the estimation method which identifies the model, but the new restrictions placed upon it. A model which is not identified cannot be estimated *because* it cannot be identified. It was the provision of the extra dimension of time which enabled the identification of the cross-section model in the Zellner *et al.* case and the predetermination of output and prices in Klein's example, not the choice of estimation method.

3.3 Elasticity of Substitution

The Cobb-Douglas production function which provided the vehicle for the path-breaking work in the subject is rather restrictive, as we have seen. To some extent this is an advantage, but it compels the isoquants to have a particular form, which may not be what occurs in practice. The shape of the isoquant varies depending upon how readily labour and capital can be substituted for each other in production. If they are not substitutable (capital and labour have to be used in fixed proportions and thus additions of capital or labour on their owen have no effect on output) the isoquants would be rectangular as is shown by isoquant *BB'* in Fig. 3.2. If on the other hand they are perfect substitutes then the isoquant would be a straight line, *AA'*. In practice we would expect a relation between these extremes, say *CC'*.

The slope of the isoquant, the marginal rate of substitution, $\partial K/\partial L$, does not tell us anything about the ease of substitution as it is consistent with an infinite number of isoquants at the production point, P. However the elasticity of substitution,

$$[\frac{d(K/L)}{(K/L)}] \ / \ [\frac{d(\partial K/\partial L)}{\partial K/\partial L}],$$

shows how factor proportions react to changes in the marginal rate of substitution.[12]   In general

$$\frac{\partial K}{\partial L} = -\frac{\partial Q}{\partial L} \ / \ \frac{\partial Q}{\partial K} \tag{25}$$

hence from (16) and (17) under profit maximization

$$\frac{\partial K}{\partial L} = -\frac{W}{R}, \tag{26}$$

the factor price ratio. Thus in the fixed proportions case the elasticity of substitution is zero, factor usage does not change in response to a change in factor prices, whereas if capital and labour are perfect substitutes the elasticity of substitution is infinity. While the Cobb–Douglas function lies between these two limits it constrains the elasticity of substitution to be unity, so it too is not as flexible as one might like。

---

[12]   The elasticity of substitution is defined in non-negative form, in effect by using the absolute value of $\partial K/\partial L$, the marginal rate of substitution, which is always non-positive。

The major development which took place to overcome this
constraint was the specification of the constant elasticity
of substitution, CES, production function by Arrow *et al.*
(1961) which permitted any elasticity of substitution and not
just unity. The Cobb-Douglas function is thus a special case
of the CES function. This new specification is of course
still restrictive as the elasticity of substitution is
constant, but this can also be relaxed with the VES, variable
elasticity of substitution, production functions developed
by Lu and Fletcher (1968) and Sato and Hoffman (1968).
We will return to the VES and other functions later (pp. 105-
113) but for the meantime let us concentrate on the CES
function. Its form is rather more complex than the Cobb-
Douglas,

$$Q = b \ [cK^{-d} + (1 - c) \ L^{-d}]^{-1/d}. \qquad (27)$$

The derivation of this function is fairly time consuming and
is clearly set out in Evans (1969) pp. 256-258, for example,
so we shall not repeat it here.[13] The general form of the
function is clear - c indicates the weighting of capital and

---

[13]
The original Arrow *et al.*(1961) article, although very well
written, is probably not the easiest description of the
rationale and mathematical background to the function.

labour, b like a_0 in the Cobb-Douglas function (6) is a
factor reflecting the scale of operation and d is a substitution parameter. The term d is not the elasticity of
substitution itself, e, but $d = (1 - e)/e$.

We said at the outset of this chapter that after
concentrating on specification in the previous chapter on the
consumption function, we would now turn our attention to
estimation. In the case of the Cobb-Douglas function we saw
that it was easy to transform an equation which was not
initially linear into a linear form by taking logarithms.
Although there were further problems posed by identification
and simultaneity we were able to suggest estimation methods
which seem generally acceptable. The CES function is not so
straightforward. We clearly cannot just take logarithms and
develop the estimation in the same way as we did for Cobb-
Douglas. Arrow *et al.* proceed by a simple use of the marginal
product conditions under profit maximization. The marginal
product of labour

$$\frac{\partial Q}{\partial L} = b^{-d} c \ (1 - c) \ (Q/L)^{1+d}. \tag{28}$$

Following (19) this is equal to W/P.

$$b^{-d} c (1 - c) \ (Q/L)^{1+d} = W/P \tag{29}$$

and rearranging

$$\frac{Q}{L} = \left[\frac{b^d}{(1-c)}\right]^e \left(\frac{W}{P}\right)^e \tag{30}$$

where e, the elasticity of substitution, is equal, as we said earlier, to $\frac{1}{1+d}$. This is susceptible to logarithmic transformation

$$\log (Q/L) = b^* + e \log (W/P) \tag{31}$$

where $b^* = e \log [b^d/ (1-c)]$.

It must be borne in mind at this point that Arrow *et al.* were primarily concerned to show that the Cobb-Douglas assumption of a unit elasticity of substitution was inappropriate. This they purport to show by using a cross-section of 19 countries from which the results in Table 3.3 are derived.[14] These results show that in 9 cases out of 24 the estimated elasticity of substitution is significantly less than unity and in all but one case the elasticity is less than unity although not necessarily significantly so. Thus although the unit elasticity is not rejected in all cases it is sometimes, which is of course quite sufficient justification for abandoning the constraint that all elasticities of substitution shall be unity.

---

[14] If a cross-section from different countries had not been used and all data taken from the same market the model would not have been identified as W/P would be the same for all firms.

Unfortunately Arrow *et al.'s* results are not necessarily acceptable. Fuchs (1963) pointed out that the range
of countries used was very great; some could be classified
a developed and others as less-developed. It is arguable
that one might not expect both groups to be governed by the
same production function. He shows, however, that while it
is reasonable to accept a common elasticity of substitution
it is not reasonable to expect the constant term in (32), b^*,
to be the same for both groups. If a dummy variable is inserted into the equation

$$\log \ (Q/L) \ = \ b^* + b_1^* \ D + e \ \log \ (W/P) \tag{32}$$

where $D = 1$ for developed countries and $= 0$ for less-developed
countries a new set of estimates is obtained. These are shown
on the right-hand side of Table 3.3.   In this case only 9 of
the 24 industries have elasticities of substitution less than
unity and none of them are significantly less at 5 per cent
and one is significantly larger. The position has therefore
changed as finding only 1 'significant' difference out of 24
does not lead us to reject the unit elasticity hypothesis of
the Cobb-Douglas function. However, this is not to say that
the CES function is to be rejected. This is only one set of
data; in his study of Nigerian manufacturing industry
Iyaniwura (1974) gives estimates for 6 of his 12 industries
for the years 1965-9 and these are shown in Table 3.4.

Table 3.3   The CES production function - elasticity of substitution

Industry	Estimate by Arrow et al. (1961)	Rank	Estimate by Fuchs (1963)	Rank
Dairy products	0.721 (0.073)**	1	0.902 (0.080)	4
Tobacco	0.753 (0.151)	2	1.215 (0.208)	21
Sugar	0.781 (0.115)	3	0.898 (0.183)	3
Knitting mills	0.785 (0.064)**	4	0.948 (0.083)	7
Textile spinning and weaving	0.809 (0.068)	5	0.976 (0.104)	9
Iron and steel	0.811 (0.051)	6	0.756 (0.112)	2
Basic chemicals	0.831 (0.070)*	7	1.113 (0.104)	20
Fats and oils	0.839 (0.090)	8	1.058 (0.181)	15
Fruit and vegetable cannings	0.855 (0.075)	9	1.086 (0.098)	19
Leather finishing	0.857 (0.062)*	10	0.975 (0.100)	8
Lumber and wood	0.860 (0.066)*	11	1.083 (0.141)	18
Printing and publishing	0.868 (0.056)*	12	1.021 (0.085)	11
Electrical machinery	0.870 (0.118)	13	1.026 (0.214)	12
Furniture	0.894 (0.042)*	14	1.043 (0.090)	13
Miscellaneous chemicals	0.895 (0.059)	15	1.060 (0.088)	16
Bakery products	0.900 (0.065)	16	1.056 (0.105)	14
Ceramics	0.901 (0.044)*	17	1.308 (0.217)	17
Metal products	0.902 (0.088)	18	1.006 (0.166)	10
Grain and mill products	0.909 (0.096)	19	1.324 (0.167)	24
Clay products	0.919 (0.098)	20	0.658 (0.197)	1
Cement	0.920 (0.149)	21	1.308 (0.217)	23
Pulp and paper	0.965 (0.101)	22	0.912 (0.175)	5
Glass	0.999 (0.084)	23	1.269 (0.096)**	22
Non-ferrous metals	1.011 (0.120)	24	0.935 (0.197)	6

* Significantly different from unity at 5%
** at 1%

Table 3.4   Elasticity of substitution in Nigerian industry - CES production function estimated by Arrow et al. method

	1965	1966	1967	1968	1969
Bakery Products	1.029 (0.240)	0.691 (0.337)	0.960 (0.261)	0.592 (0.288)	0.858 (0.284)
Textile Industry	1.026 (0.174)	0.815 (0.739)	0.739 (0.318)	1.007 (0.229)	0.704 (0.183)
Sawmills	1.283 (0.137)	1.288 (0.150)	0.763 (0.267)	0.476 (0.341)	0.905 (0.277)
Printing and Publishing	1.026 (0.169)	0.875 (0.189)	0.770 (0.195)	1.015 (0.210)	1.024 (0.237)
Chemical Products	1.359 (0.233)	0.522 (0.465)	0.967 (0.213)	0.929 (0.293)	1.300 (0.242)
Metal Products	0.263 (0.152)	0.292 (0.226)	0.590 (0.181)	0.468 (0.172)	0.254 (0.197)

Source: Iyaniwura (1974)

Table 3.5 *Elasticity of substitution in Norwegian industry*

Industry	CES[a]
Meat products	1.02
Milk products	0.65[b]
Canneries	1.13
Fish-food products	0.94
Grain mills	1.56
Bakeries	0.93
Beverages	0.92
Textile manufacture	1.00
Footwear	1.43
Suits, coats and dresses	1.03
Other textile and apparel products	1.34
Lumber mills	0.70[b]
Wood and cork products	0.86
Furniture	0.90
Wooden fixtures	0.97
Paper industry	1.16
Printing industry	0.65[b]
Industrial chemicals	2.58[b]
Fish oil and meal products	0.64
Other chemicals	1.38
Clay and glass products	1.01
Cement products	1.39[b]
Basic metal industries	1.03
Metal products[c]	0.86
Non-electrical machinery	0.78
Electrical machinery	0.81
Transport equipment	0.29[b]

[a] non-constant returns to scale are allowed for.
[b] coefficient differs from unity by more than twice its computed standard error.
[c] not elsewhere specified.
Source: Griliches and Ringstad (1971).

Many of the computed elasticities are widely different from
unity, but the equations are frequently poorly determined
so it is difficult to generalize. However, it is clear that
the assumption of unit elasticities does not apply in all
cases. This result is confirmed by Griliches and Ringstad
(1971) where out of 27 Norwegian industries studied only six
show elasticities which deviate from unity by more than
twice their standard errors. As is clear from Table 3.5, there
is no particular industrial pattern to this finding.

The drawback of the direct approach to estimating the
CES production function is that we do not obtain estimates
of the parameters b and c. While this is not always essential
we may often want to distinguish between the scale effect,
b , and the distribution between the two factors, c. Kmenta
(1967) suggests using a Taylor series expansion to linearize
the CES function in order to estimate it.[15]

---

[15]
    This expansion is an important idea and is explained in
Ahlfors (1953), pp. 140-146 and Olmsted (1959) pp. 240-253
for example. It can be thought of in the following manner.
It is fortunate that most analytic functions can be represented through a convergent power series. The Taylor series is a
convergent power series which is extremely useful because its
terms are very amenable to incorporation in linear models. A
function $f(x)$ can be written as the series

$$f(x) = f(x_0) + f'(x_0)(x - x_0) + \frac{f''(x_0)}{2}(x - x_0)^2 + \ldots$$

$$+ \frac{f^{(n)}(x_0)}{n!}(x - x_0)^n + \ldots.$$

If we take logarithms of the CES function we obtain[16]

$$\log Q = \log b + (-\frac{f}{d}) \, A \, (d) \tag{33}$$

where

$$A \, (d) = \log \, [cK^{-d} + (1 - c) \, L^{-d}]. \tag{34}$$

This can be linearized approximately by using a Taylor series

expansion of $A \, (d)$ round $d = 0$

$$A \, (d) = A \, (0) + dA' \, (0) + \frac{d^2}{2} \, A'' \, (0) + \ldots \tag{35}$$

where the ' denotes a first order differential, '' a second

order, etc.

---

where f', f'', $\ldots$, $f^{(n)}$ denote the first, second and nth
differentials of the function and x_0 is some origin. Thus if
we chose zero as the origin $f \, (x)$ becomes

$$f \, (x) = f \, (0) + f' \, (0) \, x + \frac{f'' \, (0)}{2} \, x^2 + \ldots$$

The advantage of this Taylor series, known as a Maclaurin
series if the origin is zero, is that even with the inclusion
of only a few terms it becomes a close approximation to $f \, (x)$
in many of the circumstances we will come across.

[16]

As was noted at the foot of Table 3.5 the CES function can
be modified to allow increasing or decreasing returns to scale.
Under these circumstances the function becomes

$$Q = b \, [cK^{-d} + (1 - c) \, L^{-d}] - f/d$$

where f is the returns to scale parameter.

$$A (0) = 0 \tag{36}$$

$$A' (0) = - [c \log K + (1 - c) \log L]^{17} \tag{37}$$

and

$$A'' (0) = \{c \log^2 K + (1 - c) \log^2 L - [c \log K +$$

$$(1 - c) \log L]^2\}$$

$$= c (1 - c) (\log K - \log L)^2. \tag{38}$$

Substituting into (33)[18] we obtain

$$\log Q = \log b - fc \log K - f (1 - c) \log L$$

$$+ \frac{dfc(1 - c)}{2} (\log K - \log L)^2. \tag{39}$$

We thus obtain in (39) a form which is the same as the Cobb-Douglas with the addition of the last term and hence have an interesting means of contrasting the two. (39) of course has been expressed without an error term and we must once again recall that for additive errors, u, in (39) the CES function must have a multiplicative error[19]

---

[17]
Rather than complicate the derivation by explaining this fairly complex differentiation the result is stated - a fuller explanation is given in Bridge (1971).

[18]
Neglecting higher order terms in the Taylor series by assuming that the first two are a sufficiently close approximation.

[19]
Iyaniwura (1974) compares the results of assuming additive as opposed to multiplicative errors in these production functions, but parameter estimates are not greatly affected.

$$Q = b \ [cK^{-d} + (1 - c) \ L^{-d}]^{\ -f/d} e^u.\qquad (40)$$

Griliches and Ringstad, pp. 71-72, compare estimates of (9)
with those of (39) for their 27 Norwegian manufacturing
industries. On the whole the addition of the $(\log K - \log L)^2$
term does little to improve the estimates - the standard
error of estimate falls in only 11 cases. Furthermore the
Cobb-Douglas estimates are little changed by the addition of
the further variable in the remaining 16 instances.

3.4   Further developments

Although interest still centres on the Cobb-Douglas and
CES forms of the production function, these by no means represent the limits that research has reached.   A thorough
survey and analysis of recent work runs beyond the scope of
this book, but the directions of it and the motivations for
it are clear. In the first place the problem is to try to
approximate a non-linear relation in a straightforward manner.
This entails that the form of the function to be estimated
has a relatively small number of parameters so that there are
sufficient degrees of freedom for the estimates to be well
determined and the estimation technique employed to be
manageable. Secondly it must be possible for the specification
to cope with varieties of assumptions about the nature of
returns to scale and the elasticity of substitution while

maintaining plausible marginal productivities for the
various factors. Thirdly, it is often desirable to consider
the role of other inputs besides labour and capital. While
these two factors between them receive the entire rewards
from the value added in production other factors can
affect the size of that value-added, most importantly
material inputs. This is shown clearly by Griliches and
Ringstad (1971).

However, let us proceed by taking these three points in
turn. First, approximating the shape of a non-linear relation
- we noted in the last section that Kmenta's (1967) approximation to the CES function involved adding terms to the basic
Cobb-Douglas form. This has been further developed by
Christensen *et al.*(1973) into the translog or 'transcendental
logarithmic' production function

$$\log Q = b_0 + b_1 \log K + b_2 \log L + b_3 \log K \log L$$

$$+ b_4 (\log K)^2 + b_5 (\log L)^2 + u. \qquad (41)$$

If $b_3 = b_4 = b_5 = 0$ then this is the Cobb-Douglas function and
if $b_4 = b_5 = -b_3/2$ then it is the Kmenta approximation to the
CES. Clearly, therefore it can be used to give a close

approximation to a wide range of curvilinear relations.[20]

Griliches and Ringstad point out that (41) can be used to

test whether the elasticity of substitution is in fact con-

stant as the CES model suggests. Using all the firms in their

sample from Norwegian manufacturing industry they obtain

$$\log V = 1.6 + 0.958 \log L + 0.241 \log K* - 0.026 (\log L)^2$$
$$\quad\quad\quad (0.040) \quad\quad\quad (0.033) \quad\quad\quad (0.011)$$

$$-0.010 (\log K*)^2 + 0.019 \log L \log K* \,^{21}$$
$$(0.007) \quad\quad\quad\quad (0.016)$$

$$(42)$$

and then test $H_0 : b_4 = b_5 = -b_3/2 = c_3$, where c_3 is the

coefficient in the Kmenta approximation (39) if we rewrite

it as

$$\log V = c_0 + c_1 \log K + c_2 \log L + c_3 (\log K - \log L)^2.$$

$$(43)$$

20
    These, of course, need not be production functions and
there is an interesting application to several areas relating
to economic growth in Japan and the United States in
Jorgenson and Nishimizu (1978).

21
    V is value-added rather than quantity of output, which is
a common transformation avoiding difficulties from variations
in the nature of material inputs. Their capital variable $K*$
is a capital flow variable representing the cost of capital
services in the current period rather than the value of the
capital stock.

Using a simple Chow test[22] they obtain an F value of 11.6

(with 2 and 5,355 degrees of freedom) which is considerably

larger than the upper 5 per cent point of the distribution,

3.0. Griliches and Ringstad go on to point out that the

estimated coefficients of b_3 and b_4 are not significantly

different from zero at the 5 per cent level and therefore

try re-estimating the function with them set equal to zero,

obtaining

$$\log V = 1.7 + \underset{(0.029)}{0.995} \log L + \underset{(0.009)}{0.204} \log K* - \underset{(0.003)}{0.017} (\log L)^2.$$

$$(44)$$

The determination of each of the remaining variables is

greatly improved in (44) compared to the full specification

(42) and the improvement on the Cobb-Douglas form is clearly

shown.

---

[22] This test is fully explained in Goldberger (1964) pp. 176-177. It tests the hypothesis that a variable or group of variables adds nothing to the explanation of the dependent variable, this is equivalent to saying that the coefficients of variables are not significantly different from zero. The test is in the form of an F-statistic using the residual sum of squares from the regression on all the variables, RSS_u, and the residual sum of squares from the regression with the particular variable or variables omitted (thus constraining their coefficients to be zero), RSS_c,

$$F_{(N_c, \, N-K)} = \frac{(RSS_c - RSS_u)/N_c}{RSS_u/(N-K)}$$

where N_c is the number of variables constrained to have a zero effect under the null hypothesis, N is the number of observations on the data; and K is the total number of variables in the unconstrained regression.

This model also illustrates the second point which we made concerning assumptions about returns to scale, elasticities of substitution and other properties of production functions. The elasticity of scale in this case is estimated to be $1.199 - 0.034 \log L$ which means not only that returns to scale are not constant but their nature depends on scale. The range of elasticities varies from 1.114 for the smallest size of firms (3 to 9 employees) to 0.993 for the largest size group (100 or more employees). Hence there are increasing returns to scale when firms are small and virtually constant returns at the larger levels of operation. This important result confirms the general view of economic theory – that there are economies of scale in production but that these die away as the scale increases.[23]

Although Griliches and Ringstad conclude (p. 92) that the suggestion that the elasticity is not unity is '"not proven" rather than "not guilty"' considerable steps have been made elsewhere to estimate variable elasticities of

---

[23] This finding on economies of scale is not a quirk of the particular estimation method or specification. Griliches and Ringstad estimate five versions of the Cobb-Douglas and CES functions and obtain values of the scale coefficient, (measured by the sum of the output elasticities with respect to labour and capital) ranging between 1.064 and 1.070 with a maximum standard error of 0.006 showing very clearly that there are economies of scale rather than constant returns to scale.

substitution. This VES production function was developed by
Lu and Fletcher (1968), Sato and Hoffman (1968) and
Revankar (1971). Revankar finds that in five of the twelve
US industries studied the VES specification is to be preferred
to the CES. The direction of change observed is that the more
labour intensive is the industry the greater the elasticity
of substitution. This again fits in with basic economic
prejudice - sophisticated capital intensive technologies are
more likely to be difficult to change than more basic labour
intensive structures. This therefore gives isoquants of the
form shown in Fig. 3.4.[24] It is worth noting in passing that
while the VES function gives a variable elasticity of
substitution along each isoquant the elasticity is constant
along any ray from the origin such as OA.

The last development we mentioned concerned the introduction of other inputs. This is a much more simple task than the
previous two possibilities we have considered and was tackled
at any early stage in the development of the analysis of the

---

[24]
The production function has the form

$$Q = d_0 K^{d_1(1-d_2 d_3)} [L + (d_3 - 1) K]^{d_1 d_2 d_3}$$

where the elasticity of substitution, $d_4 = 1 + \dfrac{d_3 - 1}{1 - d_2 d_3} \dfrac{K}{L}$.

The values of the parameters used in Fig. 3.4 are $Q = 50$,
$d_0 = 2.5$, $d_1 = 1$ and $d_2 = 0.6$.

Figure 3.4   Isoquants from the Revankar VES model

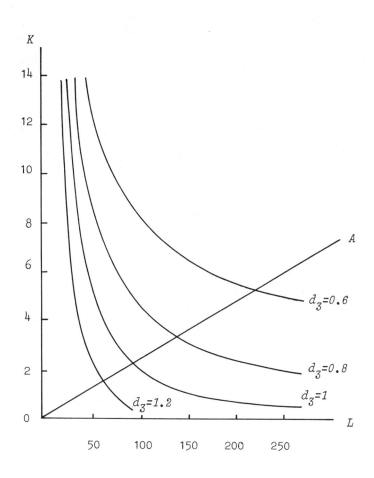

Source: Revankar (1971).

production function. In Klein's (1953) railway analysis

which we mentioned on pp. 91-92 he distinguishes between

labour, capital services, as measured by train hours, and

fuel consumption, F, giving the model

$$Q = a_0 L^{a_1} K^{a_2} F^{a_3} T_1^{a_4} T_2^{a_5} e^u \qquad (45)$$

where u is a multiplicative error term, T_1 and T_2 are

variables which allow for changes in the technical composition

of the production function, due to the average length of

journeys and the type of material carried respectively, and the

a_i are parameters. Hildebrand and Liu (1965) distinguish bet-

ween two sorts of labour input in their model

$$V = a_0 L_1^{a_1} L_2^{a_2} K^{a_3} e^u \qquad (46)$$

where L_1 and L_2 are production and non-production employees

respectively (V is value-added).[25]

This procedure of adding variables, usually appropriately

specified to avoid unpleasant consequences for estimation,

has been applied to most functions including the CES and the

translog function. In the latter case of course the cross-

product terms are also required so that if material inputs,

M, are included we have

---

[25] This model also provides another interesting approach to the problem caused by the simultaneous determination of both output and inputs.

$$\log Q = a_0 + a_1 \log L + a_2 \log K + a_3 \log M$$
$$+ a_4 (\log L)^2 + a_5 (\log K)^2 + a_6 (\log M)^2$$
$$+ a_7 \log L \log K + a_8 \log L \log M$$
$$+ a_9 \log K \log M + u. \qquad\qquad (47)$$

Griliches and Ringstad include materials explicitly in the
estimation of both the Cobb-Douglas and CES functions to test
the hypothesis that standard estimation without including
materials is satisfactory. As their original functions stand,
(42), (43), (44), for example, material inputs are subtracted
from both sides of the equation as the dependent variable is
value-added. This has several advantages and will not result
in biased results either if materials bear a fixed relation to
value added (a fixed coefficient model) or if they are
infinitely elastic. In the latter case since any combination
is possible, materials will not affect the capital and
labour parameters. In practice, of course, the actual elasticity lies between these extremes but Griliches and Ringstad
conclude that it is large enough to justify the omission of
materials from the equation.

3.5 Conclusions

In this chapter we have introduced a further area of
economic behaviour which applies not just to the whole economy
but also to individual firms. It has been very clear that

without the econometric work which has been considered the
theoretical form of production functions would remain very
ill-defined. We have seen that the ordinary least squares model
can be applied to economic models which are not linear by appropriate transformation and approximation. However, it is
also becoming clear that there are many circumstances in
which the restrictive assumptions of the OLS model do not
apply. We shall in particular move on to consider the difficulty of relations between consecutive time periods which are
posed by much economic time series analysis. In dealing with
production functions we have ignored the problem of technical
progress, which may make the study of such functions over
time very difficult because of changes in the technological
structure. We shall, therefore, look at the problem of the
renewal, expansion and development of capital over time in the
next chapter.

In looking back over this chapter we can see the way
in which empirical analysis has developed, first to give
plausible shapes to isoquants and then to take account of
returns to scale, different and variable elasticities of
substitution and the incorporation of other factors beside
labour and capital. Perhaps the most important point is the
realisation that the study of simultaneous equations and
identification will be necessary to enable the analysis of

many common economic problems. We shall therefore move on to consider first multiple equation models in Chapter 5 and simultaneity in Chapter 6.

References and Suggested Reading*

AHLFORS, L.V. (1953) *Complex Analysis,* New York: McGraw-Hill.

*ARROW, K.J., CHENERY, H.B., MINHAS, B.S. AND SOLOW, R.M.
(1961) 'Capital-labor substitution and economic eff-
iciency', *Review of Economics and Statistics,* vol. 43,
pp. 225-50.

*BRIDGE, J.L. (1971) *Applied Econometrics,* Amsterdam:
North Holland.

*CHRISTENSEN, L.R., JORGENSON, D.W. AND LAU, L.J. (1973)
'Transcendental logarithmic production frontiers',
Review of Economics and Statistics, vol. 55, pp. 28-45.

COBB, C.W. AND DOUGLAS, P.H. (1928) 'A theory of production',
American Economic Review, vol. 18 (Supplement) pp. 139-65.

*DOUGLAS, P.H. (1948) 'Are there laws of production?' *American
Economic Review,* vol. 38, pp. 1-41.

*EVANS, M.K. (1968) *Macroeconomic Activity,* Evanston:
Harper and Row.

*FUCHS, V.R. (1963) 'Capital-labour substitution: A note',
Review of Economics and Statistics, vol. 45, pp. 436-8.

GOLDBERGER, A.S. (1964) *Economic Theory*, New York: Wiley.

*GRILICHES, Z. AND RINGSTAD, V. (1971) *Economies of Scale and the Form of the Production Function*, Amsterdam: North Holland.

*HARCOURT, G.C. AND LAING, N.F. (1971) eds. *Capital and Growth*, Penguin.

HILDEBRAND, G.H. AND LIU, T.C. (1965), *Manufacturing Production Function in the United States, 1957*, Ithaca: New York State School of Industrial Relations.

IYANIWURA, J.O. (1974) 'Production functions in Nigerian manufacturing industry' PhD thesis, University of Exeter.

JORGENSON, D.W. AND NISHIMIZU, M. (1978) 'US and Japanese economic growth, 1952-74: An international comparison', *Economic Journal*, vol. 88, pp. 707-726 (December).

*KENNEDY, M.C. AND THIRLWALL, A.P. (1972) 'Technical change: a survey', *Economic Journal*, vol. 82, pp. 11-73.

KLEIN, L.R (1953) *A Textbook of Econometrics*, Evanston: Row, Peterson.

KMENTA, J. (1967) 'An estimation of the CES production function', *International Economic Review*, vol. 8, pp. 180-9.

LEONTIEF, W.W. (1951) *The Structure of the American Economy, 1919-1939: An Empirical Application of Equilibrium Analysis*, New York: Oxford University Press.

LESLIE, D. AND WISE, J. (1980) 'The productivity of hours in UK manufacturing and production industry', *Economic Journal* (March).

LU, Y. AND FLETCHER, L.B. (1968) 'A generalization of the CES production function',*Review of Economics and Statistics*, vol. 50 pp. 449-52.

MARSHAK, J. AND ANDREWS, W.H. (1944) 'Random simultaneous equations and the theory of production', *Econometrica*, vol. 12, pp. 143-205.

MOHMED-AHMED, A.E. (1979) 'An Econometric Model of the Sudan' PhD thesis, University of Exeter.

OLMSTED, J.M. (1959) *Real Variables*, New York: Appleton-Century-Crofts.

REVANKAR, N.S. (1971) 'A class of variable elasticity of sub-stitution production functions', *Econometrica*, vol. 39, pp. 61-71.

SATO, R. AND HOFFMAN, R.F. (1968) 'Production functions with variable elasticity of factor substitution: Some analysis and testing', *Review of Economics and Statistics*, vol. 50, pp. 453-60.

STONE, J.R.N. AND BROWN, J.A.C. (1963) *Input-Output Relation-ships 1954-1966*, no. 3 in *A Programme for Growth*, Department of Applied Economics, University of Cambridge, London: Chapman and Hall.

ZELLNER, A., KMENTA, J. AND DREZE, J. (1966) 'Specification and estimation of Cobb-Douglas production function models', *Econometrica*, vol. 34, pp. 727-9.

Chapter 4

INVESTMENT

In the last chapter we considered the transformation
of labour and capital into output. In this chapter we shall
consider the determinants of capital formation, not just
because this is a logical next step in studying economic
behaviour, but because investment presents an ideal area for
the development of our methods of econometric analysis. The
data which were used in the estimation of production functions
were of two forms, cross-sections of several firms in a single
time period and time series at a higher level of aggregation.
However, in both cases output in a period was determined by the
inputs employed in that same time period. There was no carry
over of determination from one period to the next (although it
is arguable that there should have been for some of the time
series data). Investment on the other hand is an inherently
dynamic process, and in estimating its determinants we shall
need to use values of variables from several previous periods.

Furthermore the existence of such inter-temporal relations
may extend to the disturbance terms of the series and we shall
hence have to consider problems of autocorrelation.

This chapter therefore begins with a short consideration
of the theory of investment behaviour and then moves on to
explain how lags may be incorporated into the system. A number
of these lag models are applied to data for the United Kingdom
and the chapter is concluded by discussion of other approaches
to the explanation of investment. An important distinction is
made between models which emphasise the role of output
(flexible accelerator models), and whose justification is generally rather ad hoc, and models which emphasise the role of
relative prices (neo-classical models) which are derived from
explicit optimising models.

4.1   Investment Behaviour

As was indicated in the previous section the level of
investment cannot be divorced in our consideration from the size
of the capital stock which it helps to build up. Investment is
thus a 'flow' concept. The capital stock, K_t, at the end of
a time period t is composed of the capital at the end of the
previous time period, K_{t-1}, less capital consumed during the
period, D_t, plus the level of total investment,

$$K_t = K_{t-1} - D_t + I_t^G. \tag{1}$$

The net investment contributing to the increase in the capital stock is thus

$$I_t^N = K_t - K_{t-1} = I_t^G - D_t. \tag{2}$$

Therefore while gross investment is necessarily non-negative, as capital consumption cannot by definition be negative, net investment will be positive, zero or negative as $I_t^G \gtreqless D_t$.

There are two problems of economic behaviour to be considered in determining the level of investment. First, what determines the desired capital stock and second, what determines the rate at which investment to achieve that desired stock proceeds? In practice these are often confused. Haavelmo (1960) points out that 'the demand for investment cannot simply be derived from the demand for capital. Demand for a finite addition to the stock of capital can lead to any rate of investment, from almost zero to infinity depending on the additional hypothesis we introduce regarding the speed of reaction of capital users'. To simplify the initial discussion let us assume for the time being that the desired stock, K_t^*, is always achieved by the end of each period.

In elementary analysis, as we saw in the previous chapter, output and capital can be assumed to have a fixed relation[1] so that

$$Q_t = aK_t^* \qquad (3)$$

or inverting the relation

$$K_t^* = bQ_t \qquad (4)$$

where $b = \dfrac{1}{a}$.

Substituting this into (2) and ignoring capital consumption

$$I_t^N = b(Q_t - Q_{t-1}) \qquad (5)$$

gives what is known as the simple accelerator model of investment.[2] Capital consumption is usually[3] assumed to be proportional to the pre-existing capital stock

$$D_t = cK_{t-1}, \qquad (6)$$

---

[1] The fixed relation between capital and output can be derived from the usual neo-classical production function under the assumption of fixed factor prices and constant returns to scale.

[2] It is an 'accelerator' because investment depends on the rate of growth of output.

[3] See Jorgenson and Stephenson (1967) for a clear justification.

thus a simple investment function can be obtained by substituting (4) and (6) into (1) and rearranging

$$I_t^G = bQ_t - b(1 - c) Q_{t-1}.$$ (7)

Investment is thus a function of current and lagged output.

In Fig. 4.1 we have set out the time path of both gross
fixed investment in manufacturing industry in the United
Kingdom and the index of production in manufacturing industry.[4]
The clearest feature of the data is the strong cycle in investment matched by a series of steps in production. It is also
clear that the step up in production occurs before the rapid
recovery in each investment upturn. The relation between the
two variables is therefore obviously going to have to incorporate a lag or lags if it is to be closely determined. If we
estimate equation (7) by ordinary least squares we obtain

$$I_t^G = \underset{(5.02)}{-2.47Q_t} + \underset{(5.04)}{11.94Q_{t-1}}$$

$$R^2 = 0.649 \quad DW = 0.266 \quad SEE = 77.92$$

(standard errors are shown in parentheses).[5]

---

[4]
  Both variables are measured quarterly.

[5]
  Since there is no constant term in this equation the variation
used in calculating R^2 is measured round the origin and not
round the sample mean of I_t^G.

Figure 4.1   Fixed Investment and Production in manufacturing
industry in the United Kingdom, 1955-78, quarterly

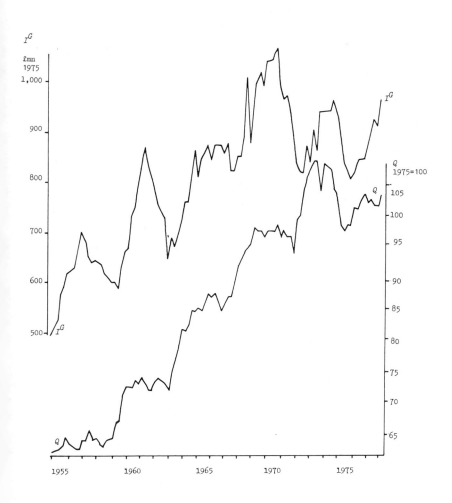

Source: *Economic Trends*, Annual Supplement, 1979.

Clearly this equation is unsatisfactory although we have explained 65 per cent of the variation in investment, first
because it suggests that b is negative and secondly, as the
Durbin–Watson statistic indicates, there is strong positive
autocorrelation.

One reason for the poor performance of (7) is that it is
assumed that the desired capital stock K_t^* is actually achieved.
In practice it is usually felt more reasonable to assume that
only a proportion d of the discrepancy between the desired
capital stock in a particular time period and the capital
stock existing in the previous period can be obtained

$$K_t - K_{t-1} = d \ (K_t^* - K_{t-1}) \quad (0 < d < 1). \tag{8}$$

Using (8), (3) and (6) we can reformulate (7) as

$$I_t^G = dbQ_t - db \ (1 - c) \ Q_{t-1} + (1 - d) \ I_{t-1}^G, \tag{9}$$

so that the partial adjustment of the capital stock results in
the addition of a lagged dependent variable to the right–hand
side of the equation. Not surprisingly this improves the
estimates of the investment function:

$$I_t^G = \underset{(2.42)}{2.05Q_t} - \underset{(2.53)}{0.61Q_{t-1}} + \underset{(0.05)}{0.85I_{t-1}^G}$$

$$R^2 = 0.920 \quad SEE = 37.43$$

However, the improvement lies mainly in the overall fit as indicated by R^2. In terms of the individual coefficients all that the equation appears to tell us is that investment this quarter and investment last quarter are highly related. Moreover, the correlation between Q_t and Q_{t-1} has meant that their individual effects are difficult to disentangle - a typical case of multicollinearity.

A second limitation to this model pointed out by Hines and Catephores (1970) is that the desired capital stock depends only on actual output and not on expected output. In their model they assume that expectations about output are also made on an adaptive basis and hence introduce a longer lag on output into the equation. A simple function like (9) clearly still does not provide a very satisfactory solution; it does not give greatly improved estimates of b, c and d. We must therefore look to more complex explanations.

4.2 A distributed lag model of investment

The general form of investment function developed in the previous section, where investment is a function of output (sales) over the current and previous periods and investment itself over previous periods, is a common feature of many investment functions - see for example Eisner (1960), de Leeuw (1962), Almon (1965) and ch. 4 in Evans (1969). While other variables are added to the equation in some examples, the general form of (9) is

$$e \ (L) \ I_t^G = f \ (L) \ Q_t,\tag{10}$$

where $e \ (L)$ and $f \ (L)$ are functions in the lag operator L.[6]

In equation (9) $e_o = 1$, $e_1 = (1 - d)$, $f_o = db$, $f_1 = -db \ (1 - c)$ and all other values of e_i and f_i are zero.

An early and very celebrated use of distributed lags in investment is Koyck (1954). (It is a pathbreaking book in the field of distributed lags as a whole.) The function known as the 'Koyck lag' (there is a very considerable further discussion in the book) suggests that the capital stock is related to output in the form of a geometric lag after the current quarter.[7]

---

[6]
The lag operator L is a convenient shorthand.   Its definition is that

$$L^i Q_t = Q_{t-i}$$

and hence the general expression

$$f \ (L) \ Q_t = f_0 \ L^0 Q_t + f_1 L^1 Q_t + f_2 L^2 Q_t + \cdots$$
$$= f_0 Q_t + f_1 Q_{t-1} + f_2 Q_{t-2} + \cdots$$

[7]
Koyck's equation is in logarithms.

$$K_t = a_o Q_t + a_1 Q_{t-1} + a_1 b\, Q_{t-2} + a_1 b^2 Q_{t-3} + \cdots$$
$$+\; a_1 b^{i-1} Q_{t-i} + \cdots \tag{11}$$

$$= a_o Q_t + a_1 \sum_0^\infty b^i Q_{t-i-1} \quad (0 < b < 1). \tag{12}$$

Lagging (13) by one period and multiplying by b

$$bK_{t-1} = a_o\, bQ_{t-1} + a_1 \sum_0^\infty b^{i+1}\, Q_{t-i-2} \tag{13}$$

and subtracting (13) from (12)

$$K_t - bK_{t-1} = a_o Q_t + (a_1 - a_o b)\, Q_{t-1} \tag{14}$$

enables us to express (11) in the form

$$I_t^N = a_o\, Q_t + (a_1 - a_o b)\, Q_{t-1} - (1 - b)\, K_{t-1} \tag{15}$$

It is not, however, generally believed that the simple
system of geometrically declining weights is necessarily the
best representation of lags in behaviour. In particular there
are specific causes of the delay between a level of output and
the consequent investment. In the first place decision-making
is not immediate, the firm likes to see what sales and profits
it has made before deciding upon investment and hence there
will be higher weights on output over the previous three to
twelve months than over the current quarter. In the second
place it takes several months and even years to construct many
forms of capital equipment and buildings, and hence current

investment may merely be part of a large project which was decided upon and commenced several time periods ago. There are thus decision and construction lags which suggest that the pattern of the weights in the lag distribution rises in the first place as we move back through previous periods and then falls. (Equation (11) in fact permits a peak at a lag of one quarter.) Evans (1969) goes further than this and suggests that the peak of the decision lag will occur before the peak of the construction lag and hence the lag distribution will have two peaks and will take the form of what he describes as an 'inverted W' as shown in Fig. 4.2.   The actual distribution which Evans estimates (Evans (1967), p. 155) has a rather smoother form with two peaks of equal 'height' in quarters 1 and 6 and only a relatively limited decline between them (the weight in period 4 - the minimum value between the peaks is higher than that in the ninth and subsequent periods). This is drawn as the line in bold dashes in Fig. 4.2, where it should be noted that the relation is between investment and output directly, and not between the capital stock and output.

These complications to the lag distribution have repercussions for estimation. We could just include all the lagged values we wish to consider in the equation and see what happens to the ordinary least squares estimates.

Figure 4.2 Time Path of Investment Response to a Change in Sales

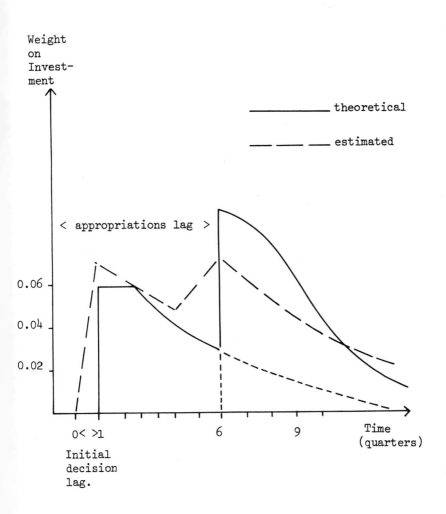

Source: Evans (1967) p. 152 and Evans (1969)

However, if these were a large number of lagged values
we might have very few degrees of freedom and would be likely
to suffer from considerable collinearity, making the estimates
rather imprecise and unstable.   To get over this problem, use
is usually made of some form of constraint on the coefficients
of the lag distribution.   In the Koyck case only three parameters were used to describe the entire distribution, a_o, a_1
and b.

The simplest solution is to decide on the form of the
distribution, such as giving equal weights or an inverted V
as suggested by de Leeuw (1962).[8]   In those two cases there
is only one parameter to estimate in the distribution. Other
distributions may be estimated by including further parameters.
Evans' inverted W, for example is estimated as

$$I_t^G = b_o + b_1\, Q_{t-1}/K_{t-1} + b_2\, Q_{t-5.5} + b_3\, K_{t-5.5}$$
$$+ b_4\, F_{t-5.5} + b_5\, R_{t-5.5} \tag{16}$$

---

[8]
  de Leeuw describes the weights in the inverted V as 'the
first half of the (weights) are proportional to the rising
series 1, 2, 3, ..., $[k]/2$ (for even values of k) and the last
half proportional to the declining series $[k]/2$, $([k]/2)-1$,
..., 3, 2, 1.' His investment function also includes further
variables,

$$I_t^G - b\ (L)\ I_t^G = a_1 b\ (L)\ CR + a_2 b\ (L)\ F +$$
$$a_3 b\ (L)\ R + b\ (L)\ u$$

where $V_{t-5.5} = \frac{1}{2} (V_{t-5} + V_{t-6})$ and the two capital stock
variables each incorporate a Koyck lag, the first starting
after one quarter and the second after $5\frac{1}{2}$ quarters, thus giving the inverted W. However, it may be that one only has an
approximate view of the exact form of the distribution such as
the position of the peak or peaks, in which case a different
technique must be applied.

An alternative approach is to choose the form of the lag
distribution and estimate the parameters of that from the
sample of observations on the individual variable separately
first.   Then using these previously calculated weights on
the variable the full investment equation can be estimated.
Almon (1965) used this method and fitted a polynomial distributed lag[9] to output before estimating the investment
equation as a whole.

---

w₁ere $b(L)$ is the inverted V distribution, CR is defined as
capital requirements (which are related to a capacity utilis-
ation index), F is internal funds – undistributed profits plus
depreciation allowances, R is the industrial bond yield and u
is an error term.

[9]
In view of the relative complexity of this lag structure we
shall begin our explanation by indicating what shapes of lag
distribution this permits and only then proceed to a formal
definition of 'polynomial' lags.

The use of this form of estimation for the lag distribution requires the choice of only two parameters, p, the
order of the polynominal and, k, the number of past periods
over which the weights in distribution are non-zero. (It is
also possible to constrain the shape of the distribution so
that one or both of the weights on the end periods of the
distribution are zero.)[10] This enables us to fit a very wide
range of shapes, as is illustrated in Fig. 4.3. A zero order
polynomial gives a rectangular distribution and a first order,
a triangular distribution of the weights. Successive higher
orders allow curves with one, two, three, etc. turning points.
The actual shape is generated by the data and in Fig. 4.3 we
have merely assumed that the weights are largely positive. The
problem is to choose the most appropriate shape and length of
distribution, but *a priori* information may be limited.   While
there are criteria which can be used to aid this choice it is
not an easy one to make and Thomas (1977) has shown that poor
choices can lead to very erroneous results. The general method
of approach is to consider only a low order polynomial, $p \leq 4$,
which is consistent with the theoretical pattern which the
distribution can have. Thus unless the distribution may be
rectangular or triangular this involves a choice between,
second, third and fourth order polynomials. In order to show
the effects of this we have estimated first to fourth order
Almon lags for our data for the UK. The estimates are shown in

---

[10]
    For $p \geq 2$

Table 4.1   Alternative Almon Lag Distributions on Output

Weights $t=0$	(1)	(2)	(3)	(4)	(5)	(6)	(7)	(8)	(9)	(10)
Order of Polynomial	1	2	3	4	5	6	4	4	4	4
$t=0$	1.13 (0.10)	1.16 (1.31)	-4.81 (2.89)	-5.59 (4.53)	-3.52 (3.99)	1.65 (1.92)	0.0	-2.55 (1.51)	0.0	0.0
1	0.13 (0.10)	1.15 (0.80)	2.28 (0.92)	3.19 (4.14)	1.27 (2.66)	1.96 (0.53)	2.61 (0.35)	1.87 (0.56)	1.68 (0.41)	1.93 (0.20)
2	1.13 (0.10)	1.14 (0.29)	5.83 (2.06)	6.37 (3.15)	4.51 (2.98)	2.27 (0.77)	3.78 (0.49)	4.18 (0.54)	2.75 (0.54)	3.03 (0.31)
3	1.13 (0.10)	1.13 (0.26)	5.84 (2.06)	5.30 (3.15)	5.76 (1.65)	2.52 (0.99)	3.82 (0.47)	4.80 (0.75)	3.27 (0.46)	3.43 (0.34)
4	1.13 (0.10)	1.12 (0.76)	2.30 (0.91)	1.39 (4.15)	4.61 (3.00)	2.64 (0.84)	3.02 (0.34)	4.16 (0.75)	3.31 (0.32)	3.26 (0.32)
5	1.13 (0.10)	1.11 (1.28)	-4.78 (2.84)	-4.00 (4.48)	0.64 (2.66)	2.55 (0.56)	1.71 (0.14)	2.68 (0.59)	2.92 (0.36)	2.67 (0.24)
6					-6.59 (3.96)	2.19 (0.56)	0.17 (0.12)	0.78 (0.38)	2.15 (0.56)	1.77 (0.14)
7						1.48 (0.85)	-1.27 (0.32)	-1.11 (0.33)	1.08 (0.71)	0.71 (0.05)
8						0.37 (0.99)	-2.31 (0.45)	-2.55 (0.47)	-0.23 (0.71)	-0.37 (0.12)
9						-1.23 (0.78)	-2.65 (0.48)	-3.13 (0.55)	-1.74 (0.51)	-1.35 (0.22)
10						-3.39 (0.50)	-1.99 (0.34)	-2.42 (0.42)	-3.38 (0.50)	-2.10 (0.30)
11						-6.16 (1.88)	0.0	0.0	-5.07 (1.39)	-2.47 (0.33)
12										-2.33 (0.30)
13										-1.55 (0.19)
SEE	71.6	72.1	70.2	70.6	69.5	57.84	62.1	61.34	57.7	57.3

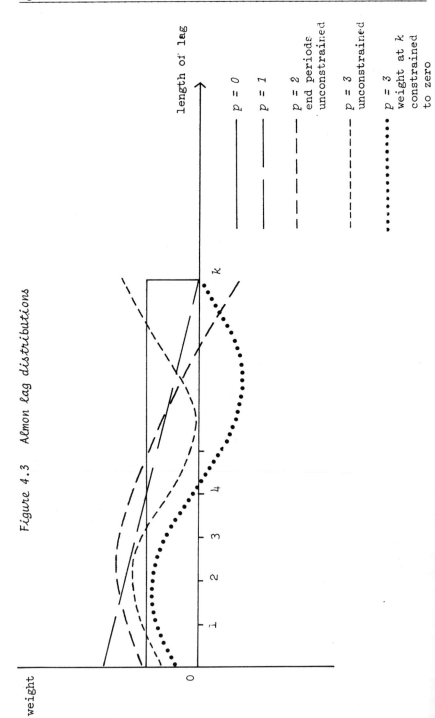

Figure 4.3   Almon lag distributions

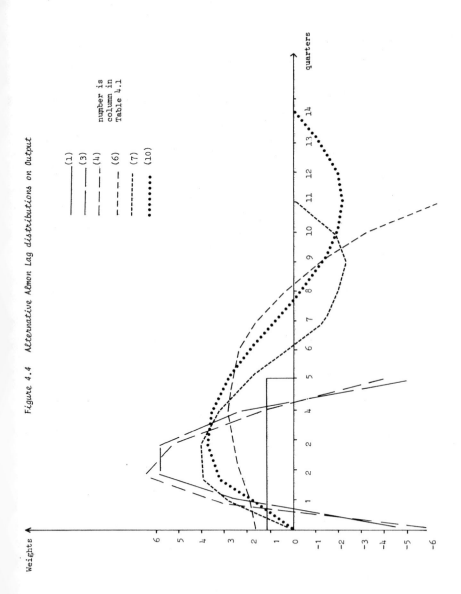

Figure 4.4 Alternative Almon Lag distributions on Output

Table 4.1 and the distributions are graphed in Fig. 4.4. We
can also see the effects of constraining the end periods to
zero and altering the number of periods with non-zero weights.
Beyond a certain point adding further periods is counter-
productive – often the weights are near zero and R^2 falls.
However the choice of p and k is not independent, the most
suitable length depends upon the order of the polynomial. It
is also important to realise that R^2 maximization (allowing
for degrees of freedom) should not be the sole criterion. The
shape of the distribution and the nature of the effect of the
lagged variable on investment must be plausible – to repeat
the general remark we made in the first chapter; it is
essential to make sure that the estimates make economic as
well as statistical sense. The resulting distributions shown
in Fig. 4.4 for the United Kingdom are not as clearly suitable
as the constrained distributions of Evans (1967) and others we
have mentioned for the United States.

We should, however, set out the means of calculation
of the Almon lag structure. Taking the simplest form of (10)
for this purpose

$$I_t^G = \sum_{j=0}^{k} b_j \, Q_{t-j} \qquad\qquad (17)$$

this approach involves assuming that the b_j can each be approximated by the series $a_0 + a_1 j + a_2 j^2 + \ldots a_p j^p$

where p is the order of the polynomial to be used.

Thus $\quad b_0 = a_0$

$$b_1 = a_0 + a_1 + a_2 + \ldots + a_p$$
$$b_2 = a_0 + 2a_1 + 2^2 a_2 + \ldots 2^p a_p$$
$$b_k = \sum_{i=0}^{p} k^i a_i. \qquad\qquad (18)$$

However, we need to estimate the a_i and this can be done by calculating weighted averages of the Q_{t-j} of the form $W_i = \sum_{j=0}^{k} j^i Q_{t-j}$ where k is defined as in (17). Thus

$$W_0 = \sum_{j=0}^{k} Q_{t-j},$$
$$W_1 = \sum_{j=0}^{k} j Q_{t-j}$$
$$W_2 = \sum_{j=0}^{k} j^2 Q_{t-j}, \text{ etc.}$$

A new equation can now be set up

$$I_t^G = a_0 W_0 + a_1 W_1 + a_2 W_2 + \ldots + a_p W_p + u_t \qquad (19)$$

and the a_i estimated by ordinary least squares. The b_j can then be calculated by substitution in (18). (A fuller explanation of this can be found in Almon (1965).) Fortunately computer programs are readily available to perform these calculations (see Chapter 10).

Two further points should be borne in mind lest we lose sight of some of the requirements for the explanation of investment expenditure in the complexities of distributed lags. They are first that in our discussion we have totally neglected the existence of the disturbance term in the relation, and second that we have introduced a number of further variables into the analysis but not considered their relevance. Some of these are financial variables such as cash flow and the long run rate of interest, both of which can be expected to influence investment as they reflect the availability of internal funds to firms and the cost of raising money from outside. We shall take these two points in order in the next two sections.

4.3   The Error Structure

If, for an equation such as (19), we feel that the disturbances are all drawn independently from a distribution with zero mean and a single unknown variance, it is appropriate to estimate the equation by ordinary least squares as before. If, however, our estimating equation is a transformation of the structure of the model then this may not be the case. Take the Koyck transformation for example; in this case if (11) should also have included an error term, e_t, where $E[e_t] = 0$ and $E[e_t e_{t-s}] = \sigma_e^2$ when $s = 0$ and $= 0$ when $s \neq 0$, the estimating equation (15) becomes

$$I_t^N = a_0 Q_t + (a_1 - a_0 b) Q_{t-1} - (1 - b) K_{t-1} + e_t - be_{t-1}.$$

$$(20)$$

Hence we have a moving average error term [11] and the errors between consecutive time periods are related.

In general the problem is that if the estimating equation is of the form

$$I_t^G = b_0 + b_1 \Sigma w_i Q_{t-i} + u_t, \tag{21}$$

u_t may still have $E[u_t] = 0$ and $E[u_t^2] = \sigma_u^2$ but $E[u_t u_s] \neq 0$ when $t \neq s$. We could therefore describe an autoregressive process of the form

$$u_t = \sum_{i=1}^{l} a_i u_{t-i} + e_t$$

where e_t does conform to the assumptions we set out above for the error in (11) and the a_i are the autogressive coefficients of orders 1 to l, not all of which may be non-zero.[12]

---

[11]
    The 'error' term in (20), $u_t = e_t - be_{t-1}$, is an average of two disturbances in the structural equation (11), e_t and e_{t-1}. It is a 'moving' average because its value changes with t, see Mayes and Mayes (1976) pp. 94-98 for example.

[12]
    Moving average models can be represented by autoregressive models of the appropriate order.

Autocorrelation, however, should not merely be regarded as a nuisance.[13] Its existence in the calculated residuals as indicated by the Durbin-Watson statistic (in the case of first-order autocorrelation) or the Box-Pierce statistic (see chapter 2 pp. 46-7) may merely mean that the model is misspecified and that this misspecification is reflected in autocorrelated errors. If the true model is (9) but we estimate (7) we will tend to observe first-order autocorrelated errors.

There is a more general relation between autocorrelation and lag-structures which may actually prove helpful in estimation. Taking the first-order case, if the model is of the form

$$I_t^G = b_0 + b_1 Q_t + b_2 Q_{t-1} + b_3 I_{t-1}^G + e_t \qquad (22)$$

in a similar manner to (9) then the autocorrelated model

$$I_t^G = c_0 + c_1 Q_t + e_t^* \qquad (23)$$

$$e_t^* = d_1 e_{t-1}^* + u_t \qquad (24)$$

is merely a constrained version of (22). Substituting from (24) in (23)

$$I_t^G = c_0 + c_1 Q_t + d_1 e_{t-1}^* + u_t \qquad (25)$$

---

[13]
    There is a useful exposition of this point by Hendry and Mizon (1978).

and then using the fact that from (23)

$$d_1 e^*_{t-1} = d_1 I^G_{t-1} - d_1 c_0 - d_1 c_1 Q_{t-1},$$

(23) and (24) are formally equivalent to

$$I^G_t = (c_0 - d_1 c_0) + c_1 Q_t - d_1 c_1 Q_{t-1} + d_1 I^G_{t-1} + u_t. \qquad (26)$$

Hence the autocorrelated model is a constrained version of (22) and while there are four parameters to be estimated in (22) there are only three in (25).

We saw this use of constraints on the lag distributions when considering the work on the consumption function by Davidson *et al.* (1978) in Chapter 2 and the same form of analysis has been applied to investment behaviour by Bean (1979). He begins by estimating a form of (10) allowing for unrestricted non-zero lag coefficients for the previous ten quarters on both investment and output using quarterly data for the UK over the period 1957Q3 – 1975Q4,[14]

$$\ln I^G_t = \begin{array}{c} -1.04 \\ (0.7) \end{array} + \sum_{i=1}^{10} b_i \ln I^G_{t-i} + \sum_{i=0}^{10} c_i \ln Q_{t-i}$$

$$+ \sum_{i=1}^{3} d_i Si - \begin{array}{c} 0.003t \\ (1.2) \end{array} \qquad (27)$$

$$\text{SEE} = 0.046 \qquad x^2_1(8) = 27.2 \qquad x^2_2(3) = 3.8$$

---

[14] The variables are actually in logarithms of seasonally unadjusted values and quarterly dummies and a time trend to take account of technical progress are also included in the equation.

i	b_i	c_i	d_i
0	–	0.3 (0.8)	–
1	0.43(3.0)	0.42(0.9)	−0.34(2.2)
2	0.25(1.6)	−0.06(0.1)	−0.24(2.2)
3	0.19(1.2)	0.56(1.2)	−0.36(2.4)
4	0.25(1.6)	−1.04(2.2)	
5	−0.28(1.7)	1.19(2.4)	
6	−0.11(0.7)	−0.29(0.5)	
7	−0.05(0.3)	−0.12(0.2)	
8	0.11(0.7)	−0.7 (1.4)	
9	−0.08(0.5)	0.56(1.1)	
10	0.07(0.05)	−0.15(0.4)	

where $x_1^2(n_1)$ and $x_2^2(n_2)$ are the $\chi^2(n)$ statistics for testing for, respectively, parameter stability in future periods and the absence of autocorrelation of higher orders (as explained in Chapter 2 pp.54-7), the Si are the seasonal dummy variables and t-ratios are shown in parentheses. It is easy to show that the lag structure on I^G can be simplified but Bean goes further than this by imposing constraints not only on the lag coefficients of I^G and Q separately, but also jointly.

The final equation which Bean selects is

$$\Delta_4 \ln I_t^G = + \underset{(6.2)}{0.82} \Delta_4 \ln Q_t + \underset{(8.6)}{1.33} \Delta_4 \ln Q_{t-5} + \underset{(4.7)}{0.4} \Delta_4 \ln(I_t^G / Q_{t-5})$$

$$+ \underset{(3.4)}{0.19} \sum_{i=1}^{4} \ln(I_{t-i}^G / Q_{t-i-5}) - \underset{(5.1)}{1.03} \ln(I_{t-4}^G / Q_{t-9})$$

$$+ \underset{(3.6)}{0.07} \Delta_4 D - \underset{(3.4)}{0.25} \Delta\ln R_{t-5}^* - 0.04 \Delta\ln C_{t-5}$$

$$- 0.12 \, CA_{t-6} \qquad\qquad (28)$$

$$\text{SEE} = 0.036 \quad x_1^2(9) = 6.5 \quad F(8,38) = 1.96$$

(constant and seasonal terms are included in the regression
but their values are not quoted; the equation is also estimated
subject to a fourth-order autoregressive process, whose
coefficient a_4 = 0.49 (3.5)). We can see immediately that this
model is better determined - the standard error of estimate
has fallen and the t values are increased showing that we
have defined the separate aspects of the structure more
closely. The actual form of the equation does not, however,
have immediate meaning and introduces four new variables D,
R, C and CA. The Δ_4 transformation indicates the change over
the previous year $\Delta_4 X_t = X_t - X_{t-4}$; as we saw in the case
of consumers' expenditure this differencing procedure conforms with the short-run pattern of the data. The remaining
terms reflect the requirement of a bimodal lag like that of
Evans (1969) although the justification here (p. 10) is that
'Investment in vehicles and some types of plant and machinery
can take place fairly rapidly once the decision to invest has
been made. On the other hand construction work or the purchase

of capital goods which are made to order is likely to be subject to substantial gestation delays.'   The effect of this
distribution is shown in Table 4.2. The additional variables
are a dummy variable, D, which has the value 1 in 1968Q4, -1
in 1969Q4 and 0 otherwise, to capture the effects of the anticipated removal of the special bonus on investment grants
at the end of 1968; R^*, which is the rate of interest on bank
borrowing to reflect nominal interest rates; C, the real cost
of capital; and CA, the difference between the proportion
of those respondents with sufficient capacity to meet demand
and those experiencing capacity shortages.[15]

Bean's model (27) as reformed in (28) shows how closely
we can 'explain' the level of investment by lag distributions
on output and investment itself as set out in (10). The
particular formulation of (28) is perhaps best explained by
considering three ways in which output may influence investment: (i) *changes* in output will result in changes in
investment as represented by the current change in output
$\Delta_4 \ln Q_t$ and its change over the previous year, $\Delta_4 \ln Q_{t-5}$;[16]

---

[15]
   The data are obtained from the CBI 'Industrial Trends
Survey.'

[16]
   Note that this is different from the accelerator, equation
(5) where the change in output affects the *level* of investment.

Table 4.2   Impulse Response of Change in Output

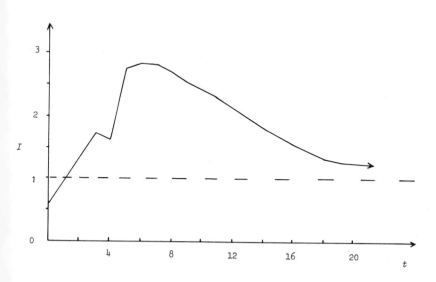

Percent change in Investment for 1 per cent change in output

Time period		Time period	
0	0.621	10	2.437
1	0.977	11	2.279
2	1.321	12	2.103
3	1.738	13	1.952
4	1.635	14	1.814
5	2.744	15	1.676
6	2.82	16	1.552
7	2.826	17	1.451
8	2.705	18	1.360
9	2.566	19	1.279

Source: Bean (1979)

(ii) the change in the *ratio* of investment to output affects

the change in investment, $\Delta_4 \ln(I_t^G/Q_{t-5})$ and $\Delta_4 \ln(I_{t-4}^G/Q_{t-9})$

- implying that in the long run there is an equilibrium ratio

between output and investment, in the same way that there

was between output and capital in equation (3); (iii) lastly

there is a cumulative effect of movements in the investment/

output ratio $\sum_{i=1}^{4} \ln(I_{t-i}^G/Q_{t-i-5})$. These forms of dynamic con-

trol in the path of a relation are sometimes known, following

the terminology of the control engineers, as differential,

proportional and integral control respectively. The choice of

the distributed lag structure rests on a number of criteria.

First that the underlying long-run relation, round which the

short-run fluctuations take place, should make economic sense.

Here it is $I^G/Q = \exp(a + 5.66g)$.[17] Second, that the full

length of the distribution should be included. We can test

whether further values should be included by including longer

lags in general form, (27). Third, that the forecast statistic

shows that the relation is stable outside the sample period

and that the autocorrelation statistic suggests that no sys-

tematic influence has been omitted. Lastly, the actual form of

(28) should be chosen to give meaning in the control framework

we have outlined and to limit the effects of multicollinearity

---

[17] The term g is the rate of growth and a is a constant.

which are present in the equation as far as possible.

As we said at the end of section 4.2 we must consider the inclusion of further variables, particularly financial determinants; this is done in the next section. In this section we have shown that there are complex lag structures in the investment relation. Furthermore it has become clear that we must pay close attention to the autoregressive structure of the residuals, because poorly specified lag structures will cause autoregressive error processes of several orders.

4.4 The Inclusion of Further Variables and Different Approaches to Investment Behaviour

Part of the problem with the type of investment model that we have considered up to this point is that it merely specifies a relation between output and investment and does not take into account other factors which are involved in the decision making of the firm, like prices, for example. More importantly it is not derived from explicit optimising behaviour on the part of firms. In the previous chapter we considered the output decision itself and input decisions related to factor prices. Since investment is actually creating one of these factors, capital, there is clearly a rather more complex structure which could be incorporated. The most important work in this field is that of Jorgenson and his

colleagues who develop what might be described as a neo-

classical approach.[18] There are, however, many other authors

who introduce various other decision variables into the

analysis.   Since we are not trying to provide a survey here,

but merely trying to establish a number of major points of

economic and econometric interest, we shall not attempt to

refer to these models comprehensively.[19] We shall concentrate

on two specific aspects of the problem namely the influence

of the availability of internal and external funds to the

firm.

We have already come across these two influences in the

models of de Leeuw (1962) and Evans (1969) as well as Bean

(1979). The argument for their inclusion is very simply that

although previous output (or sales) determines the general

level of investment through appropriate lag distributions the

ability to carry out the desired investment programme depends

on the availability of sufficient funds. Thus if internal

---

[18]
    See Jorgenson (1963; 1965; 1967); Jorgenson and Stephenson
(1967); Jorgenson and Siebert (1968); and Jorgenson, Hunter
and Nadiri (1970a, b).

[19]
    There are good surveys to be found in Bridge (1971) and
Jorgenson (1971). Further reading is also suggested at the
end of this chapter.

funds to the firm, in the form of retained profits are larger, then it is possible to invest more. In the same way, if the market rate of interest for commercial borrowing is cheaper, firms will tend to invest more.[20] These are not the only financial indicators available; others, such as the debt-asset ratio give an indication of the firm's ability to borrow. Experience in including these variables has been mixed, but in general it is clear as Bean's results (equation (28)) show, for example, that some extra financial factors can contribute to the explanation of investment.

The work of Jorgenson provides a rather more interesting alternative approach. He argues (see Jorgenson and Stephenson (1967) pp. 170–182 for example) that the theory of investment behaviour depends upon the neo-classical theory of the optimal

---

[20]
This is shown clearly by Hines and Catephores (1970) in their preferred equation (8.17A, p. 220) also using UK quarterly data but for an earlier period

$$I_t^G = 15.61 + \underset{(0.084)}{0.691}\ I_{t-1}^G + \underset{(0.734)}{1.696\Delta}\ Q_{t-3} + \underset{(0.282)}{1.230}\ Q_{t-4}$$

$$- \underset{(6.193)}{28.822\Delta}\ R_{t-6} - \underset{(2.887)}{13.559}\ R_{t-7}$$

$$\bar{R}^2 = 0.944 \quad SEE = 6.949$$

Average lag on output is 9.236 quarters, standard errors are shown in parentheses and R is the quarterly average of the flat yield on $2\frac{1}{2}$ per cent Consols.

accumulation of capital. This involves maximizing the
present value of the firm subject to a suitable production
function, which he chooses to be the Cobb-Douglas and subject
to a simple proportionate requirement for depreciation in the
same form as our equation (6). The present value of the firm,
V, can be defined as

$$V = \int_0^\infty [S(t) - T(t)] \, e^{-rt} dt \qquad (29)$$

where $S(t)$ is the gross profit $(S = PQ - WL - BI^G)$, the
revenue from sales less the current labour and capital costs.
B is the price of investment goods, and $T(t)$ is total taxation where

$$T = f_1 [PQ - WL - (f_2 cB + f_3 rB - f_4 \dot{B}) \, K]. \qquad (30)$$

cK (from (6)) is depreciation and BcK is this expressed in
value terms (f_2 is the proportion of this which represents the
tax payable). Similarly f_3 is the proportion of the total
value of capital, rBK, which represents the tax payable on it
and f_4 is the parameter giving the tax on capital gains $\dot{B}K$ (the
dot denoting the change over time, dB/dt).

When we find the maximum of (29) subject to the constraints of depreciation and the production function

$$\frac{\partial Q}{\partial K} = \frac{C}{P} = \frac{B}{P}\left(\frac{1 - f_1 f_2}{1 - f_1}\ c + \frac{1 - f_1 f_3}{1 - f_1}\ r - \frac{1 - f_1 f_4}{1 - f_1}\ \frac{\dot{B}}{B}\right)$$

$$(31)$$

where C is the 'flow' price of capital,[21] B being the 'stock' price. Using the result we derived in Chapter 3 equation (19) for the Cobb-Douglas production function we obtain

$$\frac{\partial Q}{\partial K} = a_2\ Q/K = \frac{C}{P}$$

$$(32)$$

(the Cobb-Douglas function being $Q = a_o\ L^{a_1}\ K^{a_2}$). The desired level of the capital stock can thus be written as

$$K^* = a_2\ \frac{PQ}{C}\ .$$

$$(33)$$

Jorgenson then goes on to suggest that actual investment is a distributed lag of previous desired investment so that taking depreciation into account

$$I_t^G = d(L)\ (K_t^* - K_{t-1}^*) + cK_t.$$

$$(34)$$

The term $d(L)$ is actually in the form of lags on both variables as in (10) so that we obtain a lag distribution in both K^* and I^G in the same manner as we have observed in section 4.2

$$e\ (L)\ (I_t^G - cK_t) = f\ (L)\ \Delta PQ/C.$$

$$(35)$$

---

[21]
    The definition of the flow price is important. As C incorporates the effects of relative prices, given the assumption of a Cobb-Douglas production function, Jorgenson can show that relative prices have the same effect on desired capital stock as does output.

In Jorgenson and Stephenson (1967) only e_1, e_2, f_4, f_5, f_6, and f_7 are non-zero and for the manufacturing sector in the United States using quarterly data over the period 1947-1960 they obtain

$$
I_t^G = \underset{(0.00077)}{0.00305} \; \Delta PQ/C_{t-4} + \underset{(0.00076)}{0.00153} \; \Delta PQ/C_{t-5}
$$

$$
+ \underset{(0.00070)}{0.00190} \; \Delta PQ/C_{t-6} + \underset{(0.00080)}{0.00270} \; \Delta PQ/C_{t-7}
$$

$$
+ 1.20525 \; (I_{t-1}^G - cK_{t-1}) - 0.36316 \; (I_{t-2}^G - cK_{t-2})
$$

$$
+ \underset{(0.00178)}{0.02084} \; K_t
$$

$$
R^2 = 0.96440 \tag{36}
$$

where $c = 0.02084$. This presents a clear difficulty for estimation because of the need to predetermine c. Jorgenson achieves this by estimating c from the capital stock and gross investment series. As our very first equation, (1), shows the definitional relation between investment, depreciation and the capital stock must hold. The resulting value for c is then substituted into $I_{t-i}^G - cK_{t-i}$ and (36) is estimated. If the calculated value of c from the last term in (36) does not conform with the initial estimate the procedure is continued iteratively until convergence is achieved.

This work by Jorgenson which is applied to some 17 industries by Jorgenson and Stephenson (1967) compares very favourably with the other models we have considered. Jorgenson and Siebert (1968) show how a simplified version compares and despite subsequent criticism by Eisner and Nadiri (1968), which was shown to be somewhat weakly founded by Bischoff (1969), it stands up well to criticism. Bean (1979) shows for example that a neo-classical specification is not markedly worse than his preferred equation, (28). The attractiveness of the neo-classical approach is that it integrates investment into a theory of optimal behaviour for the firm rather than having the rather *ad hoc* basis of the distributed lag model; it specifically takes account of the cost of capital.

4.5   Conclusions

The study of investment behaviour has brought out some important features of applied econometric work. In the first instance we have seen that all models, whether of the flexible accelerator or neo-classical form result in the need to incorporate complicated distributed lag relations. In many cases the existence of these lags makes direct estimation impossible either because of severe collinearity between the lagged values of the variables or serious loss of degrees of freedom in unconstrained models. We further noted that the existence of complex lags was likely to pose difficulties for the error structure of the model. The main reason that

Bischoff (1969) used to reject Eisner and Nadiri's (1968)
questioning of the assumption by Jorgenson that returns to
scale and the elasticity of substitution are unity, was that
they had ignored the autoregressive process in the errors.
Indeed Jorgenson's own results do not take into account the
full moving average nature of the errors.

Despite these difficulties of the lag-structures and
the error processes it is necessary to decide upon a
preferred specification of the model. Bean (1979) provides
a good example of the type of analysis we have already discussed in the work of Davidson *et al.* (1978) and Hendry and
Mizon (1978). In this approach, having decided on the basis
of the theory what the general form of the model is going to
be, the short-run dynamic structure is established in the
light of the particular set of data. Examining the stability
of the model in time periods outside the set of data used for
estimation, considering the autoregressive structure of the
residuals and looking at the effect of the inclusion of
further variables, enables us to achieve the desired result.
Bean also shows that competing specifications can be tested,
albeit inconclusively upon occasion by using the method
suggested by Pesaran and Deaton (1978) although we have not
considered this here.

In conclusion the reader should consider the work of Boatwright and Eaton (1972), first because they consider an improvement to the Jorgenson type of neo-classical model using UK data, but mainly because they use their estimated model to examine the effects on investment of three different investment incentive schemes. These operate through changes in the taxation function, equation (30). Boatwright and Eaton show that the new system of initial and investment allowances being introduced by the UK government in October 1979 would, if it had been applied in 1967, have resulted in investment being $4\frac{1}{2}$ per cent lower than it otherwise would have been in 1970. The policy would thus appear to be harmful rather than beneficial in its aim of increasing investment.

Boatwright and Eaton also provide a good starting point for further reading through their examination of the Jorgenson model (they substitute a CES production function for the Cobb-Douglas) and their comparison of three different methods of estimating the lag distribution.

References and Suggested Reading*

ALMON, S. (1965) 'The distributed lag between capital
    appropriations and expenditures.' *Econometrica*, vol. 33,
    pp. 178-196.

*BEAN, C.B. (1979) 'An econometric model of manufacturing
    investment in the UK', Government Economic Service
    Working Paper No. 29.

BISCHOFF, C.W. (1969) 'Hypothesis testing and the demand for
    capital goods'. *Review of Economics and Statistics*,
    vol. 51, pp. 354-368.

*BOATWRIGHT, B.D. AND EATON, J.R. (1972) 'The estimation of
    investment functions for manufacturing industry in the
    United Kingdom'. *Economica*, vol. 39, pp. 403-418.

BRIDGE, J.L. (1971) *'Applied Econometrics'*, Amsterdam:
    North-Holland.

DAVIDSON, J.E.H., HENDRY, D.F., SRBA, F., AND YEO, S. (1978)
    'Econometric modelling of the aggregate time series
    relationship between consumers' expenditure and income
    in the UK' *Economic Journal*, vol.88, pp. 661-692.

DE LEEUW, F. (1962) 'The demand for capital goods by manufac-
    turers: a study of quarterly time series' *Econometrica*,
    vol. 30, pp. 407-423.

EISNER, R. (1960) 'A distributed lag investment function.'
    Econometrica, vol. 28, pp. 1-30.

EISNER, R. AND NADIRI, M.I. (1968) 'Investment behaviour and neo-
classical theory.' *Review of Economics and Statistics*,
vol. 50, pp. 369-382.

EVANS, M.K. (1967) 'A study of industry investment decisions',
Review of Economics and Statistics, vol. 49, pp. 151-164.

EVANS, M.K. (1969) *'Macroeconomic Activity'*, New York: Harper
and Row.

HAAVELMO, T. (1960) *A Study in the Theory of Investment*,
University of Chicago Press.

HENDRY, D.F. AND MIZON, G.E. (1978) 'Serial correlation as a convenient simplification, not a nuisance'. *Economic Journal*,
vol. 88, pp. 549-563.

HINES, A.G. AND CATEPHORES, G. (1970) 'Investment in UK manufacturing industry' in Hilton, K. and Heathfield, D. (eds.)
The Econometric Study of the UK , London: Macmillan.

JORGENSON, D.W. (1963) 'Capital theory and investment behaviour'
American Economic Review, Papers and Proceedings, vol. 53,
pp. 247-59.

JORGENSON, D.W. (1965) 'Anticipations and investment behaviour'
in Duesenberry, J.S., Fromm, G., Klein, L.R. and Kuh, E.
(eds.). *'The Brookings Quarterly Econometric Model of the
UK Economy'*. Chicago: Rand McNally.

JORGENSON, D.W. (1967) 'The theory of investment behaviour' in
Ferber, R. (ed.) *'Determinants of Investment Behaviour'*.
New York: National Bureau of Economic Research.

JORGENSON, D.W. (1971) 'Econometric studies of investment behaviour: a survey'. *Journal of Economic Literature*, vol. 9,
    pp. 1111-47.

JORGENSON, D.W., HUNTER, J. AND NADIRI, M.I. (1970*a*) 'A comparison of alternative econometric models of quarterly investment behaviour', *Econometrica*, vol. 38, pp. 187-212.

JORGENSON, D.W., HUNTER, J. AND NADIRI, M.I. (1970*b*) 'The predictive performance of econometric models of quarterly investment behaviour', *Econometrica*,vol. 38, pp. 213-24.

JORGENSON, D.W. AND SIEBERT, C.B. (1968) 'A comparison of alternative theories of corporate investment behaviour'.
    American Economic Review, vol. 58, pp. 681-712.

JORGENSON, D.W. AND STEPHENSON, J.A. (1967) 'Investment behaviour
    in US manufacturing, 1947-1960'. *Econometrica*, vol. 35,
    pp. 169-220.

KOYCK, L.M. (1954) *Distributed Lags and Investment Analysis*
    Amsterdam: North Holland.

MAYES, A.C. AND MAYES, D.G. (1976) *Introductory Economic Statistics*, Wiley.

PESARAN, M. AND DEATON, A. (1978) 'Testing non-nested non-linear
    regression models'. *Econometrica*, vol. 46, pp. 677-94.

THOMAS, J.J. (1977) 'Some problems in the use of Almon's technique in the estimation of distributed lags'. *Empirical
    Econometrics*,vol. 2, pp. 175-193.

Chapter 5

MONEY

In recent years the importance of money in the running of the economy has become an issue which has generated considerable heat in exchanges between economists. The generally Keynesian approach to macro-economic policy which prevailed in the post-war period has come under increasing attack from those who support the 'monetarist' approach to the determination of prices and real output.[1] What it would be nice to do in this chapter is to compare the econometric evidence for the Keynesian and monetarist positions and suggest what the resolution of the problem is in the light of empirical reality. However, the main reason that there is still controversy is that there is no clear empirical evidence one way or the other. What we shall do, therefore, in this chapter is consider some of the major characteristics of the supply and demand for money, with the emphasis on the latter.

The money market provides an interesting step forward in

---

[1]
The main protagonist of this argument is usually thought to be Milton Friedman (see for example Friedman (1956; 1959)).

our development of econometric analysis through the consideration of multiple equation models. In the first instance
it can be argued that the demand for money must be treated
as part of a general demand for a portfolio of financial
assets. Secondly, it is argued that additional equations should
be included to determine the supply as well as the demand for
money and other real variables which are jointly affected by
the movements in the money market - real incomes and the price
level, for example.

The existence of more than one equation does not necessarily pose any problems for estimation. If equations are
completely independent then they can be treated independently.
Problems start when other endogenous variables are specified
as determinants of a particular variable in the model. If
these endogenous variables are determined in the same time
period we are then involved with the problems of simultaneity.
If, however, they are predetermined then it is possible to use
the methods we have already considered with an appropriate
recursive structure to the model. In this chapter we shall not
actually estimate any simultaneous equation models, but we
shall show how simultaneity affects the single equation specification of the demand for money. Also we shall examine a
three equation recursive model of the US economy which links
money, prices and real incomes. Lastly we shall consider the

use of 'St Louis' models as a type of reduced form equation approach to the problem. Simultaneity will be introduced in the next chapter when we consider wages and prices.

5.1   The Demand for Money

In the traditional Keynesian framework there are three motives for holding money – first in order to facilitate the desired level of transactions, second as a precaution against unexpected events, and last as a speculation against a fall in the price of alternative assets. The transactions demand is usually thought of as being directly related to the value of the transactions to be undertaken (see Laidler (1977) for an excellent exposition of the various theories of the demand for money and an overview of their applications). Since the precaution is against unexpected variations in the money required this is determined in a similar way,

$$M_d = aYP \qquad\qquad (1)$$

where M_d is the demand for money (precautionary and transactions only in this case), Y is real income and P, the price level.[2] Speculative demand on the other hand relates to asset

---

[2]

Some authors incorporate an interest rate term in (1), see Tobin (1956) for example.

holding and the rate of return available so it is a function
of the expected rate of interest, R, - the higher the rate of
interest expected, the more attractive it is to lend one's
wealth, say by buying bonds - and the wealth available which
can be held as money or other assets, W. Thus the total
demand for money from all three motives can be written in
simple form as

$$M_d = aYP + b(R)WP. \tag{2}$$

In practice the formulation actually estimated tends to
differ from (2) first because of the difficulties involved
in measuring and defining the appropriate wealth variable,
and second because there may be more than one rate of interest
which is appropriate. In the simplest case more than one
interest rate will be required if money is broadly defined
to include some money holdings which themselves attract a rate
of interest, bank deposit accounts for example. The more
narrowly defined money is, the less is the importance of the
speculative motive relative to the transactions and precautionary motives. It is important to note right at the outset that
there are enormous variations in the definitions of money used,
from currency, through M_1 where non-interest bearing deposits
with the main banks are added and M_3 where deposits with other
banks and interest bearing deposits are also included to what
Melitz and Sterdyniak (1979) define as M_4 (M_3 plus national

savings deposits and private sector claims on local authorities) and M_5 (M_4 plus deposits with building societies and
finance companies). The issue is further complicated by considerable differences between countries where variations in
the nature of the banking system entail different definitions
of even M_1 and M_3. In an effort to reduce the problem the
majority of the evidence considered in this chapter relates
to the UK. Even with this limitation, the importance of
differences between definitions can be seen in Fig. 5.1 where
quarterly changes in M_1 and M_3 (seasonally adjusted) are shown
for the UK over the period 1973-77. The two series have
rather different time paths and are unlikely to be explicable
by the same factors.

The alternative specification by Friedman (1956) which
we referred to at the beginning of this chapter is different
in concept although estimated versions sometimes have little
to distinguish them from estimated versions of (2). The first
main difference concerns the definition of the wealth available for the holding of money. In (2) only current claims and
fixed assets are considered, whereas Friedman points out that
claims can be made against the expected value of future incomes, which is referred to as 'human wealth'. Secondly, the
holdings of money are chosen like any other good so that at
the margin the return from holding money is equal to the

return from alternative holdings. The cost of holding money
is the yield foregone on alternative assets where yield is composed of the rate of interest payable and the change in capital value. In the case of government securities the price of
the security and the interest rate payable on it are inversely
related, so, following Laidler (1977), the expected yield is
$R - \frac{1}{R}\frac{dR}{dt}$ where the second term gives the increased (decreased)
return if the price rises - $dR/dt < 0$ - (falls - $dR/dt > 0$).
Furthermore any asset denominated in money terms will fall
in value according to the rate of inflation, so this second
specification can be expressed as

$$M_d = c(W^*, \; R - \frac{1}{R}\frac{dR}{dt}, \; \frac{1}{P}\frac{dP}{dt}, \; \frac{WH}{WN}) \; P \qquad (3)$$

where the wealth variable W^*, reflects the inclusion of human
wealth, WH, as well as non-human wealth, WN. The ratio WH/WN
is included because Friedman felt that human wealth could not
be marketed so easily. Thirdly we should also note that
Friedman assumes a stable demand for money which Keynes did
not, because of the speculative motive.

In practice specifications have adopted points out of
both (2) and (3). The wealth variable is normally replaced
either by income, representing a more transactions-based view
to the demand for money, or by permanent income. Since permanent income is the expected income and wealth is the discounted

Figure 5.1   Quarterly Changes in Money Stock, United Kingdom
              (seasonally adjusted, 1973-7)

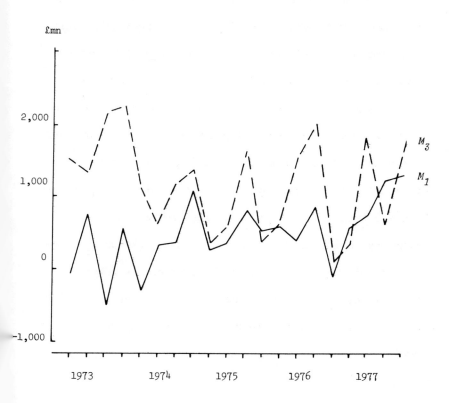

Source: *Bank of England Quarterly Bulletin*

present value of future incomes, variations in the two will move together (with a constant discount rate). Of the studies we shall consider, Coghlan (1978) and Rowan and Miller (1979) use Total Final Expenditure, Hacche (1974) uses both Total Final Expenditure and Personal Disposable Income, Courakis (1978) and Hendry and Mizon (1978) use Personal Disposable Income, whereas Laidler and Parkin (1970) use permanent income and Artis and Lewis (1976) use both a permanent income concept and GDP. This particular choice of 'income' variable is very much influenced by the definition of money used in each model. Total Final Expenditure is clearly more appropriate for a transactions demand, whereas personal disposable income may be more appropriate for personal sector M_3. GDP as a measure of output may be suitable if money is regarded in some sense as a factor of production. For the sake of simplicity we shall therefore develop the analysis of the demand for money by reference to a single model, that of Laidler and Parkin (1970).

5.1.1 A model of the demand for money

Laidler and Parkin (1970) incorporate permanent income by suggesting an adaptive expectations model

$$Y^e_t - Y^e_{t-1} = d(Y_t - Y^e_{t-1}), \tag{4}$$

where Y^e is expected income. The demand equation they use is merely

$$M_d = a_1 + a_2 \, Y^e + a_3 \, R, \tag{5}$$

where M includes time as well as demand deposits with banks, so combining (4) and (5)

$$M_{dt} = a_1 \, d + a_2 \, dY_t + a_3 \, R_t - a_3 \, (1 - d) \, R_{t-1}$$

$$+ \, (1 - d) \, M_{dt-1}. \tag{6}$$

A second change which has been introduced in all the specifications is to suggest that (5), or whatever direct demand equation is being used, represents the desired money holding, not the actual one, and that there is a partial adjustment of the actual to the desired. Denoting the desired stock by M^*_{dt} the adjustment mechanism is

$$M_{dt} - M_{dt-1} = f \, (M^*_{dt} - M_{dt-1}). \tag{7}$$

If the demand equation is of the form

$$M^*_{dt} = b_1 + b_2 \, Y + b_3 \, R \tag{8}$$

combining (7) and (8) gives

$$M_{dt} = b_1 \, f + b_2 \, fY + b_3 \, fR + (1 - f) \, M_{dt-1}. \tag{9}$$

If both permanent income and partial adjustment are posited then this is equivalent to combining (4) and (7) with (5) where M_{dt} is replaced by M^*_{dt}

$$M_{dt} = a_1 \, df + a_2 \, dfY_t + a_3 \, fR_t - a_3 \, f \, (1 - d) \, R_{t-1}$$

$$+ \, (2 - f - d) \, M_{dt-1} - (1 - f) \, (1 - d) \, M_{dt-2}$$

$$(10)$$

as in Laidler and Parkin (1970).

However, (10) ignores the role of P_t and is expressed in nominal terms. Parkin and Laidler use not just M_{dt}/P_t to overcome this problem, but also express both the money stock and real income in per capita terms

$$(\frac{M_d}{PN})_t = a_1 \, df + a_2 \, df \, (\frac{Y}{N})_t + a_3 \, fR_t - a_3 \, f \, (1 - d) \, R_{t-1}$$

$$+ \, (2 - f - d) \, (\frac{M_d}{PN})_{t-1} - (1 - f) \, (1 - d) \, (\frac{M_d}{PN})_{t-2}$$

$$(11)$$

where N is the size of the population. This division by population allows for the fact that we have discussed the demand for money on the basis of the individual and hence removes a source of aggregation bias. The division by P, however, imposes the constraint that the elasticity of money demand with respect to the price level is unity, an assumption some authors would wish to test (eg Courakis (1978)).

The model in equation (11), presents an interesting problem when we come to estimation – there are five unknowns a_1, a_2, a_3, f and d, but six variables to determine them. The model is 'over-identified'[3] and direct estimation by ordinary least squares will not produce efficient estimators of the parameters. Laidler and Parkin try to identify the model by introducing a constraint. If f is constrained equal to unity the coefficient on $(\frac{M_d}{PN})_{t-2}$ is zero (ie it is omitted from the regression) and the following results are obtained

$$(\frac{M_d}{PN})_t = 0.126 + \underset{(2.55)}{0.074} (\frac{Y}{N})_t - \underset{(0.92)}{0.015R_t} + \underset{(0.01)}{0.002R_{t-1}}$$
$$+ \underset{(9.36)}{0.964} (\frac{M_d}{PN})_{t-1}$$

$R^2 = 0.852$ ESS = 0.0071 where ESS is the error sum of squares and t-statistics are shown in parentheses. Solving for d from the coefficient for $(M_d/PN)_{t-1}$, $d = 0.036$ and hence $a_2 = 2.05$. Note, however, that the problem of identification is still present as, using the coefficient of R_t and R_{t-1}, we obtain a value of 0.002/0.015 = 0.133 for $(1 - d)$ and hence 0.866 for d. If d is constrained equal unity as an alternative the estimated equation is hardly changed

---

[3] We shall discuss 'identification' in more detail in the next chapter, but here the problem is clear – if we have more unknowns than we have variables to determine them the model is *under*-identified; if it has the same number it is *identified*, and if it has more as in equation (11) it is *over*-identified.

$$(\frac{M_d}{PN})_t = 0.127 + 0.074 \ (\frac{Y}{N})_t - 0.014R_t + 0.964 \ (\frac{M_d}{PN})_{t-1}$$

$$R^2 = 0.852 \quad ESS = 0.0071$$

but the parameters of the model a_3 and f are now -0.40 and
0.036 respectively (a_2 is still 2.05). Furthermore if both
f and d are constrained and equal to unity, $a_2 = 0.205$ and
$a_3 = 0.049$.

Clearly these are not a very happy set of results as
Laidler and Parkin themselves admit (they go on to produce
improved estimates) and they do not enable us to get a clear
idea of the nature of the demand for money. The interest rate
seems to have little effect and it might be perverse, the
income elasticity is high with a very long lagged adjustment
(implausibly long Laidler and Parkin feel) or very low with
complete adjustment. These discrepancies indicate that the
lag structure of the model is extremely important and subsequent work, especially the Hacche (1974), Courakis (1978),
Hendry and Mizon (1978), Williams (1978) controversy, high-
lights this. These authors also take account of the fact
that the argument of equations (4) - (11) ignores the form of
the error term in the relation. Such errors will occur in both
the formation of expectations and the demand for money and
thus the resulting error in (11) is likely to be complex.

5.2   A Controversy over the Structure of Lags in the Demand for Money

Following the work of Laidler and Parkin which was discussed in the previous section, somewhat improved estimates
were obtained by Goodhart and Crockett (1970) and Price
(1972). However, Hacche (1974), looking at the problem shortly
afterwards, discovered that relationships which had been established using data up to 1971 (Laidler and Parkin's data
were quarterly 1956 (2) - 1967 (4))no longer seemed to hold
(for the M_3 definition of money).[4] Hacche re-estimated the
demand for money to obtain an improved explanation of the
period after 1970. Since 1970 much of the research into the
demand for money has been concerned with the issue of the
stability of that demand.

Hacche's initial specification may not seem very different from those we have considered in the previous section,
merely multiplicative instead of additive:[5]

$$\ln M^*_{dt} = a_1 + a_2 \ln Y_t + a_3 \ln P_t + a_4 \ln R_t$$

$$\ln M_{dt} - \ln M_{dt-1} = f \left(\ln M^*_{dt} - \ln M_{dt-1} \right) \qquad (12)$$

---

[4]   There is an interesting diagrammatic presentation of the increasing forecasting errors in Artis and Lewis (1974).

[5] R is actually $1+R$ to prevent a doubling of the interest rate
from say 1 per cent to 2 per cent having the same effect as a
doubling from 10 per cent to 20 per cent. Hacche, p. 286,
admits that this really implies that R rather than $\ln(1+R)$
should have been used.

giving

$$\ln M_{dt} = a_1 f + a_2 f \ln Y_t + a_3 f \ln P_t + a_4 f \ln R_t$$

$$+ (1 - f) \ln M_{dt-1}, \qquad (13)$$

where a_3 is constrained equal to unity and (13) rewritten as

$$\ln(M_d/P)_t = a_1 f + a_2 f \ln Y_t + a_4 f \ln R_t$$

$$+ (1 - f) \ln (M_{dt-1}/P_t). \qquad (14)$$

Up to this point there is no controversy, but his next two
steps involve a very interesting consideration which is common
in econometric estimation (Laidler and Parkin used it in the
model we described in the previous section) - namely, the
model estimated and the model specified are not identical.
In many cases the change is either unimportant or a straightforward re-specification. Hacche's changes do not fall into
this category given our previous remarks about the importance
of the exact nature of the lag-structure as pointed out by
Laidler and Parkin. The first step was to take first differences and the second to allow for first-order autocorrelation
in the differenced model. Neither of these transformations is
uncommon, the first was taken to remove trends in the
variables and the second to take account of autocorrelation in
the residuals of the transformed model.

Taking first differences imposes a particular form of lag-structure, namely for a typical variable X_{it} with coefficient a_i, in the original model it constrains the coefficient on the lagged value to be $-a_i$.

$$(a_i \, \Delta X_{it} = a_i \, (X_{it} - X_{it-1}) = a_i \, X_{it} - a_i \, X_{it-1}.)^6$$

Secondly specifying a first-order autoregressive pattern on the differences implies a further constraint namely that the variables now become

$$a_i \, (\Delta X_{it} - c \, \Delta X_{it-1}) = a_i \, [(X_{it} - X_{it-1}) - c \, (X_{it-1} -$$

$$X_{it-2})]$$

$$= a_i \, X_{it} - a_i \, (1 + c) \, X_{it-1} +$$

$$a_i \, c X_{it-2}^{7}$$

where c is the autoregression coefficient in

$$e_t = c e_{t-1} + u_t$$

e_t being the error in the original equation ((14) in this case) and u_t an error which has the desired $E \, [u] = 0$ and $E \, [uu']$ $= \sigma^2 I$.

In the case of the dependent variable $a = 1$.

Since there is a lagged dependent variable the nature of the lags on M_d/P is even more complex.

Courakis (1978) and Hendry and Mizon (1978) both point out that these two constraints on the equation are testable hypotheses.

We can specify a general log-linear model of the demand for money using the same explanation variables Y, P and R and a lagged dependent variable

$$\ln M_{dt} = a + \sum_{i=0}^{k} (b_i \ln Y_{t-i} + c_i \ln R_{t-i} + d_i \ln P_{t-i}$$
$$+ f_i \ln M_{t-1-i}) + e_t. \qquad (15)$$

Hendry and Mizon estimate (15) using $k = 4$ and obtain

i	$\ln Y_{t-i}$	$\ln R_{t-i}$	$\ln P_{t-i}$	$\ln M_{dt-1-i}$	a
0	0.22	0.90	0.59	0.92	−2.40
	(0.13)	(0.39)	(0.25)	(0.22)	(3.63)
1	0.05	−0.82	−0.71	−0.05	
	(0.15)	(0.66)	(0.42)	(0.28)	R^2
2	0.14	−0.99	0.94	−0.17	0.9995
	(0.15)	(0.76)	(0.59)	(0.28)	
3	0.01	1.28	−0.99	−0.22	SEE
	(0.15)	(0.81)	(0.60)	(0.29)	
4	0.20	−0.63	0.24	0.30	0.0096
	(0.13)	(0.68)	(0.39)	(0.23)	

(standard errors in parentheses)

Few of the individual coefficients are different from zero at the 5 per cent level not least because of the strong multi-collinearity in the variables. Upon comparison with Hacche's restrictions they conclude that the 'common factors' across the coefficients of the four lag distributions in (15) (unity in the case of first differences and $'c'$ in the case of first order autocorrelation) are not all consistent with the data. They do, however, conclude that the restriction of the order of the lags is justified and present as their preferred specification

$$\Delta \ln(M_d/P)_t = 1.60 + 0.21 \; \Delta \ln Y_t + 0.81 \Delta \ln R_t + \\ (0.65) \; (0.09) \qquad (0.31)$$

$$0.26 \; \Delta \ln (M/P)_{t-1} - 0.40 \; \Delta \ln P_t - \\ (0.12) \qquad (0.15)$$

$$0.23 \; \ln (M_d/PY)_{t-1} - 0.61 \; \ln R_{t-4} + \\ (0.05) \qquad (0.21)$$

$$0.14 \; \ln Y_{t-4} \\ (0.04)$$

(16)

$$SEE = 0.0091 \quad R^2 = 0.69$$

Equation (16) is a very different form of specification from that used originally by Hacche, (14), as it contains both levels and differences. The term in $\Delta \ln P_t$ allows short-run deviations due to the rate of inflation from the constraint that the long-run elasticity with respect to the price level is unity, and $\ln (M_d/PY)_{t-1}$ reflects the effect on current demand of 'previous disequilibria in the relationship between the levels of "real" money and "real" income'.[8,9] Equation 16) can be solved for the consequent coefficients on

---

Recalling from the approach of Marshall and Pigou (see Laidler 1977) pp. 59-63) that $MV = PY$ (where V is the 'income' velocity of circulation) M/PY is a measure of $1/V$.

$\ln M_{dt}$, $\ln R_t$, $\ln Y_t$ and $\ln P_t$ which it implies:

i	$\ln Y_{t-i}$	$\ln R_{t-i}$	$\ln P_{t-i}$	$\ln M_{dt-1-i}$
0	0.21	0.81	0.60	1.03
1	0.02	−0.81	−0.63	−0.26
2			0.26	
3				
4	0.14	−0.61		

In effect this form omits the unimportant variables from the unconstrained equation (15) and expresses the remainder in a manner where their independent influences on the demand for money can be clearly distinguished.

Courakis (1978) shows two further aspects of the Hacche model and the demand for money during the period 1953 (4) - 1975 (2) in the UK. First using maximum likelihood estimation, he tests specifically the hypotheses that: (a) Hacche's first differences autocorrelated model is to be preferred to the equation in levels but autocorrelated; (b) Hacche's constraints on the coefficients are to be preferred to including the same variables without constraint; and (c) not only the first difference specification should be dropped but also the autocorrelation.[10] (In all cases the

---

[9] Hendry and Mizon also point out that the fourth order lags may represent poor seasonal adjustment - a point mentioned in Chapter 2, pp. 51-52.

[10] Courakis also tests further specific hypotheses.

long run elasticity of money demand to the price level is constrained to unity as Hacche suggests.) For hypotheses (a) and (b) Courakis does not find any evidence for preferring Hacche's specification and it is only when data from 1974 (1) – 1975 (2) are included that even (c) is preferred, ie only when data which Hacche did not have when he performed his original calculations are included.

Secondly, Courakis shows the enormous variation in results that is obtained when the specifications in (a) and (b) are estimated and when the date period is varied (Table 5.1). With variations such as these Courakis calls into question whether we can really produce any estimates of the demand for money in the United Kingdom which allow us to make any sensible judgements as to whether the Keynesian framework is to be preferred to the Monetarist one or about many of the other conflicting ideas in this area. This is to say the least a rather disheartening conclusion, but fortunately it has not deterred subsequent investigators from pursuing the matter further and suggesting alternative specifications and estimates in which they are prepared to put faith. It does, however, make it very clear why there should be so much controversy over this topic. Two of these alternative models are discussed in the next section.

5.3   The Demand for Money in the 1970's

The last two sections have both cast doubt on the existence of stable demand functions for money in the UK over recent years. Laidler and Parkin (1970) concluded that considerable further work should be undertaken in examining lag structures and yet after extensive study Courakis (1978) was still not optimistic about the determination of the demand for money in its broader definition as M_3. In this section two further recent models are considered, Coghlan (1978) and Rowan and Miller (1979), where the authors do feel that it is possible to identify a *stable* demand for money as the narrower aggregate, M_1.[11] However, these two models are by no means identical and it will be interesting to see whether on the basis of two or three more years' data and further estimation whether either or both of these specifications can be shown to be misspecified or at least unduly optimistic about their level of stability. Previous history would certainly suggest this.

---

[11] These are not the only models of the UK monetary sector with interesting results for determining the nature of the demand for money. We shall consider another (Artis and Lewis 1976) in the next section on simultaneity. As we have stressed throughout, this book is not a survey of econometric evidence on each topic but a presentation of interesting econometric results and controversies to show the range of applications of the subject. Artis and Lewis (1976) find that instability is maintained in the 1970's whether one uses M1 or M3 as the definition of money and even if the likely effects of Competition and Credit Control are taken into account - an interesting contrast to the results quoted in this section. Coghlan (1978) has a useful table summarizing various other authors' findings (p. 60).

Table 5.1 Long-run income and interest rate elasticities

Model	Data period ends	Income	Interest Rate
Hacche (1974)	1971(3)	0.823	-0.504
	1973(4) *	2.067	-0.321
	1975(2)	0.173	-0.176
Hypothesis (a)	1971(3)	2.141	-4.165
	1973(4)	3.985	-8.136
	1975(2)	0.112	-0.488
Hypothesis (c)	1971(3)	1.921	-3.475
	1973(4)	4.015	-8.409
	1975(2)	*	*

Source: Courakis (1978).

* Partial adjustment coefficient, f, lies outside the range $0 < f < 1$; elasticities were not calculated.

The two studies both consider the demand for M_1 and use
Total Final Expenditure as their 'income' or 'scale' variable
and the TFE deflator as the relevant price series.[12] The
choice of short-run interest rate is, however, different
with Coghlan choosing the local authority three-month rate
and Rowan and Miller the three-month Euro-dollar rate. Rowan
and Miller, writing after Coghlan, have the advantage of being
able to test his hypotheses against their own and to examine
comparative forecasting ability.

The overall results turn out to be very interesting.
Coghlan suggests two estimating equations which are really
just developments of the models we have seen in the previous
section, without the imposition of rigid lag-structures,
which he shows to be a cause of previous apparent instability,

$$M_{dt} = a_1 Y_t + a_2 Y_{t-3} + a_3 P_{t-1} + a_4 P_{t-2} + a_5 P_{t-3} +$$

$$a_6 P_{t-6} + a_7 R_t + a_8 M_{dt-1} + u_t \qquad (17)$$

$$\Delta M_{dt} = b_1 \Delta Y_t + b_2 \Delta Y_{t-1} + b_3 \Delta Y_{t-2} + b_4 \Delta P_{t-1} + b_5 \Delta P_{t-2} +$$

$$b_6 \Delta P_{t-3} + b_7 \Delta R_t + b_8 \Delta R_{t-1} + b_9 \Delta R_{t-2} + v_t, \qquad (18)$$

---

[12]
Rowan and Miller use expectations as is explained on the
next page.

Rowan and Miller on the other hand, first deliberately choose
a simple specification as they are suspicious of the
stability of the more detailed lag-structures. They then
examine a number of specific hypotheses about the most
suita__e variables to be included. In the first place they
examine the use of expected values of P, P^e, from the series
obtained by Rowan and Edwardes (1978); secondly they compare
the use of different interest rates; thirdly they examine
whether interest rates should be nominal or 'expected' real
rates $(R_t - \dot{P}^e_t$, where $\dot{P}^e$ is the expected rate of inflation);
fourthly whether $\dot{P}^e$ should be included separately in the
equation; fifthly whether there is an adjustment to errors
in price expectation; and lastly what effect the introduction
of Competition and Credit Control, CCC, had on the model –
quite a formidable list. They suggest two specifications, one
using a dummy variable to account for the influence of CCC
during the period 1971(3)-1973(4) and the other merely omitting the CCC period from the data. This generates the
following model:

$$\ln M^*_{dt} = c_1 + c_2 \ln Y_t + c_3 \ln R_t + c_4 \ln \dot{P}^e_t \ (+ \ c_5 D)$$

$$\ln M_{dt} - \ln M_{dt-1} = d \ (\ln M^*_{dt} - \ln M_{dt-1}) + e \ln \ (P/P^e)_{t-1},$$

$$(19)$$

where D is a dummy variable for the CCC period and estimating equation

$$\ln(M_{dt}/M_{dt-1}) = f_1 + f_2 \ln Y_t + f_3 \ln R_t + f_4 \ln P_t^e +$$

$$f_5 \ln(P/P^e)_{t-1} + f_6 \ln(M_{dt-1}/P_t^e) \ (+ f_7 D).$$

$$(20)$$

The coefficients, t-statistics, long run elasticities and forecasts are given in Table 5.2. Clearly there is little to choose between their forecasting ability (1977(3) excluded) and the general conclusions for the price elasticity of around 0.7 and an interest rate elasticity of -0.1 ie a very low value ((18) is preferred to (17) by Coghlan), but a serious difference remains in the 'income' elasticity, at unity for Coghlan and 0.6 for Rowan and Miller. Both values are plausible and the previous evidence we have examined and other work do not give any real indication of which to accept. They do, however, suggest that 'stable' demand functions for M_1, at least, can be estimated.

5.4 Simultaneity

At the beginning of this chapter two further consider-ations were mentioned which may affect the determination of the demand for money. The first of these is the determinants of the supply of money and the second the demand for other assets; both of these will bias our estimates of the demand

Table 5.2   Alternative Estimates of the Demand for Money

Coefficient	(17)	(18)	(20)	(20)*
1	0.41(3.89)	0.31(2.47)	2.44(2.93)	3.09(3.49)
2	-0.25(2.37)	0.41(3.36)	0.37(3.67)	0.41(3.93)
3	1.34(4.89)	0.23(2.00)	-0.79(4.12)	-0.88(4.16)
4	-2.13(4.99)	1.07(4.06)	-0.22(5.03)	-0.26(5.24)
5	1.85(4.13)	-0.89(3.25)	0.90(3.47)	0.99(3.21)
6	-0.95(3.14)	0.59(1.92)	-0.64(7.10)	-0.76(6.80)
7	-0.05(5.08)	-0.05(2.91)	0.03(3.54)	
8	0.84(17.35)	-0.01(0.69)		
9		-0.07(4.04)		
R^2	0.997	0.65	0.59	0.59
DW	2.19	1.96	1.83	1.66
SEE	0.013	0.014	0.015	0.014
Long run elasticities				
Y	1.01	0.99	0.60	0.54
P	0.78	0.77	0.66	0.66
R	-0.31	-0.12	-0.08	-0.08
Forecasts (% error)				
1976 1	1.26	0.17	-0.46	-0.36
2	1.30	-0.47	-2.43	-2.54
3	1.36	0.82	-2.69	-2.50
4	1.57	1.20	0.86	0.99
1977 1	1.95	2.49	-0.24	-0.26
2	1.43	0.93	-1.23	-1.32
3	-0.44	-0.00	-5.68	-5.89
Mean absolute error				
1976(1)-77(3)(%)	1.33	0.87	1.93	1.98

* Excluding the CCC period

Source: Rowan and Miller (1979).

for money if they are ignored. Artis and Lewis (1976) tackle

the problem of simultaneous influences of the money supply.

They suggest that one of the reasons that the traditional

demand for money functions have performed poorly in recent

years is because the money stock has not been so clearly

demand determined in the period. There have been factors such

as 'the government's budget deficits and the Bank [of

England]'s abolition of controls upon advances contributing

initially to a substantial disequilibrium between money supply

and demand. Variations in reserve requirements and other

institutional changes in 1971 enabled further disturbances

from the supply side to occur'.

Two models are presented to incorporate the influences

of supply which are treated as 'exogenous'. In the first place

it is postulated that there is a desired ratio of money to

income

$$(\frac{M}{Y})^*_t = a_1 + a_2 Y_t + a_3 R_t + u_t; \qquad (21)$$

the adjustment of the actual money to income ratio is, however,

not just a partial adjustment to desired levels but is also

affected by supply factors, S, independent of the demand

factors:

$$\left(\frac{M}{Y}\right)_t - \left(\frac{M}{Y}\right)_{t-1} = b_1 \left[\left(\frac{M}{Y}\right)_t^* - \left(\frac{M}{Y}\right)_{t-1}\right] + b_2 S_t + v_t \qquad (22)$$

and hence by substitution

$$\left(\frac{M}{Y}\right)_t = b_1 a_1 + b_1 a_2 Y_t + b_1 a_3 R_t + b_2 S_t +$$

$$(1 - b_1) \left(\frac{M}{Y}\right)_{t-1} + w_t. \qquad (23)$$

There are three supply factors considered: (i) the banks' capacity to create money as indicated by the availability of 'high powered' money[13] (its change $\Delta H_t = H_t - H_{t-1}$ is included in the equation but not shown here); (ii) the government's domestic borrowing requirement, B; and (iii) a dummy variable reflecting the severity of directives concerning advances made by the Bank of England to banks, D. Taking a broad definition of money, M_3, over the period 1963(2)–1973(1) they obtain

$$\left(\frac{M}{Y}\right)_t = \underset{(1.09)}{0.174} + \underset{(5.78)}{0.736} \left(\frac{M}{Y}\right)_{t-1} + \underset{(3.31)}{0.0015} \left(\frac{Y}{N}\right)_t - \underset{(2.34)}{0.019 R_t} +$$

$$\underset{(1.59)}{0.202 B} + \underset{(2.41)}{0.013 D}$$

$R^2 = 0.834$,   DW = 2.18 (t-statistics in parentheses).

The rate of interest is in relative terms for this broad definition of money. These results show a clear influence of

---

[13]
    High powered money is equal to currency held by the public and by banks, bankers' balances at the Bank of England including Special Deposits.

independent supply factors and more importantly show that
a *stable* demand for money function can be obtained once these
influences are incorporated.

Artis and Lewis also consider a second means of adjustment of the money market to disequilibrium between supply and
demand. In (21)-(23) it is income through which the adjustment
takes place, the obvious alternative is the rate of interest
which can act as the market clearing mechanism like other
'prices'. In this case therefore it is the rate of interest
which is the dependent variable and not the money stock

$$R_t = -0.769 + 2.207 \ Y_t - 1.559 \ M_t$$
$$\quad\quad (7.82) \quad (5.78) \quad\quad (4.27)$$

$$R^2 = 0.801 \quad DW = 0.76 \quad\quad\quad\quad\quad\quad (24)$$

with implied elasticities of 1.42 for income and -0.64 for the
interest rate - not the same results as we observed from
Coghlan (1978) and Rowan and Miller (1979), but then they
were considering M_1 and not M_3. Artis and Lewis also estimate
equations for M_1 which give implied elasticities of 1.22 and
-0.75, still rather different from those in the previous
section.

The inclusion of supply factors in Artis and Lewis's
model illustrates two interesting features of simultaneity:

first that it is possible to reformulate the model and
re-estimate by a technique which does not involve simultaneous equation methods. By using a reduced form and incorporating the supply influences in both (23) and (24)
it proved possible to use single equation methods. The
second feature is that the existence of simultaneity
problems was indicated by the instability of the demand for
money function. Hendry and Mizon (1978) and Coghlan (1978)
felt that this instability could be solved by a more careful
specification of the short-run dynamic structure of the
model, whereas Rowan and Miller (1979) as well as Artis and
Lewis have opted for the inclusion of supply factors or
other special influences on market behaviour. Clearly the
optimal result may very well be a combination of the two,
but it is unlikely that much further progress can be made
without specifying a full model of the monetary sector
allowing for the behaviour of banks and the Bank of England
as well as the demand for money.

Two further possibilities can, however, be considered
in the current context. First that further equations can be
introduced to explain the whole network of relations between
money, prices and real incomes without encountering the
problem of simultaneity (Laidler, 1974) and secondly that it

is possible to explain the relation between changes in money
and changes in activity by use of a 'reduced form' model such
as those of the St Louis form.

5.5   A Small Monetarist Model

Just because a model has more than one equation it does
not mean that it is necessarily simultaneous. Laidler (1974)
specified a three equation model for the United States over the
period 1953-72 to explain the relation between money, real
income and inflation. Although the variables are interrelated
he is able to use ordinary least squares to estimate the
model because of its temporal structure. The model is
deliberately simple for analytical clarity and his first equation explaining the money market is a simple quantity theory
– that the demand for money is proportional to the price level
and a function of real income

$$\Delta \ln M = a\Delta \ln Y + \Delta \ln P \qquad\qquad (25)$$

(the supply of money is exogenously determined) ie unlike our
earlier discussions the rate of interest has no role to play.

Real income is divided into two components: a full
employment trend $\overline{Y}$ and the deviation from it Y^*. Prices are
formed as a function of Y^* in the previous period and the

expected rate of inflation

$$\Delta \ln P_t = b \ln Y^*_{t-1} + \Delta \ln P^e_{t-1}. \tag{26}$$

This is a form of expectations augmented Phillips curve. If there is excess demand for labour $Y^* > 0$ the price level will be bid up and conversely if $Y^* < 0$ (ie $b > 0$). Expectations are formed adaptively (cf equation (4))

$$\Delta \ln P^e_t = c \Delta \ln P_t + (1 - c) \Delta \ln P^e_{t-1} \tag{27}$$

where $0 < c < 1$. However the whole model can be rearranged into a two equation reduced form by solving for $\dot{P}^e$ and writing

$$\Delta \ln Y_t = \frac{1}{a} \Delta \ln M_t - \frac{1}{a} \Delta \ln P_t \tag{28}$$

$$\Delta \ln P_t = b \ln Y^*_{t-1} - (1 - c) b \ln Y^*_{t-2} + \Delta \ln P_{t-1}. \tag{29}$$

This rearrangement also enables us to see the role of money in the model, which is the only exogenous variable in the model other than the full employment level of real income. Given initial values of Y^*_{t-1}, Y^*_{t-2} and ΔP_{t-1} it is the money stock which determines the path of income relative to $\overline{Y}$ and hence inflation.

This structure is recursive and not simultaneous so it is possible to estimate the two equations separately by ordinary least squares. No current endogenous variable appears on the right-hand side of (29) only lagged values and $\Delta \ln P_t$

does not depend on any current values as its value is not

similtaneously determined. Equation (28) is then estimated as

$$\Delta \ln Y_t = 1.125 \ (\Delta \ln M - \Delta \ln P)$$
$$ (26.59)$$

$$R^2 = 0.974 \quad DW = 0.571$$

(t-value in parentheses)

thus constraining the coefficient on $\Delta \ln M$ equal to that on

$-\Delta \ln P$.[14] Equation (29) is also estimated as[15]

$$\Delta \ln P_t - \Delta \ln P_{t-1} = 0.233 \ \ln Y^*_{t-1} - 0.157 \ \ln Y^*_{t-2}$$
$$\phantom{\Delta \ln P_t - \Delta \ln P_{t-1} = } (3.42) \phantom{\ln Y^*_{t-1}} (2.28)$$

$$R^2 = 0.381 \quad DW = 1.33.$$

We can now solve for a, b and c, the parameters of the

original structure (25)-(27), and Laidler goes on to show that

even this very simple model follows the path of real income,

inflation and the rate of change of inflation quite closely.

In particular it is good at predicting the turning points in

the series.

---

[14]
   Laidler actually tests this constraint and finds that it is
not rejected by the data if unconstrained estimation is used.

[15]
   Again the constraint on $\Delta \ln P_{t-1}$ is tested and not rejected.

Laidler develops the model further, but this does not cast much more light on the nature and applicability of the monetarist position. What it does show is that it is possible to get a simple representation of the relation between money, real income and inflation in the United States using a monetarist basis. This elementary monetarist framework is as we mentioned at the outset a difficult hypothesis to test. What we shall do in the next section is to consider rather more complex 'St Louis' monetarist models of the economy and see what conclusions we can draw from them.

5.6   St Louis' Models of the Economy

In the last section a simple complete model of the relation between money, real incomes and inflation was presented. It was developed, however, not because it was thought to provide an accurate representation of the behaviour of the economy but because it provided a clear analytical framework which was consistent with the evidence. From the point of view of our specific argument here, it also showed how further equations could be introduced without problems of simultaneity. In this section the analysis is taken a step further forward by showing a 'monetarist' model of the US economy where the prime contention is that 'changes in the money stock are a primary determinant of changes in total spending, and should thereby be given major emphasis in economic stabilization programmes'. (Andersen and Carlson (1970) p. 7.) The model is known as the 'St Louis' model after the affiliation of the authors with the Federal Reserve Bank of St Louis. The same model can also be applied to the UK – and has been done so by Artis and Nobay (1969) and Matthews and Ormerod (1978) although they do not support the use of such models.

The St Louis model, as set out by Andersen and Carlson (1970) has five behavioural equations and three identities

(i)   Total spending $\Delta YP_t = f_1 \, (\Delta M_t, \, \ldots, \, \Delta M_{t-k},$

$$\Delta E_t, \, \ldots, \, \Delta E_{t-k}) \qquad (30)$$

(ii)   Price $\Delta P_t = f_2 \, (D_t, \, \ldots, \, D_{t-k}, \, \Delta P_t^e)$ (31)

(iii)   Demand Pressure $D_t = \Delta YP_t - (\overline{Y}_t - Y_{t-1})$ (32)

(iv)   Anticipated price $\Delta P_t^e = f_3 \, (\Delta P_{t-1}, \, \ldots, \, \Delta P_{t-k})$

$$(33)$$

(v)   Interest Rate $R_t = f_4 \, (\Delta M_t, \, \Delta Y_t, \, \ldots, \, \Delta Y_{t-k},$

$$\Delta P_t, \, \Delta P_t^e) \qquad (34)$$

(vi)   Identity $\Delta YP_t = \Delta P_t + \Delta Y_t$ (35)

(vii)   Unemployment rate $U_t = f_5 \, (G_t, \, G_{t-1})$ (36)

(viii)   GNP gap $G_t = (\overline{Y}_t - Y_t)/\overline{Y}_t$ (37)

where variables not explicitly defined in (30)-(37) are defined as before, E, being 'high-employment government expenditure',

k is the undefined maximum lag, which may vary from equation to equation.

Equation (30) is the same idea as that expressed by Laidler (1974), shown here as (25), since the cumulative effect of the fiscal policy variable is expected to be zero. Equation (31) is also of the same form as (26) with demand pressure defined in (32) and price expectations (antici- pations) are formed (33) as a more complex lag on previous actual price changes. The interest rate (34) is endogenous as in the Artis and Lewis (1976) model, equation (24), on the basis of the same equilibrating mechanism between supply and demand for money. To avoid undue complication we shall merely concentrate on equation (30) as this embodies the main mone- tarist contention - 'changes in money stock are a primary determinant of changes in total spending'which we set out on p. 192.

Equation (30) is estimated over the period 1953(1)-1969 (4) using quarterly data with Almon lags on the two variables ΔM_{t-i} and ΔE_{t-i}.

Almon lags were explained in the previous chapter, p. 128. A fourth order polynomial is used here with the lag coefficients constrained equal zero at $i = -1$ and $i = 5$.

The coefficients obtained are

i	0	1	2	3	4	Σ
ΔM_{t-i}	1.22	1.80	1.62	0.87	0.06	5.57
	(2.73)	(7.34)	(4.25)	(3.65)	(0.12)	(8.06)
ΔE_{t-i}	0.56	0.45	0.01	−0.43	−0.54	0.05
	(2.57)	(3.43)	(0.08)	(3.18)	(2.57)	(0.17)

$R^2 = 0.66$ SEE = 3.84   DW = 1.75   constant = 2.67(3.46)

t-statistics in parentheses.

From these figures it appears that the changes in the
money stock have a rapid influence on total spending, whereas
fiscal measures have a small short-run effect, but almost no
effect after five quarters. Not only is this result quite
robust but it forecasts well; Andersen and Carlson compare it
with the Wharton Model (Evans and Klein (1968)), summarised
here in Table 5.3.

Table 5.3   Forecast Errors St Louis and Wharton Models US$ bn.

Nominal GNP	Wharton	St Louis
1963 1	−4.6	0.4
2	−0.2	0.3
3	1.3	1.5
4	0.9	2.1
1964 1	0.9	1.7
2	1.1	0.1
3	1.5	1.7
4	0	−1.7
Mean Error	0.11	0.76
RMSE[a]	2.00	1.49

Source: Andersen and Carlson (1970)
a   Root Mean Square Error = $\sqrt{\Sigma \hat{e}^2 / N}$ where N is the number of
forecasting errors, $\hat{e}$.

If such a model is to be believed it has immense advantages over the more standard econometric models in terms of simplicity and cost. The Wharton model quoted had 43 exogenous variables compared with 3 for the St Louis model.

The model can be transferred satisfactorily to the UK and Matthews and Ormerod (1978) obtain[16]

i	0	1	2	3	4	Σ
ΔM_{t-i}	0.081	1.25	1.14	0.827	1.41	4.701
	(0.15)	(2.49)	(2.89)	(1.57)	(2.42)	(7.12)
ΔE_{t-i}	0.606	−0.105	0.066	0.167	−0.754	−0.019
	(2.81)	(0.52)	(0.31)	(0.76)	(2.92)	(0.25)

$R^2 = 0.64$ SEE = 2.91   DW = 1.87

a remarkably similar result. The equation also forecasts well with an absolute forecasting error 3.86 per cent and an RMSE of 4.16 per cent of GDP over the period 1975(1)-1976(2) using the actual values of M and E. This compares with an absolute error of 2.20 for the NIESR macro-model and an RMSE of 3.14 per cent of GDP over the same period. However, Ormerod and Matthews suggest that in the UK case the model is not very robust to changes in the definition of variables and that if definitions of the money stock are varied and allowance is

---

[16]
    M is 'high powered' money (see definition on p.185 and E is the full employment public sector budget deficit.

made for the introduction of CCC both monetary and fiscal
variables have an insignificant effect on total spending.
The failure of Artis and Nobay (1969) to obtain similar
results for the UK is a case in point.

There are of course a number of very fundamental
issues which should be explored in evaluating these St Louis
models, which space precludes here. In particular the use
of such 'reduced form' models without a specification of the
structure of economic behaviour renders them liable to the
charge that the economy becomes merely a 'black box'. There
is a general prejudice among economists that they prefer to
put a heavy weight on an understanding of economic relations
rather than on close statistical correlations. It is all too
easy to confuse 'association' with 'causation' in the analysis
of economic time series. There may be biases in the estimated
coefficients if other exogenous variables have been omitted
from the equation. Moreover, it may be thought that the right-
hand side variables are not really exogenous in the system.

5.7   Conclusions

It is clear from the first part of this chapter that the
controversy over the determinants of the demand for money is
far from concluded. Although it is possible to obtain relatively stable functions from past data it is by no means clear

that the fairly complex short-run dynamic structures required
will be maintained in the future. Furthermore it is clear
that some allowance needs to be made for the introduction
of Competition and Credit Control in 1971 and for other
'exogenous' influences on the market by the authorities. In
these circumstances it is no longer clear that estimation of
a single equation model is appropriate.

The form of the demand for money function did little
to resolve whether a Keynesian approach should be preferred to
a monetarist one as the actual estimated equations had many
common features. The last two sections therefore tackled the
monetarist controversy more directly by considering the nature
of 'monetarist' models of the US and UK economies. Although
these models performed comparably with traditional macro-
econometric models there was no clear evidence that their
rather different results should be preferred. The St Louis
equation also shows signs of instability when the data period
is extended into the mid-1970's and when the definitions of
variables are varied. Clearly here is an interesting controversy to follow as new evidence and new results are obtained.
While there are obvious attractions of avoiding simultaneous
equations it is clear that they must be considered in some
contexts and so this concept will be introduced in the next
chapter.

References and Suggested Reading*

*ANDERSEN, L.C. and CARLSON, K.B. (1970) 'A monetarist model
    for economic stabilization', *Federal Reserve Bank of
    St Louis Review*, (April) pp. 7-24.

ARTIS, M.J. and LEWIS, M.K. (1974) 'The demand for money:
    stable or unstable', *The Banker* (March) pp. 239-247.

*ARTIS, M.J.and LEWIS, M.K. (1976). 'The demand for money in
    the United Kingdom' *Manchester School* (June) pp. 147-181.

ARTIS, M.J. and NOBAY, A.R. (1969) 'Two aspects of the mone-
    tary debate' *National Institute Economic Review* (August).

*COGHLAN, R.T. (1978) 'Transactions demand for money', *Bank
    of England Quarterly Bulletin* (March) pp. 48-60.

COURAKIS, A.S. (1978) 'Serial correlation and a Bank of
    England study of the demand for money: an exercise in
    measurement without theory', *Economic Journal* (September).

EVANS, M.K. and KLEIN, L.R. (1968) *The Wharton Econometric
    Forecasting Model* (2nd enlarged edition) Philadelphia:
    University of Pennsylvania.

*FRIEDMAN, M. (1956) 'The Quantity Theory of Money, a restate-
    ment', in M. Friedman (ed.) *Studies in the Quantity
    Theory of Money* Chicago: University of Chicago Press.

FRIEDMAN, M. (1959) 'The demand for money - some theoretical
    and empirical results', *Journal of Political Economy*
    (June) pp. 327-351.

GOODHART, C.A.E. and CROCKETT, A.D. (1970) 'The importance

   of money' *Bank of England Quarterly Bulletin* (June)

   pp. 159-198.

HACCHE, G. (1974) 'The demand for money in the United Kingdom:

   experience since 1971', *Bank of England Quarterly*

   Bulletin (September) pp. 284-330.

*HENDRY, D.F. and MIZON, G.E. (1978) 'Serial correlation as a

   convenient simplification, not a nuisance: a comment on

   a study of the demand for money by the Bank of England'

   Economic Journal (September).

LAIDLER, D.E.W. (1974) 'The influence of money on real income

   and inflation: a simple model with some empirical tests

   for the United States 1953-72', *Manchester School*

   pp. 367-395.

LAIDLER, D.E.W. (1977) *The Demand for Money* (2nd edn.) New

   York: Dun-Donnelley.

LAIDLER, D.E.W. and PARKIN, J.M. (1970) 'The demand for money

   in the United Kingdom 1956-1967: preliminary estimates',

   Manchester School (September) pp. 187-208.

*MATTHEWS, K.G.P. and ORMEROD, P.A. (1978) 'St Louis models

   of the UK economy',*National Institute Economic Review*

   (May), pp. 65-69.

MELITZ, J. and STERDYNIAK, H. (1979) 'An econometric study of

   the British monetary system', *Economic Journal* (December).

PRICE, L.D.D. (1972) 'The demand for money in the United
    Kingdom - a further investigation' *Bank of England
    Quarterly Bulletin* (March) pp. 43-55.

ROWAN, D.C. and EDWARDES, W.H. (1978) 'Inflation and the term
    structure: the UK experience' in *Pioneering Economics:
    International Essays in Honour of Giovanni Demaria*, Padua:
    Edizioni Cedam, pp. 939-972.

*ROWAN, D.C and MILLER, J. (1979) 'The demand for money in the
    United Kingdom, 1963-1977', University of Southampton
    Discussion Paper in Economics and Econometrics 7902.

TOBIN, J. (1956) 'The interest elasticity of transactions
    demand for cash', *Review of Economics and Statistics*,
    (August).

WILLIAMS, D. (1978) 'Estimating in levels or first differences:
    a defence of the method used for certain demand for money
    equations', *Economic Journal*, (September).

Chapter 6

WAGES AND PRICES

In the last chapter it became increasingly apparent that estimates of the demand for money, where money is broadly defined, would need to take account of supply factors and the demand for other liquid assets. This would in many cases involve the estimation of a system of simultaneous equations. This chapter is therefore devoted to a simultaneous equation problem - the determination of wages and prices. The particular choice of the wage-price interaction has been made for a number of reasons. First, because in its simplest form it is a two equation model which enables the nature of the problem of simultaneity to be set out clearly and simply. Second, because this particular problem was one of the first areas in which simultaneous equation methods were used and hence there is an interesting path of historical development. But lastly and perhaps most importantly, because the whole subject of the determination of wages, prices and the inflationary process is a crucial issue in current economic policy.

The disadvantage of tackling a subject which is thought
to be of great importance is the sheer size of the literature
available, Laidler and Parkin (1975) in a comprehensive survey
make some 414 references, but their complete bibliography is
much longer. In this chapter therefore we shall restrict our
considerations to four topics: (i) the Phillips curve, (ii)
the breakdown of the Phillips relation and attempts to reinstate it, (iii) do incomes policies work?, and (iv) do trades
unions cause inflation? Even so our coverage of these points
will be highly selective. These topics are all interesting
steps in the development of the understanding of the inflationary process.

During the late 1950s and the first half of the 1960s
it had proved possible to estimate wage and price functions
for the UK, US and other major industrialized countries which
were well determined and seemed to give adequate forecasts.
However, in the last four years of the 1960s these relations
appeared to collapse and a new period of intense research
ensued to replace them. Our first two sections therefore
develop first the initial equations of the period 1955-1967
and second the explanation of the equations which sought to
replace them.

The third and fourth sections of this chapter examine
particular issues which have attracted considerable interest
in the course of the debate on the determinants of inflation.
The process of inflation, whatever its cause, is generally
thought to be a spiral of wage rises leading to increases in
prices as a result of the increase in costs and these price
rises in turn leading to increases in wages because of the
desire to maintain real incomes. The purpose of incomes
policies (which may also include measures for the control of
prices) is to break the spiral. In Sectin 6.3 we examine
whether, historically, incomes policies in the UK have broken
the spiral by restraining the rate of increase in wages or
whether they merely create a temporary hold-up in the spiral
and that wages (and prices) catch up the rises they would
otherwise have made when the incomes policies are ended.
Section 6.4 on the other hand examines a specific hypothesis
about the causes of inflation, namely, whether trades unions
can alter the pace of inflation. In the course of the first
two sections, we will naturally have to examine causes of
inflation if we are to discuss plausible specifications of
the determinants of wages and prices.

6.1   Early Models of Inflation: the Phillips Curve

The 'inflationary spiral' mentioned in the introductory
remarks to this chapter is usually thought of as a two equation

model with one equation explaining the rate of change of
wages and the other the rate of change of prices. There is
not usually an attempt to explain either the wage level or
the price level as such. The basic form of the spiral is
that the rate of change of wages is explained by the rate of
change of prices and a number of other factors and that
correspondingly the rate of change of prices is explained by
the rate of change of wages and some further variables (some
of which may have also occurred in the wage equation).
However, it is easy to be misled by this degree of uniformity
as there is not only wide scope for differences in the choice
of other variables to include in the equations, but also in
the definitions of wages and prices and even in the measurement of rates of change. It is therefore important in considering models to make a careful note of their particular definitions.

The form of these two-equation models is best demonstrated by considering the work of Dicks-Mireaux (1961) (which
is reproduced in a useful set of readings on inflation, Ball
and Doyle (1969)).His model has the form

$$W_t = a_1 + a_2 P_{t-i} + a_3 D_{t-j} + a_4 Q_t + e_{1t} \tag{1}$$

$$P_t = b_1 + b_2 W_{t-k} + b_3 M_{t-l} + b_4 Q_t + e_{2t} \tag{2}$$

where W = percentage change in wages; P = percentage change
in prices; D = a measure of the pressure of demand for labour;
Q = percentage change in output per head; and M = import
prices; the occurrence of i, j, k and l implies the existence
of lags in the relation (which may be complex) and e_1, and e_2
are disturbances.

Here wages are defined as average wages and salaries
per person employed, and so are a per capita earnings variable
rather than a wage rate. Prices are at factor cost on final
output. The rate of change is measured as annual percentage
change between twelve month averages ie if P^*_{tq} is the value
of the price index in year t quarter q the value of P_t in
equation (2) is calculated as

$$P_t = 100 \ [(\sum_{q=1}^{4} P^*_{tq} / \sum_{q=1}^{4} P^*_{t-1,q})-1].$$

The pressure of demand for labour is related to the gap
between unfilled vacancies and unemployment as a percentage
of the labour force and changes in it are, according to
Dicks-Mireaux, 'broadly similar to changes in the percentage
level of unemployment' (p. 301 in Ball and Doyle).

The explanation of the additional factors in the
inflationary spiral are that wages can be higher if output
per head increases and that wages will be bid up if there is

pressure of demand for labour. In the price equation prices
will rise with costs, which have a labour and an import
element; however, cost increases will be offset by productivity. The preferred estimates actually exclude Q_t from the
wage equation as it adds nothing to the explanation. The
equations, as estimated by ordinary least squares over the
period 1946-1959, are

$$W_t = \underset{(0.51)}{3.72} + \underset{(0.11)}{0.38} P_t + \underset{(0.08)}{0.14} P_{t-1} + \underset{(0.66)}{2.44} D_{t-\frac{1}{4}} \qquad (3)$$

$$R^2 = 0.91$$

$$P_t = \underset{(1.03)}{1.95} + \underset{(0.15)}{0.35} W_t + \underset{(0.03)}{0.20} M_{t-\frac{1}{4}} - \underset{(0.14)}{0.52} Q_t \qquad (4)$$

$$R^2 = 0.95$$

(t is measured in years so $t-\frac{1}{4}$ means a lag of one quarter).
Standard errors are shown in parentheses.

Equations (3) and (4) are well determined with the exception of lagged price in the wage equation. (No measures
of serial correlation in the residuals are given.) However,
both equations contain current endogenous variables among
their determinants hence leading to possible simultaneous
equation bias in the ordinary least squares estimates.

This is overcome by the use of Two Stage Least Squares[1] which provides consistent estimates of the parameters. The bias arises because the current endogenous variable among the explanatory variables is not independent of the errors in that equation – an assumption which is necessary for the appropriate use of OLS.[2]

The 2SLS estimates are

$$W_t = \underset{(0.63)}{3.90} + \underset{(0.13)}{0.30} P_t + \underset{(0.10)}{0.16} P_{t-1} + \underset{(0.82)}{2.78} D_{t-\frac{1}{4}} \qquad (5)$$

$$P_t = \underset{(1.39)}{2.47} + \underset{(0.04)}{0.27} W_t + \underset{(0.04)}{0.21} M_{t-\frac{1}{4}} - \underset{(0.16)}{0.54} Q_t . \qquad (6)$$

None of the parameters in the equation are changed dramatically by the use of 2SLS but some of the changes are noteworthy.

---

[1]
The name Two Stage Least Squares, 2SLS, is given because ordinary least squares, OLS, is used twice in the estimation procedure. On the first occasion the current endogenous variable is regressed on the predetermined and exogenous variables in the model (P_{t-1}, $D_{t-\frac{1}{4}}$, $M_{t-\frac{1}{4}}$ and Q_t) and then the estimated values from that regression are used to create a new variable which replaces the current endogenous variable in the original equation and the second stage is the estimation of this new formulation by OLS.

See for example Mayes and Mayes (1976) pp. 175-176, 179-183.

The price coefficient in the wage equation is decreased by
25 per cent and the wage coefficient in the price equation is
also decreased by a similar amount. Hence the strength of
the inflationary spiral appears considerably weaker when simultaneity is taken into account. Only about 1/3 of any change
is passed on immediately (in the longer run of course there
is always the effect of price lagged one period to be incorporated).

Dicks-Mireaux emphasizes that his model only provides
a short-run explanation of the behaviour of wages and prices.
Furthermore he explicitly points out (p. 307 that 'The deliberate exclusion of lagged explanatory variables from the
short-term relationships gives strong grounds for suspecting
autocorrelation in the residuals of the estimated equations ..
Consequently the estimated standard errors of the coefficients
may contain considerable bias, although the coefficients
themselves may be unbiased.' Although it is unfortunate that
Dicks-Mireaux did not actually test for the presence of autocorrelation, this is an extremely perspicacious remark (as
will be seen in Section 6.3 in the discussion of the Lipsey
and Parkin (1970) model). Not only is the wage-price spiral
a pair of simultaneous relations but one with important lag
structures.

Although we have begun this chapter with Dicks-Mireaux's
(1961) model it is by no means the start of the story. It was
the culmination of work published in Dow (1956), Dow and
Dicks-Mireaux (1958) and Dicks-Mireaux and Dow (1959). However, it provides the first clear exposition and estimation
of the two, simultaneous, price and wage relations, where the
price relation is based on a mark-up over costs and the wage
relation on the excess demand for labour. This latter
relation had already been developed in the work of A.W.
Phillips (1958) and is consequently now known as the 'Phillips
curve'.

The Phillips curve is of the form

$$w = a + bU^c \qquad\qquad (7)$$

where w is the percentage rate of change of wages[3] expressed
as

$$w_t = 100 \ \left(\frac{W_{t+1} - W_{t-1}}{2W_t}\right)$$

---

[3] The central first difference is used as the most appropriate
measure of the percentage change in wage rates during year t
because W_t measures the average of wage rates during year t; use
of the uncentred difference $100 \ (W_{t+1} - W_t)/W_t$ would, for example, approximate the change in a year comprised of the second
half of t and the first half of $t + 1$.

W being the index of wages in year t and U is the percentage
of the labour force unemployed. The relation is expected to
be highly non-linear and the resultant estimate is shown
in Fig. 6.1. As unemployment nears zero, wage inflation increases more and more rapidly and similarly, at the other
extreme of the curve, despite increasingly high levels of
unemployment, wages hardly fall – reflecting a long held
belief that wages are sticky downwards.

Phillips estimates the relation over the years 1861-1913
using a two step procedure. First he groups the observations
by the unemployment percentages $0 < U \leq 2$, $2 < U \leq 3$,
$3 < U \leq 4$, $4 < U \leq 5$, $5 < U \leq 7$ and $7 < U \leq 11$ and finds the
average values for unemployment and the change in money
wages in each of those groups. These values are shown by the
points in Fig. 6.1. The second step is then to estimate b and
c using the first four observations (ie U in the range 0-5
per cent) by ordinary least squares on the logarithmic
transformation of (7)

$$\log (w - a) = \log b + c \log U, \tag{8}$$

choosing a by trial and error to obtain the best fit on the
last two observations (U in the range 5-11 per cent).[4]

---

[4] This method is also necessary because some values of $(w - a)$
are negative when $U > 5$ per cent.

Figure 6.1   The Phillips curve

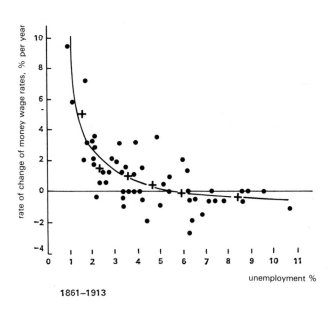

1861–1913

• denotes the original observations ✚ the points used in fitting the line

Source: Phillips (1958).

With the benefit of hindsight Phillips' method might
seem unduly complex and inefficient, but he gives a very clear
explanation of the averaging procedure. The relation, (7),
is not expected to be constant over the trade cycle. In
general, in the upturn, wage rates will increase faster than
the relation suggests while in the downturn they will increase slower, because employers will be bidding more
vigorously for labour in a rising market than a falling
market at any given level of unemployment. The intervals used
for estimation will include both years when unemployment
was rising and years when it was falling hence a series of
'loops' in the time series of observations, the most striking
of which, that for 1868-1879 is shown in Fig. 6.2.

The estimated equation is

$$w = -900 + 9.638U^{-1.394}.$$

As can be seen from Fig. 6.1 this entails constant money
wages at about $5\frac{1}{2}$ per cent unemployment and an equilibrium
growth of money wages at the level of productivity – about 2
per cent per year during the period 1861-1913 at $2\frac{1}{2}$ per cent
unemployment.   This relation, with its clear shape, meaning
and correspondence with the data was justifiably hailed as
a very important step.   It suggests that by appropriate
management of aggregate demand, a government has a measurable

trade-off between inflation and unemployment. The belief in this trade-off had a powerful influence on economic policy during the 1960s. However, there are two drawbacks to the analysis, in the first place the rather unusual estimation method may obscure the relation, and secondly there are events which it does not explain (which were known in 1958).

The first difficulty was initially tackled by Lipsey (1960) who re-specified the model using ordinary least squares to estimate the parameters directly. In order to preserve the non-linearity and to take account of the short-run dynamics when including the individual observations in their time series, the specification is necessarily more complicated

$$w = a + bU^{-1} + cU^{-2} + du + ep, \qquad (9)$$

where u and p are the proportionate changes in unemployment and prices. The introduction of u merely reflects the lag structure, but p, which occurred in the original Dicks-Mireaux specification (equation (1)) represents a substantial shift in thinking. Nevertheless, the distinction is largely between the short-run relation, which was Dicks-Mireaux's concern and the long-run which was Phillips'. When (9) is estimated Lipsey obtains

$$w = 1.21 + 6.54\ U^{-1} + 2.26\ U^{-2} - 0.019\ u + 0.21\ p$$
$$R^2 = 0.85$$

Figure 6.2   The 1868-1879 'loop' round the Phillips curve

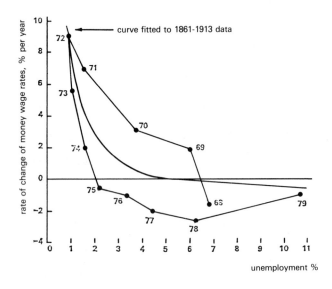

Source: Phillips (1958).

which in terms of its long-run values and the relation between U and w is not very dissimilar from that estimated by
Phillips.

The events which are not explained by the Phillips
curve are a rather more important drawback. In the first place
the period after 1913 showed data outside the previous range
of experience. Wages increased by more than 25 per cent in
1918 and 1919 and fell by around 20 per cent in 1921 and 1922
whilst unemployment was less than 1 per cent in some of the
war years and greater than 20 per cent in 1931-33. Surprisingly the new data appear to fit quite well with the exception
of 1921, 1922 and 1940, but this is largely because of their
relatively extreme nature which clusters round the near vertical and near horizontal segments of the curve. This impression is aided by the scale change in the graph used to
illustrate them. Phillips does not, however, test the hypothesis that these new observations are consistent with the
pre-1914 relation and Lipsey (1960) suggests that if the
data for the years 1923-39 and 1948-57 are examined they show
a shift in the curve

$$w = 0.74 + 0.43 \ U^{-1} + 11.18 \ U^{-4} + 0.038 \ u + 0.69 \ p$$
$$R^2 = 0.91$$

In particular the post-1923 relation is rather more sharply
curved than the original 1863-1913 function, showing that
at levels of unemployment greater than 3 per cent wage inflation was greater than previously while for levels less
than 3 per cent it was lower. Even so this may be spurious
because, as Fig. 6.3 shows, the inter-war and post-war data
sets have distinctly different sample spaces, the former all
reflecting high unemployment (> 10 per cent) and the latter
low unemployment (< 2 per cent). It might be more appropriate
to assume that the two periods were distinct and curves estimated during the two periods separately have a rather different profile.

There is thus some basis for arguing that the Phillips
curve may not have been stable after 1913. Phillips, himself,
spends a few pages discussing lags and the influence of retail
and import prices to explain deviations in the post-war data.
However, when the second half of the 1960s is encountered
the relationship begins to break down altogether - we shall
see in the next section one suggestion for reinstating the
relation through the incorporation of expectations. The
Phillips relation also shows fairly substantial variations
between countries. OECD (1970) shows wage (and price)
relations for Canada, France, Germany, Japan and the US as
well as the UK, but unfortunately all the specifications are

Figure 6.3   Inter-war and post-war observations of
Phillips relation

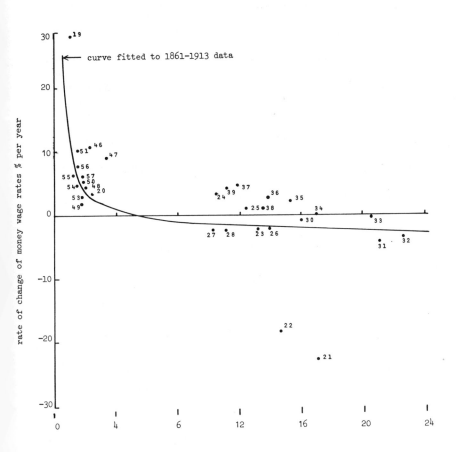

Unemployment %

Source: Phillips (1958).

different so it is difficult to make a clear comparison.
However, one characteristic does emerge, namely that if a
relation between excess demand and wage inflation is going
to be estimated using annual (or quarterly for that matter)
observations it must take explicit account of the variables
which explain the 'looping' or business cycle phenomenon.
If it does not then the Phillips curve will suffer from
'omitted variables bias' as the omitted variables, particularly prices and lagged prices are not independent of excess demand as measured by labour market variables.

It is these considerations which take us to models of
the form used by Dicks-Mireaux, which first incorporate
cyclical variables other than excess demand for labour,
and secondly take specific account of the fact that while
the change in prices as such is a determinant, it is also
clearly a simultaneously determined endogenous variable.
We have now come full circle and are in a position to ask
(a) why did the Phillips curve break down? and (b) what should
replace it? We should also note the problem of the measurement of excess demand for labour, which Phillips proxied by
unemployment and to which Dow and Dicks-Mireaux (1958)
devoted so much attention.

6.2   The Breakdown of the Phillips Curve and some Attempts to reinstate it
6.2.1   *The measurement of the demand for labour*

There are two readily available measures of the demand for labour; the first is the level of unemployment and the second is the number of notified vacancies. Both of these are only indicators and both suffer from bias which is related to the cycle in economic activity. There is no compulsion to notify vacancies nor is it necessarily the case that all those who are 'unemployed' register as such, especially in the case of married women. Furthermore, firms may be holding excess labour because under-employment is thought less costly than redundancy and then the retraining of new staff when demand picks up. This problem has been picked up very effectively by Taylor (1974) where his main contention is 'that empirical work on the unemployment-wage inflation trade-off has been persistently hampered by the use of inadequate and inappropriate data.' (p. 2) In particular he emphasizes the estimation of hidden unemployment and labour hoarding.

Using biannual data for the period 1954(1)-1971(1) for the UK Taylor (1974) obtains

$$w_t = 2.04 + 0.64\ U_t + 1.01\ p_{t-1}$$
$$\quad\ (1.52)\ \ (0.91)\ \ \ \ (5.48)$$

$$R^2 = 0.51 \quad DW = 1.29$$

(11)

(t ratios in parentheses)

for a linear version of the Phillips relation with the
addition of a single lag in the price term, which is a version of equation (1). The variables in (11) are defined as:
w = rate of change of average hourly earnings of manual
workers corrected for overtime working in the UK; U = rate
of registered unemployment; p = rate of change of retail
prices; where the rate of change is calculated as

$$100 \ (W_{t+2} - W_{t-2})/W_t \quad \text{for wages and similarly for prices.}$$

However when the rate of labour hoarding, U^*, is included in
the equation the estimates become

$$w_t = 4.76 + 0.82 \ U_t - 0.50 \ U^*_t + 0.89 \ p_{t-1}$$
$$ (3.10) \quad (1.27) \qquad (2.88) \qquad (5.24)$$
$$R^2 = 0.60 \quad DW = 1.53 \tag{12}$$

Thus while in (11) the unemployment variable is insignificant
and has the 'wrong' sign, and the relation appears to be
largely between prices and wages, the addition of labour
hoarding has a substantial effect. The equation gives a
dampening rather than expanding spiral – the price coefficient
is less than unity in (12) – and while the registered unemployment coefficient is still positive and insignificant the
labour hoarding variable is negative *and* significantly
different from zero at the 5 per cent level. (Taylor also
examines individual industries for the UK and a similar set

of hypotheses for the US, in both cases including a further
variable to take account of labour disputes.)

While (11) does not show any apparent Phillips curve,
although such a relation is reinstated by (12), it should
be noted that both equations entail a linear Phillips 'curve',
which Phillips very specifically considers is unlikely, and
is of course impossible at high rates of inflation as it
would require negative unemployment.

6.2.2   A *real wage model*

It was suggested at the outset of this chapter that the
treatment of wages and prices provided a series of landmarks
in the development of econometrics and applied economics for
that matter. Not only was there the Phillips curve with its
introduction of a specific non-linear relation, estimated by
an iterative method which managed to obtain a long-run relation
by filtering out short-run dynamic variation through aggregation by size class, and the use of simultaneous methods b
Dicks-Mireaux, but in a further development by Sargan (1964)
a major step forward was made towards the modelling of
dynamic simultaneous equation relations.

Sargan's model is based on the wage and price equations
from the Klein, Ball, Hazlewood and Vandome (1961) econo-

metric model of the UK – itself a very important step in the history of econometric modelling in the United Kingdom. The basic form of the equation used by Sargan (p. 37) was

$$W_t - W_{t-1} = a_0 + a_1 (P_{t-1} - P_{t-4}) + a_2 U_{t-1}$$

$$+ a_3 (W_{t-1} - P_{t-1}) + a_4 F_t + a_5 t \qquad (13)$$

where W_t is the wage-rate index in quarter t, P is the index of retail prices, U is the percentage index of the number of wholly unemployed (expressed as a percentage of the 1948 value), F_t is a dummy variable to take account of the change in the trend in wages caused by the wage freeze at the end of the 1940s. (F_t = 0 up to 1951(4) and t - 16 thereafter, t = 1 in 1948(1) and the data period ends at 1960(4). Dicks-Mireaux (1961) has money wages rising less than prices and hence real wages falling as is shown in equations (3) and (4). Sargan argues that wage bargainers will attempt to rectify any fall in real wages, hence the inclusion of $W_{t-1} - P_{t-1}$ as a separate variable.

Sargan estimates the parameters of (13) by maximum likelihood assuming that the error u_t, is of the form

$$u_t = bu_{t-1} + e_t. \qquad (14)$$

This method is called 'autoregressive least squares' by Sargan and the estimates are shown in (15). However, this ignores the simultaneity which we have argued is important. Sargan takes account of it by using instrumental variables where the instruments are indexes of total import prices, and export prices, the current value of total exports, consumption, and government expenditure on goods and services (all lagged one quarter except consumption which was lagged two quarters), F_t and t.[5]

Table 6.1   Estimation of equation (13)

Coefficients	(15) Autoregressive least squares	Method used (16) Autoregressive Instrumental variables
a_1	−0.015 (0.090)	+0.062 (0.262)
a_2	−0.017 (0.007)	−0.289 (0.145)
a_3	−0.497 (0.148)	−0.388 (0.512)
a_4	+0.391 (0.161)	+0.283 (0.456)
a_5	+0.038 (0.056)	+0.049 (0.110)
b	+0.231 (0.159)	+0.441 (0.597)
s^2	0.846	1.022
χ^2	9.17 4 DF	0.51 2 DF

[5]
Instrumental variables take account of simultaneity because, while they are closely correlated with the particular endogenous variable on the right-hand side of the equation they are supposed to be largely uncorrelated with the error term, and thus represent most of the influence of the variable but without the bias.

In Table 5.1 s^2 is the estimate of the error variance and χ^2
is a likelihood ratio test of the autoregressive restriction,[6]
standard errors are shown in parentheses.

The major difference between (15) and (16) is in the
estimate of the coefficient on unemployment. In the instrumental variables case the value is considerably greater: however, given the lack of other differences and the much larger
standard errors in (16), Sargan accepts (15), thus implying
that simultaneity is not important. This is not surprising
as there is no clear current effect of prices on wages.

Sargan refines the initial model and his preferred
specification of the model of wages *and* prices (p. 44 and
p. 46) is

$$\ln W_t - \ln W_{t-1} = -\underset{(0.008)}{0.018} \ln U_{t-4} - \underset{(0.119)}{0.375} (\ln W_{t-1} - \ln P_{t-1})$$
$$+ \underset{(0.064)}{0.106} (\ln W_{t-1} - \ln W_{t-2})$$
$$- \underset{(0.157)}{0.524} (\ln W_{t-2} - \ln W_{t-3}) + \underset{(0.0008)}{0.0019t}$$

$b = 0.441\ (0.186)$

$s^2 = 0.353 \times 10^{-4}$

$\chi^2 = 0.12\ (4\ \text{DF})$ *(17)*

---

[6] The logarithm of the ratio of the likelihoods of the unrestricted and restricted models multiplied by 2 is distributed
as χ^2 with the same number of degrees of freedom as there are

$$\ln P_t - \ln W_t = \underset{(0.054)}{0.012} \ (\ln WE_t - \ln W_t) + \underset{(0.014)}{0.198} \ (\ln M_{t-2}$$

$$- \ln W_t) + \underset{(0.706)}{0.875} \ \ln T_t - \underset{(0.052)}{0.115} \ \ln Q_t^{\cdot} - \underset{(0.0008)}{0.0018t}$$

$b = 0.587 \ (0.115)$

$s^2 = 0.745 \times 10^{-4}$

$\chi^2 = 0.55 \ (4 \ DF)$ (18)

Equation (17) was estimated by ALS and (18) by AIV using the same set of instruments as was described for equation (16); (18) also includes 1961 in the data period. The new variables introduced in (18) are WE, average weekly earnings; M, index of total import prices; T, ratio of consumers' expenditure at market price to its factor cost value; Q, ratio of index of industrial production to number employed in the same industry. The earnings variable was introduced to allow for the difference between wage rates and earnings, although this wage drift does not appear to have a significant effect on real wages; M and Q were included in our original discussion of the price equation (equation (2)) and T introduces the effect of interest taxes. (Since (2) was expressed in terms of money variables, T was not included, but Sargan's important consideration of bargainers' attempts to maintain real wage trends explains its introduction in (18)).

---

restrictions; see Maddala (1977) pp. 179-180.

The first step in considering the consequences of this model is to set out the (static) equilibrium equations from (17) and (18)

$$\ln W - \ln P = 0.00491t - 0.0443\ln U \tag{19}$$

and [7]

$$\ln P - \ln W = 0.198 \, (\ln M - \ln W) + 0.875 \, \ln T$$
$$- 0.115 \, \ln Q - 0.0018t \, . \tag{20}$$

From (19) we can see that real wages have been increasing in equilibrium at approximately 2 per cent per year which is in turn similar to the general rate of increase in productivity which occurred during the period. This gives a basic consistency to the model. The *real* wage/unemployment trade-off is that a doubling of unemployment will reduce the real wage by 3 per cent ($-0.443 \times \ln 2 = 0.0307$). For the nominal effects we must solve (19) and (20) for $\ln W$ and $\ln P$

$$\ln W = \ln M + 5T - 0.22\ln U + 0.015t - 0.85\ln Q \tag{21}$$

$$\ln P = \ln M + 5T - 0.18\ln U + 0.010t - 0.58\ln Q \tag{22}$$

---

[7] The actual values of equation (20) are in Sargan's words (p. 47) 'almost identical' to the values shown which are for a simplified version of (17).

The relation between unemployment and money wages is now that doubling unemployment eventually lowers the money wage by 15 per cent, but this of course is not a Phillips curve as that involves the rate of change of money wages and unemployment. Sargan also shows that this effect on the level of money wages has a mean lag of 18 quarters and that 50 per cent of the effect will occur within 13 quarters but 90 per cent only by 43 quarters. Thus a change in unemployment will not alter the rate of change of money wages permanently, but it will take a very long time for the once and for all effect to diminish into insignificance. This model therefore is strikingly different from the Phillips and Dicks-Mireaux relations.

6.2.3   The Role of Expectations

Although the wage-price model set out in equations (1) and (2) puts equal weight on wages and prices it is clear from the discussion so far that the emphasis has been on the wage equation. This is not unnatural as it was the wage equation which ceased to provide a reasonable explanation at the end of 1966. Many reasons for this breakdown have been suggested, such as the effect of cycles mentioned in 6.2.1, but we shall concentrate on only one of them, relating directly to the simultaneity of the model, namely the influence of prices on wages.

Parkin, Sumner and Ward (1976), PSW, argue that wage
bargainers are concerned not so much with the rate of inflation since their last bargain but with the rate expected
in the future, thus actual prices should be replaced in (1)
by 'expected' prices:

$$w = a + bD + cp^e, \qquad\qquad (23)$$

where w is the rate of wage inflation, D is the level of
excess demand and p^e is the expected rate of inflation. (The
productivity term is temporarily suppressed for ease of
exposition.) Furthermore they argue that the value of c is
unity. Thus the Phillips curve will be shifted vertically
by the amount p_t^e in each time period t. If p_t^e is not a linear
function of p_t then (1) will be misspecified and consequently
it may not be possible to establish the parameters of the
Phillips relation. With one or two exceptions it is arguable
that during Phillips' original estimation period expectations
of inflation were sufficiently stable that the parameters a
and b could be established, or alternatively that Phillips'
averaging procedure removes the variation in p^e. The first
argument might also legitimately be applied to post-war data
up until the end of 1966. Since that date much higher and more
variable rates of price inflation have been experienced beginning with the 1967 devaluation of sterling, and hence one
might expect considerable variation in price expectations.

These suggestions do not determine whether the co-efficient c is unity, and this value is extremely important for the implied form of the long-run relation between excess demand and nominal wage inflation. If wages were the only element of costs and $c = 1$ the Phillips curve would be vertical. Similarly if $c \neq 1$ the effective slope of the curve will be $(a + bD)/(1 - c)$. (This is clearly explained, with prices substituted for wages, in Trevithick and Mulvey (1975).) The value of c is empirically testable given an assumption about what determines expected prices. Solow (1969) assumed a simple 'adaptive' model,

$$p_t^e - p_{t-1}^e = d(p_{t-1} - p_{t-1}^e) \qquad (24)$$
$$0 < d \leqslant 1,$$

and concluded that $c < 1$. His estimates lie in the range of $0.37 \leqslant c \leqslant 0.55$ (using a price rather than a wage equation).

Saunders and Nobay (1972) used a more complex derivation of expectations from lags on past prices and concluded (p. 284) 'it can be shown that the adaptive expectations scheme yields a parameter for price expectations which is biased downwards, thus falsely implying the existence of a Phillips trade-off albeit a steeper one, between inflation and unemployment. We have demonstrated that an alternative expectations scheme yields the same reduced form as an adaptive expectations

model but implies a structural parameter for price-expec-
tations which is substantially higher and nearer in the
region of unity.' Adaptive expectations have the disadvantage
that even if inflation is constant, expectations only adjust
asymptotically to that rate if $0 < d < 1$ in (24). However,
Saunders and Nobay were reacting to the work of Lipsey and
Parkin (1970) and Parkin (1970) rather than that of Solow
(1969).

Lipsey and Parkin (1970) effectively assume that $p^e = p$,
while Parkin (1970) applies an adaptive model of the same
form as (28). Both articles, however, begin their titles
with the words 'incomes policy' and we shall therefore consider
them in the next section, 6.3, and restrict ourselves here
to the more highly developed version of the expectations
hypothesis estimated in Parkin, Sumner and Ward (1976). Like
Saunders and Nobay, PSW conclude that c is approximately unity
but they use a very different means of determining expectations,
deriving them directly from CBI and Gallup survey data in the
manner pioneered by Carlson and Parkin (1973).

PSW disaggregate prices and also take account of taxes,
giving for quarterly data over the period 1956(2)-1971(4),

$$w = 5.9108 - 1.9973 \ U + 0.5027 \ p_1^e + 0.2029 \ p_2^e + 0.2944 \ p_3^e$$
$$- 0.2944 \ r_1^e - 0.7056 \ r_2^e \ (+ \ IP)$$
$$\overline{R}^2 = 0.432 \quad DW = 1.689 \tag{25}$$

where w is the proportionate rate of change[8] in basic weekly
wage rates of all workers (quarterly average of monthly
observations); U is number of wholly unemployed expressed as
a percentage of the estimated total number of employees
(Great Britain), (quarterly average of monthly observations);
p_1^e is the expected proportionate change in the wholesale
price index; p_2^e is the expected proportionate change in the
export unit value index; p_3^e is the expected proportionate
change in the general index of retail prices; r_1^e is the expected proportionate change in the ratio of take home pay to
gross pay; r_2^e is the expected proportionate change in employers
pay roll taxes; and IP refers the inclusion of two dummy
variables to take account of incomes policy.

(The question of the effects of incomes policies is
specifically considered in Section 6.3.) Furthermore it should
be noted that the coefficients of p_1^e, p_2^e and p_3^e are *constrained*
to sum to unity and those of r_1^e and r_2^e to minus unity; the
coefficient of r_1^e is constrained minus that of p_3^e. The con-

---

[8] Proportionate rate of change in this equation is defined
for a variable V_t as $\ln \ (V_t/V_{t-1}) \times 400$.

straints are imposed because, when the equation was esti-

mated in un-constrained form, the sign of the r_2^e was

perverse, $r_1^e + r_2^e = -0.1906$ and only the coefficient of p_1^e

was significantly different from zero at the 5 per cent level

(partly due to collinearity between the price variables).

PSW also present an equation which uses the expected

real wage paid by employers (ie including employers' payroll

taxes) and expected take home pay as measures of the excess

demand for labour instead of unemployment. The second of these

variables does not, however, prove to be well determined.

Overall (25) does seem to reinstate the Phillips relation

and suggests that the level of unemployment consistent with

price stability is 1.7 per cent. However, this is not the end

of the story as this equation does not take specific account

of either simultaneity or the lag-structure. This is also the

drawback of Lipsey and Parkin (1970) and since these issues

are the central point of this chapter we shall now move on

to consider their analysis in detail.[9]

6.3   Incomes Policy and the Price-Wage Spiral

This section forms the heart of the chapter, not so much

because incomes policies indicate a solution to the problem of

---

[9]
  This is not to imply that this is the last word on the role
of expectations. Other models have been estimated, one noteworthy set being those using rational expectations, Minford
and Brech (1979) for example.

inflation, but because the main controversy over their

effect centres on a model of the form of equations (1) and

(2). This model, presented in Lipsey and Parkin (1970) and

extensively discussed in Parkin and Sumner (1972) shows the

full importance and difficulty of this simultaneous equation

problem. The model, estimated over the period 1948(3)–1968(2),

is

$$p_t = 1.374 + 0.562\ w_t + 0.085\ m_{t-1} - 0.145\ q_t$$
$$\ (2.51)\ \ \ (5.53)\ \ \ \ \ (4.60)\ \ \ \ \ \ \ (3.48)$$

$$R^2 = 0.697 \quad DW = 0.946 \tag{26}$$

$$w_t = 4.147 - 0.891\ U_t + 0.482\ p_t + 3.315\ n_t$$
$$\ (4.26)\ \ \ (1.77)\ \ \ \ \ (5.76)\ \ \ \ \ (2.09)$$

$$R^2 = 0.616 \quad DW = 0.742 \tag{27}$$

where p, w, m, q and n are proportionate rates of change of
the form

$$v_t = (V_{t+2} - V_{t-2})/[\tfrac{1}{2}\ (V_{t+2} + V_{t-2})] \times 100.$$

P is the index of retail prices, W is the all industry index

of weekly wage rates, U is the percentage of the civilian

labour force unemployed, N is the percentage of the labour

force unionized, M is the import unit value index, and

$Q = R/E$, R being the index of industrial production and E the

number of employees under a similar definition of industrial

production. (Exact definitions together with data sources

are given in Parkin and Sumner (1972) p. 110). The equations
are estimated by OLS; t-statistics are shown in parentheses.

The argument of the paper is that if incomes policies
are effective then they will break the existing inflationary
spiral and the parameters of (26) and (27) will change.
Specifically therefore allowance should be made for a structural shift between periods where an incomes policy was in
force ('policy on') and ones when it was not ('policy off').
The policy on years are defined as 1948(3)-1950(3), 1956(1)-
1956(4), 1961(3)-1964(3), 1964(4)-1968(2). Lipsey and Parkin
re-estimate (26) and (27) for policy on and policy off and
the results appear to confirm the expected structural change:

Policy on

$$p = 3.874 + 0.014\ w + 0.001\ m_{t-1} - 0.198\ q$$
$$\quad\ (5.65)\quad (0.10)\quad\ \ (0.04)\quad\quad\ (2.68)$$

$$R^2 = 0.241 \quad DW = 1.088 \tag{26a}$$

$$w = 3.919 - 0.404\ U + 0.227\ p + 3.746\ n$$
$$\quad (2.27)\quad (0.56)\quad\ (0.93)\quad\ (1.61)$$

$$R^2 = 0.138 \quad DW = 0.724 \tag{27a}$$

Policy off

$$p = -\ 0.140 + 0.851\ w + 0.073\ m_{t-1} - 0.092\ q$$
$$\quad\ (0.16)\quad (5.52)\quad\ (2.93)\quad\quad\ (1.90)$$

$$R^2 = 0.843 \quad DW = 1.274 \tag{26b}$$

$$w = 6.672 - 2.372\ U + 0.457\ p + 0.136\ n$$
$$\quad\ (5.79)\quad (3.64)\quad\ (6.25)\quad\ (0.07)$$

$$R^2 = 0.856 \quad DW = 1.231 \tag{27b}$$

Although the coefficients for q and particularly n are poorly determined in the policy off period, the unemployment coefficient is significantly different from zero and negative. The wage coefficient in (26b) is much higher than that obtained by Dicks–Mireaux, 0.35, in equation (4), but the price coefficient in the wage equation (27b) is similar to those in (3), 0.38 for p_t and 0.14 for p_{t-1}. Equations (26a) and (27a) on the other hand present a totally different picture: the wage equation no longer appears to tell us anything useful, except that the residuals are serially correlated; similarly the only important element in the price equation is the change in productivity. The authors conclude, not surprisingly, that incomes policies have a clear effect. There are, however, several grounds on which their model has been criticized.

(a) It is simultaneous but is estimated by OLS.

(b) It is clearly autocorrelated.

(c) It does not make a reasonable allowance for price expectations.

(d) It implies an implausible Phillips curve.

(e) Unemployment is not measured properly.

(f)   Earnings rather than wage rates should be used.

(g)   There is considerable variety in the nature of
      incomes policies and hence their effects may
      be expected to be different.

Since a whole book and several further articles have been
written on these criticisms we can only summarize some of
the major points in this section.

We have already discussed expectations in the previous
section and the measurement of unemployment and the drawbacks
of positing that the Phillips curve is linear in Section 6.2.1.

In the Lipsey-Parkin model with policy off $w = 10.9 -
4.0U$ and with policy on $w = 4.6 - 0.4U$. The two curves cut at
approximately 1.8 per cent unemployment and 3.8 per cent wage
inflation. Thus according to these estimates incomes policies have only resulted in lower rates of inflation, at a
given level of unemployment, when excess demand has been high.
However the simultaneity problem might be regarded as even
more complex if we feel that incomes policy itself is
endogenous because it is only imposed when the rate of inflation is high (Wallis, 1972). Also, it needs only a trivial
calculation to observe that these equations do not coincide
with experience in more recent years. In the fourth quarter of
1979, for example, the values of w and U were 17 per cent and

6 per cent respectively. At that rate of unemployment, with policy off, a *fall* in nominal wage rates of 13.1 per cent is implied by the model.

We shall concentrate in this section on points (a) and (b) although we shall also mention the remaining criticisms (f) and (g) at the end of the section.

Godfrey (1972) has shown that if equations (26) and (27) are re-estimated by Sargan's (1964) AIV method we obtain

$$p = 0.903 + 0.731\ w + 0.052\ m_{t-1} - 0.230\ q$$
$$\quad\ (3.070)\quad (0.531)\quad\ (0.048)\qquad\quad (0.244)$$

$$b_2 = 0.528\ (0.119)\qquad s_2 = 1.444\qquad \chi^2 = 1.438\ (1\ \mathrm{DF})\qquad (28)$$

$$w = 2.957 - 0.674\ U + 0.728\ p - 1.193\ n$$
$$\quad\ (3.397)\quad (1.556)\qquad (0.336)\qquad (7.616)$$

$$b_2 = 0.641\ (0.096)\qquad s_2 = 1.044\qquad \chi^2 = 0.137\ (1\ \mathrm{DF})\qquad (29)$$

(instruments used were, in (28), constant, m_{t-1}, m_{t-2}, q_{t-1}, w_{t-1} and p_{t-1}, and in (29), constant, m_{t-1}, n_{t-1}, U_{t-1}, w_{t-1} and p_{t-1}). The autoregression coefficients, b in both equations are highly significant so it is clear that auto-correlation should be allowed for. Furthermore, the parameter values are changed fairly substantially and their standard errors increased. The only 'significant' variable is price in the wage equation. The wage, import price and productivity

coefficients in (28) change by 30 per cent, 40 per cent and
60 per cent respectively and the unemployment and price
coefficients in (29) change by 25 per cent and 50 per cent
and the trade union coefficient changes sign.

Wallis (1972) shows that the autocorrelation is not
merely first order in (26) but fourth order as well. His
'preferred' specification gives maximum likelihood estimates
of

$$
p_t = \underset{(0.153)}{0.220} + \underset{(0.078)}{0.567}\ p_{t-1} + \underset{(0.076)}{0.364}\ w_{t-1} + \underset{(0.015)}{0.070}\ m_t
$$

$$
\quad - \underset{(0.023)}{0.041}\ q_t \tag{30}
$$

$$
u_t = - \underset{(0.103)}{0.459}\ u_{t-4}
$$

where u_t is the autocorrelated error. He takes this to indicate
that a partial adjustment mechanism is at work by the inclusion of the lagged dependent variable, and also suggests that
the differencing procedure which Lipsey and Parkin use may
actually be causing the fourth order autoregression coefficient of -0.5.

Wallis also makes a further interesting finding on the
simultaneity of the model. When full-information maximum

likelihood, FIML[10] is used to estimate the policy off model

the procedure fails because the matrix of coefficients on

the endogenous variables is singular (all other coefficients

in the model being insignificant). If we express the Lipsey-

Parkin model in its structural form (as was explained in

Chapter 1)

$$A\ y + Bx = u \tag{31}$$

where y is the vector of endogenous variables, x is the vector

of predetermined variables, u the vector of errors and the 2

rows of A and B are the coefficients of the respective equations

(26b) and (27b), we have that

$$y' = \begin{bmatrix} p_t & w_t \end{bmatrix} \quad x' = \begin{bmatrix} m_{t-1} & q_t & U_t & n_t \end{bmatrix}$$

$$A = \begin{bmatrix} 1 & a_{12} \\ a_{21} & 1 \end{bmatrix} \quad B = \begin{bmatrix} b_{11} & b_{12} & 0 & 0 \\ 0 & 0 & b_{23} & b_{24} \end{bmatrix}$$

The estimated values of A are[11]

$$A = \begin{bmatrix} 1 & -0.8755 \\ -1.1442 & 1 \end{bmatrix}$$

---

[10]
    This technique is explained in Maddala (1977) pp. 486-490,
but the major point to note here is that it takes account of
the error covariances between equations.

[11]
    These values are given in Desai (1976) and attributed to
D.F. Hendry.

A is singular because $-0.8755 = 1/-1.1442$.

If we consider the identification of the model while ignoring these estimates it appears that the model is *over-identified* in both equations by the *order* condition as there are two constraints on each but only one is required for exact identification.[12] The *rank* condition is also met in both cases, but clearly if any one of the coefficients b_{11} and b_{12} in the first equation is zero then the rank condition will not be met for the *other* equation and it will be under-identified. Similarly, if either of b_{23} or b_{24} is zero the rank condition will not be met for the first equation. However, Wallis' results suggest that neither equation is identified because the whole B matrix has no role.[13]

FIML introduces a further element into the problem of simultaneity which we have not yet discussed. A first order autoregression process in the disturbances of (31) can be expressed as

$$u = C\,u_{t-1} + e_t \tag{32}$$

---

[12]
See Maddala (1977), pp. 220-231, for example, for an exposition of these conditions.

[13]
The B matrix is actually a simplification, for with a first order autoregression in the residuals all the y and x variables lagged one period, should also occur in the vector x.

where C is the matrix of autoregression coefficients, the diagonal terms being the first order autoregression coefficients within equations, and the off-diagonal ones, those between equations. Desai (1976) estimates (26) and (27) by this method and obtains

$$p = -15.761 + \underset{(27.90)}{4.150}\ w + \underset{(0.63)}{0.147}\ m_{t-1} - \underset{(1.55)}{0.077}\ q \qquad (33)$$

$$w = 2.198 - \underset{(1.75)}{0.392}\ U + \underset{(16.43)}{0.508}\ p + \underset{(0.54)}{0.246}\ n \qquad (34)$$

(t-ratios in parentheses)

$$C = \begin{bmatrix} 0.544 & -0.0476 \\ (0.279) & (0.0626) \\ \\ 0.202 & 0.863 \\ (1.080) & (0.242) \end{bmatrix}$$

(standard errors in parentheses).

The coefficients of m_{t-1} and q are still not significantly different from zero which would tend to indicate underidentification. Furthermore the off-diagonal elements of C are also insignificant, showing that this will not affect the identification problem. (It should be noted that while we need only consider Ay and Bx for identification when C is diagonal, the full model to be identified is

$$Ay + Bx - CAy_{t-1} - CBx_{t-1} = e.)$$

The other major areas of criticism of the Lipsey-Parkin
explanation of the effects of incomes policies which we said
we would tackle in this section, were first, the choice of
wage-rates instead of earnings as the wage variable, and
secondly the treatment of incomes policies as if they were
all the same.   In the very same volume as Lipsey-Parkin
(Parkin and Sumner (1972)) there is an article by Smith (1972)
which identifies six separate incomes policies. These are
identified on the left hand side of table 6.1. The variables
$I_1 - I_6$ are all dummy variables taking the value unity when
the particular policy was in force and zero elsewhere.   However, Smith also used dummy variables which increased linearly
in proportion to the length of the period the policy was in
force; thus a policy lasting four quarters would have the
values $\frac{1}{4}, \frac{1}{2}, \frac{3}{4}, 1$ for the dummy variable over that period.
(This concept of variable dummies is also dealt with by Henry
and Ormerod (1978) see p. 245-6.) The other variables in
Table 6.1 are defined as: U is a four quarter average unemployment rate, w is a wage variable using four definitions as
given in the various column headings, p is the index of retail
prices, m is an index of import prices and q is industrial
output per industrial employee; w, p and m are measured
in the form $(X_t - X_{t-4})/X_{t-4}$ for quarterly data and $(X_t - X_{t-2})$
X_{t-2} for half yearly data and q is measured as the change in a
twelve month period over the previous twelve month period

(t-values in parentheses).

The model therefore has the Lipsey-Parkin form with the addition of lagged prices in the wage equation and the omission of the union strength variable. Both earnings and wage rates are shown (although weekly earnings are not), but unfortunately with the use of half yearly data for earnings and quarterly data for wage rates it is difficult to compare their performance in the model. One might be tempted to conclude that wage rates should enter the wage equation and earnings the price equation (as concluded by Henry *et al.* (1976) and P nry and Ormerod (1978) in a different form). The effects of the incomes policies are clearly different in both magnitude and significance. However, the variation in signs and in particular the occurrence of positive signs calls the specification into question.   The OLS results are much more coherent than the 2SLS picture and do suggest that the incomes policies have varying effects.

The results of Henry *et al.* (1976) are much more promising where a version of Sargan's (1964) model is used

$$\ln W_t - \ln W_{t-1} = a_0 + a_1 (\ln P_{t-1} - \ln P_{t-2}) + a_3 \ln U_{t-1}$$

$$+ a_4 (\ln E_{t-1} - \ln P_{t-1}) + a_5 t. \qquad (35)$$

Table 6.2 *Wage and price regressions: method of two-stage least squares, coefficients of explanatory variables*

Explanatory variable	Quarterly 1948(1)–1957(2)				Half-yearly 1948(1)–1967(1)			
	Weekly wages	Retail prices	Hourly wages	Retail prices	Hourly earnings including overtime	Retail prices	Hourly earnings excluding overtime	Retail prices
Constant	0.0008	-0.0291	0.0110	-0.0312	0.0182	-0.0034	0.0106	-0.0034
U^{-1}	0.0404 (3.539)	—	0.0311 (2.019)	—	0.0434 (1.349)	—	0.0460 (1.571)	—
p	0.3774 (2.835)	—	0.5670 (3.157)	—	0.5875 (2.412)	—	0.5485 (2.474)	—
p_{t-1}	0.1778 (1.610)	—	-0.0233 (0.156)	—	-0.1890 (0.903)	—	-0.0758 (0.398)	—
w	—	1.350 (9.344)	—	1.3560 (8.060)	—	0.8070 (3.840)	—	0.8137 (4.238)
m_{t-1}	—	0.0304 (1.419)	—	0.0306 (1.238)	—	0.0934 (2.894)	—	0.0906 (3.006)
q	—	-0.0104 (0.223)	—	-0.1046 (2.117)	—	-0.3966 (5.670)	—	-0.3313 (5.608)
$I_1(1948(1)$–$50(3))$	-0.0233 (9.023)	0.0293 (4.877)	-0.0203 (5.843)	0.0272 (4.033)	-0.0133 (1.594)	0.0035 (0.464)	-0.0141 (1.860)	0.0042 (0.595)
$I_2(1956(1)$–$(4))$	0.0096 (1.843)	-0.0273 (3.556)	0.0121 (1.722)	-0.0270 (3.071)	0.0067 (0.470)	-0.0130 (1.300)	0.0098 (0.754)	-0.0161 (1.653)
$I_3(1961(3)$–$2(2))$	-0.0168 (4.404)	0.0262 (3.717)	-0.0048 (0.938)	0.0066 (0.858)	-0.0079 (0.682)	0.0047 (0.554)	-0.0046 (0.434)	0.0043 (0.541)
$I_4(1962(3)$–$4(2))$	0.0057 (1.756)	-0.0006 (0.131)	0.0038 (0.863)	0.0005 (0.093)	0.0037 (0.405)	0.0012 (0.210)	0.0057 (0.680)	-0.0001 (0.017)
$I_5(1965(1)$–$6(2))$	-0.0097 (2.998)	0.0015 (2.065)	0.0088 (1.998)	-0.0126 (1.829)	0.0252 (2.637)	-0.0176 (1.777)	0.0231 (2.663)	-0.0166 (1.846)
$I_6(1966(3)$–$7(2))$	-0.0125 (3.284)	0.0167 (2.592)	-0.0071 (1.379)	0.0103 (1.319)	-0.0121 (1.069)	0.0086 (0.983)	-0.0062 (0.602)	0.0044 (0.557)
R^2	0.87	0.77	0.78	0.69	0.58	0.80	0.65	0.82

Source: Smith (1972 p. 84).

The changes from Sargan's formulation are that real earnings net of income tax and other deductions $(E/P)_{t-1}$ is used rather than real wages and real earnings gross; also P is the retail and not the consumer price index. Including dummy variables for the 1949(1)-1950(3) wage freeze, I_1, the 1966(3)-1967(2) pay 'standstill', I_2, and the phases I and II of the 1972-4 policy 1972(4)-1973(3), I_3, only, they obtained

$$\ln W_t - \ln W_{t-1} = 0.0203 + 0.476 \ (\ln P_{t-1} - \ln P_{t-2})$$
$$(0.031) \ (0.150)$$

$$- 0.0058 \ \ln U_{t-1} - 0.154 \ (\ln E_{t-1} - \ln P_{t-1})$$
$$(0.0079) \qquad (0.0621)$$

$$+ 0.0009t - 0.0014 I_1 - 0.0131 I_2 + 0.0058 I_3$$
$$(0.00036) \ (0.0054) \ (0.006) \quad (0.007)$$

$$R^2 = 0.498 \qquad DW = 1.473.$$

Since no remarks are made to the contrary this equation is presumably estimated by OLS, so we have no indication of what it would look like if estimated by AIV. Nevertheless it appears that the pay 'standstill' in I_2 had a very clear effect. Furthermore the positive sign for I_3 is explicable by the freeze's coincidence with a rapid expansion of the public sector which might also be expected to have an effect on the wage equation, though in the opposite direction to the incomes policy.

In Henry and Ormerod (1978) these results are amplified and improved, first by suggesting that there is a catching up

process after the removal of an incomes policy and secondly
by using AIV as the estimation method.

The equation specified is not identical and is

$$\ln W_t - \ln W_{t-1} = b_1 + b_2 \left(\ln P_t - \ln P_{t-1} \right)$$
$$+ b_3 \left(\ln E_t - \ln E_{t-1} \right) + b_4 D^* \qquad (36)$$
$$+ \text{ incomes policy and catch up}$$
$$\text{dummy variables.}$$

The dummy variables used are

Incomes policy	Period	
I_1	1966(3)-1967(2)	Stage II compulsory freeze
I_2	1967(3)-1969(2)	Stage III and IV zero norm
I_3	1972(4)-1973(1)	Phase I compulsory freeze
I_4	1973(2)-1974(1)	Phase 2 and Phase 3

Catch-up	Corresponding policy dummy	Period
C_1	I_1	1967(3)-1968(2)
C_2	I_2	1969(3)-1971(2)
C_3	I_3	1973(2)-1973(3)
C_4	I_4	1974(2)-1975(1)

and D^* is a further dummy variable to take account of what
appears to be a 'structural change' in the adjustment behaviour of desired real net earnings after 1975(2) (the authors
admit that they would have preferred to be able to explain

this change explicitly rather than by using a dummy variable).
The estimates obtained by AIV for the period 1961(1)-
1977(2) are

b_1	b_2	b_3	I_1	I_2	I_3	I_4
0.000	0.312	-0.199	-0.002	-0.019	-0.014	-0.002
(0.047)	(1.48)	(1.43)	(0.35)	(1.953)	(1.37)	(0.317)

c_1	c_2	c_3	c_4	D^*	ρ	$\chi^2(12)$ SE
0.000	0.029	0.009	0.002	-0.009	-0.279	27.99 0.015
(0.032)	(2.03)	(1.318)	(0.429)	(1.638)	(1.819)	

The estimates suffer from poor determination, but the
coefficients all have the expected signs. The magnitude of
the 'catch-up' variables suggested that catching up is
complete. Thus although incomes policies do reduce wage inflation while they are in force their effect is quickly
eroded afterwards. This result is an impressive step forward
in the understanding of the way in which departures from the
long-run path of real net earnings take place. However, we
should note in leaving this topic that the Phillips relation
has gone, unemployment is no longer useful as an argument in
the equation.

6.4   Do Trade Unions Cause Inflation?

The somewhat provocative title 'do trade unions cause
inflation?' reflects two important issues which have coloured
the estimation of wage-price relations. In the first place
it has been suggested that the strength of trades unions has
a positive effect on the rate of change of wages. This argument was developed by Hines (1964) and a similar variable
was included in the Lipsey and Parkin (1970) model which was
examined in some detail in the last section. We shall,
therefore, evaluate the empirical evidence for the existence
of this relation in the current section. The second issue is
that it has been assumed implicitly in the foregoing analysis
that wage bargains have been made and that the rate of price
inflation and the level of unemployment are determinants of
those bargains. We shall now take this further with an explicit model of bargaining suggested by Johnston (1974) and
Johnston and Timbrell (1974).

As we noted in the last section it is important to
decide what it is that is bargained for, wage rates, earnings
before overtime, gross earnings, net earnings after tax and
deductions, etc. Johnston and Timbrell opt for the wage
rate, and they point out that the change in the wage rate
will be influenced by the proportions of workers obtaining
a settlement in a given time-period, S.   Furthermore

they also point out that the ratio of net to gross earnings
- the retention ratio, R - affects the demand for gross pay.

They also suggest that if real wages fall below their
trend then bargainers will try to 'catch up' the lost ground.
Including a price expectations variable derived as the
average retail price inflation over the past year and using
annual data over the period 1952-71 they obtain a fair degree
of support for their hypothesis. Most importantly the inclusion of these bargaining variables acts as a substitute for
excess demand variables. To the extent that they have a
'preferred' equation they obtain

$$w_t = 1.09 + \underset{(0.22)}{0.70} S_t + \underset{(1.53)}{0.100} p_t^{e^2} - \underset{(1.35)}{2.25} R_t$$

$$R^2 = 0.755 \quad DW = 2.53 \quad 1959\text{-}1971$$

where $p_t^{e^2}$ is the square of the expected rate of inflation to
take account of a non-linear effect, t-values are shown in
parentheses.

The major issue of this section is whether indicators
of bargaining strength can be incorporated in the more
standard excess demand framework. These indicators may refer
to strikes - which was tried explicitly by Johnson and
Timbrell - or to trade union strength. The Hines indicator,

developed in a series of article (1964; 1968; 1969; 1971) was trade union pushfulness, measured as the proportion of the labour force belonging to a trade union and the change in that proportion. His results suggested that there was a clear relation both between the wars and since the last war and also at a disaggregate as well as the aggregate level. In his (1964) article Hines estimates a three-equation model,

$$w_t = a_0 + a_1 N_t + a_2 n_t + a_3 P_t + a_4 P_{t-1} + a_5 U_t$$

$$p_t = b_0 + b_1 w_t + b_2 m_{t-\frac{1}{2}} + b_3 q_t$$

$$n_t = c_0 + c_1 n_{t-1} + c_2 P_t + c_3 P_{t-1} + c_4 T_{t-\frac{1}{2}}, \qquad (36)$$

where T_t is level of money profits deflated by the rate of change of prices, by 2SLS, giving a wage equation of

$$w_t = -1.9740 + 1.5945 N_t + 0.1282 n_t + 0.6804 p_t$$
$$\qquad\quad (0.2418) \qquad (0.0409) \qquad (0.1129)$$

$$-0.0812 p_{t-1} - 0.0441 U_t$$
$$(0.0276) \qquad (0.0370)$$

$$R^2 = 0.9953 \quad DW = 1.32$$

for annual data over the period 1921-1961 excluding the war years. The specification is revised in Hines (1968) where n_t is dropped and sub-periods estimated. It is clear from the sub-periods that N_t has a larger effect in the post-war period compared with between the wars and that unemployment as little additional effect on the post-war data. The estimates in equations (27), (27a), (27b), (29) and (34) shown earlier were rather less promising as the coefficient of the change in the percentage of the labour force belonging to a union, N, was sometimes not significantly different from zero and on one occasion was actually significantly negative. Hines' results were also called into question by Purdy and Zis (1974) who pointed out that the labour force measures used were rather poorly specified and that N was a poor measure of union militancy.

Purdy and Zis begin by re-specifying the labour force to exclude those who cannot join a union: employers, self-employed and the armed forces. They then suggest that militancy may be more appropriately measured by the level of unionization rather than just its difference, and using (36) obtain for the period 1925-38, 1950-69 with 2SLS on annual data

$$w_t = -\underset{(2.758)}{1.930} + \underset{(0.069)}{0.060}\, n_t + \underset{(0.185)}{0.441}\, N_t + \underset{(0.167)}{0.123}\, p_t + \underset{(0.162)}{0.232}\, p_{t-\frac{1}{2}}$$

$$+ \underset{(0.964)}{5.582}\, U_t^{-1}$$

$$\overline{R}^2 = 0.930 \quad DW = 1.000 \tag{37}$$

$$p_t = -\underset{(0.280)}{0.185} - \underset{(0.115)}{0.021}\, q_t + \underset{(0.031)}{0.236}\, m_{t-\frac{1}{2}} + \underset{(0.069)}{0.677}\, w_t$$

$$\overline{R}^2 = 0.724 \quad DW = 1.586 \tag{38}$$

$$N_t = 10.626 - 0.258\ n_{t-1} + 0.403\ p_{t-\frac{1}{2}} - 0.0004\ T_{t-1}$$
$$\quad\ (1.624)\quad (0.039)\qquad\quad (0.059)\qquad\quad (0.0003)$$

$$\overline{R}^2 = 0.724 \quad DW = 1.192 \tag{39}$$

(standard errors in parentheses).

The equations are well determined although the n_t coefficient
is not significant in the wage equation. It also appears that
there is some evidence of autocorrelation. A further re-
specification is also introduced to eliminate the effect on
militancy of the closed shop. Clearly these results suggest
that this approach has some merit, but does it imply that
trades unions cause inflation? In one sense it obviously
does in that they form the major element in the bargaining
process from the employees' side. However, although they
do provide a greater influence on wage inflation the greater
the increase in their membership, that change in membership
is itself responsive to inflation. The Henry *et al.* (1976)
approach suggests that it is also possible to represent the
power in bargaining by the disequilibrium in real net earnings;
what Hines has emphasized is that this pressure is itself an
endogenous variable. The endogeneity in that case lies in the
link between wage rates and savings.

The critical feature throughout this chapter has been the
importance of simultaneity in the estimation of the wage-price

relations. This dependence also has an important time path

and unless both are taken into account together the results

may be very misleading. Furthermore, the wage equation gives

the most impressive example of the way in which well estab-

lished relations, in this case the Phillips curve, collapsed

around 1967 and have not been re-established with the same

degree of confidence. As a result this equation has attracted

perhaps the largest interest of any of the major macro-economic

relations and, as the current economic situation suggests, it

will continue to do so.

References and Suggested Reading*

*BALL, R.J. and DOYLE, P. (1969) *Inflation* Harmondsworth:

   Penguin.

CARLSON, J.A. and PARKIN, J.M. (1973) 'Inflation expectations'

   Economica (new series) vol. 42 (166) pp. 123-138.

DESAI, M. (1976) *Applied Econometrics* London: Phillip Allan.

*DICKS-MIREAUX, L.A., (1961), 'The inter-relationship between

   cost and price change, 1948-1959: a study of inflation

   in post-war Britain', *Oxford Economic Papers* (new

   series), vol. 13, (3), pp. 267-292 (reprinted in Ball

   and Doyle (1969).

DICKS-MIREAUX, L. and DOW, J.C.R. (1959) 'The determinants of

   wage inflation in the United Kingdom, 1946-1956' *Journal

   of the Royal Statistical Society*, series A, vol. 122 (2)

   pp. 145-184.

DOW, J.C.R. (1956) 'Analysis of the generation of price inflation' *Oxford Economic Papers* (new series) vol. 8 (3) pp. 252-301.

DOW, J.C.R. and DICKS-MIREAUX, L. (1958) 'The excess demand for labour' *Oxford Economic Papers* (new series) vol. 10 (1) pp. 1-33.

GODFREY, L.G. (1972) 'The Phillips curve: incomes policy and trade union effects' in Parkin and Sumner (1972) original version in Johnson and Nobay (1971).

*HENRY, S.G.B. and ORMEROD, P.A. (1978) 'Incomes policy and wage inflation: empirical evidence for the UK 1961-1977' *National Institute Economic Review*, no. 85 (August) pp. 31-39.

*HENRY, S.G.B., SAWYER, M.C. and SMITH, P. (1976) 'Models of inflation in the United Kingdom: an evaluation' *National Institute Economic Review* (August) (77) pp. 60-71

*HINES, A.G. (1964) 'Trade unions and wage inflation in the United Kingdom, 1893-1961' *Review of Economic Studies*, vol. 31 (3) no. 88 pp. 221-252.

HINES, A.G. (1968) 'Unemployment and the rate of change of money wage rates in the United Kingdom, 1862-1963: a reappraisal' *Review of Economics and Statistics* vol. 50 (1) pp. 60-67.

HINES, A.G. (1969) 'Wage inflation in the United Kingdom,

1948-1962: a disaggregated study' *Economic Journal*
vol. 79 (313) pp. 66-89.

HINES, A.G. (1971) 'The determinants of the rate of change
of money wage rates and the effectiveness of incomes
policy' in Johnson and Nobay (1971).

JOHNSON, H.G. and NOBAY, A.R. (1971) (eds.) *The Current
Inflation* London: Macmillan.

JOHNSTON, J. (1974) 'A model of wage determination under
bilateral monopoly' in Laidler and Purdy (1974) reprinted
from *Economic Journal,* 1972 pp. 837-852.

JOHNSTON, J. and TIMBRELL, M.C. (1974) 'Empirical tests of a
bargaining model of wage rate determination' in Laidler
and Purdy (1974) reprinted from *Manchester School,* 1973
pp. 141-167.

KLEIN, L.R., BALL, R.J., HAZLEWOOD, A. and VANDOME, P. (1961)
An Econometric Model of the United Kingdom, Oxford:
Oxford University Press.

*LAIDLER, D.E.W. and PARKIN, J.M. (1975) 'Inflation - a
survey' *Economic Journal,*vol. 85, (December) pp. 741-809.

LAIDLER, D.E.W. and PURDY, D. (1974) (eds.) *Labour Markets
and Inflation* Manchester and Toronto: Manchester and
Toronto University Presses.

LIPSEY, R.G. (1960) 'The relationship between unemployment
and the rate of change of money wage rates in the UK,
1862-1957: a further analysis' *Economica* (new series)

vol. 27 (105) pp. 1-31.

*LIPSEY, R.G. and PARKIN, J.M. (1970) 'Incomes policy - a reappraisal' *Economica* (new series) vol. 37, (146) pp. 115-138 reprinted in Parkin and Sumner (1972).

MADDALA, G.S. (1977)*Econometrics*, McGraw Hill.

MAYES, A.C. and MAYES, D.G. (1976) *Introductory Economic Statistics*, Chichester: John Wiley and Sons.

MINFORD, A.P.L., and BRECH, M. (1979) 'The wage equation and rational expectations' AUTE conference at Exeter (forthcoming in proceedings).

OECD (1970) *Inflation: the present problem*, Paris.

PARKIN, J.M. (1970) 'Incomes policy: some further results on the rate of change of money wages' *Economica* (new series) vol. 37 (148) pp. 386-401 reprinted in Parkin and Sumner (1972).

*PARKIN, J.M. and SUMNER, M.T. (1972) (eds.) *Incomes Policy and Inflation* Manchester and Toronto: Manchester and Toronto University Presses.

PARKIN, J.M., SUMNER, M.T. and WARD (1976) 'The effects of excess demand, generalized expectations and wage-price controls on wage inflation in the UK: 1956-71' in Brunner, K and Meltzer,A.H. (eds.) *The Economics of Price and Wage Controls*, North Holland.

*PHILLIPS, A.W. (1958) 'The relationship between unemployment
    and the rate of change of money wage rates in the UK,
    1861-1957' *Economica* (new series) vol. 25 (100) pp. 283-
    299 reprinted in Ball and Doyle (1969).

PURDY, D. and ZIS, G. (1974) 'Trade unions and wage inflation
    in the UK: a reappraisal' in Laidler and Purdy (1974).

SARGAN, J.D. (1964) 'Wages and Prices in the United Kingdom'
    in Hart P.D., Mills, G. and Whittaker, J.K. (eds.)
    Econometric Analysis for National Economic Planning
    (Colston Papers) London: Butterworths.

SAUNDERS, P.G. and NOBAY, A.R. (1972) 'Price expectations,
    the Phillips curve and incomes policy' in Parkin and
    Sumner (1972).

SMITH, D.C. (1972) 'Incomes policy' in Parkin and Sumner
    (1972).

SOLOW, R.M. (1969) *Price Expectations and the Behaviour of
    the Price Level* Manchester: Manchester University Press.

TAYLOR, J. (1974) *Unemployment and Wage Inflation*, London:
    Longmans.

TREVITHICK, J.A. and MULVEY, C. (1975) *The Economics of
    Inflation*, London: Martin Robertson.

WALLIS, K.F. (1972) 'Wages, prices and incomes policies:
    some comments' in Parkin and Sumner (1972).

Chapter 7

INTERNATIONAL TRADE

In sharp contrast to the sectors of the economy which we
have considered previously the international sector is
characterized by the lack of sophistication in econometric
modelling. This lack of sophistication is readily understandable
when we realise the size of the problem. If one were to take
the trade flows between the twenty-five most important countries
alone this generates 600 trade flows which have to be explained.
Disaggregation by commodity group, even into just: finished
manufactures, semi-finished manufactures, food and raw materials
and services, increases the total number of flows to 2,400.
Clearly any model which seeks to explain such a number of flows
must be straightforward if the problems of the sheer size of
data handling and estimation are to be overcome. Nevertheless
these difficulties must not result in substantial specification
errors or poor estimators if the models developed are to be of
any real use.

In the first section of this chapter we shall set out the
general form of these models and show how they are used in

258

practice by organizations such as the OECD and the IMF. In
general they can be categorized into two groups: (a) those
models which are basically of a cross-section form and explain
flows between countries with a common set of parameters (sometimes a number of years of observations are employed);
(b) those models which estimate time series functions for
individual flows and build up the overall picture in a much
less constrained manner.

In the second section we shall move on to consider a
specific problem involving the use of these models namely the
estimation of the effects of free trade areas and customs
unions on trade. Particular emphasis is laid on the effects
of the EEC both for the original six members and the enlarge-
ment to the nine.

It might appear that in one sense we are taking a step
backwards in econometric methodology in the analysis presented
in this chapter. However, the sequence of this and the two
chapters which follow, on demand analysis and models of the
macro-economy, is that in this chapter we introduce the problem
of having a large number of equations and a consequently large
amount of data. Here the equations are either unconstrained or
estimated subject to very simple constraints. Demand analysis
on the other hand presents systems of highly constrained
equations which are derived from one of the areas of economics

where the theory has been most fully and highly developed.
This series of four chapters on simultaneous equations which
we began with simple two equation wage-price models is completed by the most complex case of all where we consider
models of the whole economy.

7.1   The explanation of international trade flows

In the introduction it was suggested that the general
form of trade models is very simple. Taking the time series
approach to begin with, the volume of imports, M, is thought
to depend upon the level of real economic activity in the
importing country, Y, and the relative price of imports to
domestic products, PM/PD, in the form

$$M = a_1 Y^{a_2} (PM/PD)^{a_3}. \tag{1}$$

This can be estimated readily by logarithmic transformation if
the error term in (1) is assumed to be multiplicative

$$\log M = a_0 + a_2 \log Y + a_3 \log (PM/PD) + u \tag{2}$$

where $a_0 = \log a_1$ and u is the error term.[1]

The specification and estimation of trade models has been
preoccupied by the concept of elasticities largely because

---

[1]
There are of course other possible functional forms of this
relation, but (2) among other things has the advantage that a_2
and a_3 are themselves estimates of the income and price elasticities of import demand.

of the Marshall-Lerner condition for the effect of an exchange rate change on the balance of trade: a devaluation
will improve the balance of trade if the sum of the price
elasticity of domestic demand for imports and the foreign
price elasticity of demand for the country's exports is
greater than unity (both elasticities are traditionally defined in positive terms although of course they are both negative on a strict interpretation). In pre-war studies there
was a considerable worry that the elasticities were in fact
very small, but Orcutt (1950) showed that part of this was
due to an elementary simultaneous equations problem. If
foreign suppliers of imported goods were also price sensitive
in that the higher the price they could obtain for their
product the more they were prepared to supply, as is shown by
the line SS' in Fig. 7.1, then a shift in the demand curve DD'
such as D_1D_1' due to non-price factors would result in a price
which is higher than that associated with DD' and hence a
positive error in that time period. In general therefore, with
a given SS', errors in the import demand function and the
relative price term will be correlated. The ensuing bias is easy
to show heuristically. If the supply curve also shifts from
time period to time period due to factors which are unrelated
to shifts in the demand curve, the observations on price and
quantity will be distributed in some space such as the parrall-
elogram $ABCD$. Hence the ordinary least squares line (minimizing
the error sum of squares in the vertical dimension) will tend

Figure 7.1   Bias in the estimation of import
price elasticities

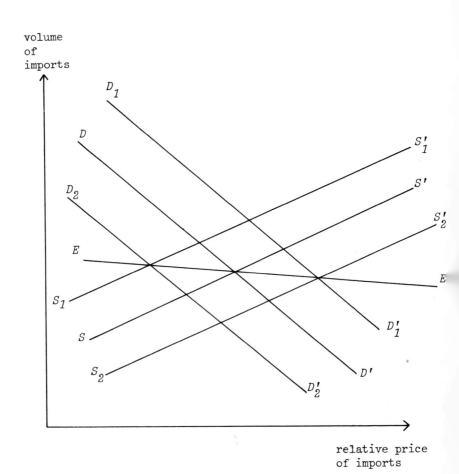

volume
of
imports

relative price
of imports

to be nearer the horizontal than the true demand curve, thus
biasing the price elasticity towards zero.

7.1.1   Elasticity pessimism

In the post-war years this problem of bias towards zero
has appeared soluble by a number of means. In the first place
it is argued that for most countries the supply of imports can
be treated as being perfectly elastic with respect to price,
in which case shifts in demand will not result in changes in
price (if the supply curve remains unchanged). The simultaneity
bias therefore disappears.

In the second place disaggregation of imports by product
category, food, raw materials, fuels, semi-finished manufactures
and finished manufactured products helps to reduce the problem.
Basic inputs such as food, raw materials and fuels are essential parts of the productive process and tend to vary much
more closely with industrial output (household income and population in the case of food) than with price. Finished manufactures on the other hand have close domestic substitutes in many
cases and hence price is an extremely important factor. With
the high levels of protection on finished products between the
wars the aggregation of the various categories of imports may
very well have contributed to the downward bias in the estimates of the price elasticity of demand.   Orcutt pointed out

that the three categories with the lowest price elasticities
also had the highest variations in price and hence would tend
to dominate the price variable.

Ball and Marwah (1962) obtain price and 'income'
elasticities from a linear import function which confirm
these results, using quarterly data for the United States over
the period 1948-58:

Import category	Income	Output	Price elas- ticity	Other vari- ables in equation	$\bar{R}^2$	Von Neuman Ratio
	elasticity					
Crude food- stuffs	–	0.49	-0.34	D	0.19	2.22
Manufac- tured food- stuffs	0.96	–	-1.87	–	0.84	1.53
Crude materials	–	0.87	-0.26	D	0.50	1.53
Semi man- ufactures	–	1.22	-1.38	S	0.72	1.31
Manufactures	–	2.47	-3.50	D	0.89	1.63
Services	0.58	–	–	t	0.85	1.76

Elasticities are measured at the sample mean, D is a dummy
variable for the Korean war, S is the stock/output ratio and t
is a time trend.

This type of aggregation problem occurs throughout macro-
economics and it has been mentioned to varying extents in each
of the chapters in this book. Furthermore it will be a topic

of major importance in Chapter 9 when we consider a model of
the whole economy. Barker (1970) provides a detailed analysis
of the causes of the aggregation bias and shows its extent in
the case of the UK. In particular he shows that shares of the
component import categories in total imports have varied
systematically over the period 1955-66 and hence that the aggregate elasticities have varied over time. Secondly, one of
the reasons why relative price effects are smaller in the
aggregate is because the high elasticity items have tended to
show smaller relative price fluctuations.

There is clearly considerable variation in elasticities
between product groups as can be seen from Barker's work with
Lecomber (1967) on the Cambridge Department of Applied Economics
'Programme for Growth', where over thirty categories are
distinguished and classed as 'competitive' or 'complementary'
according to whether or not a domestically produced substitute
is widely available. In the case of 'complementary' imports we
would expect near zero price elasticities. These results are
confirmed by those from a ninety-nine category break-down of
manufactures for the UK in Mayes (1971). (In both cases the import
functions used are linear in logarithms.) The problem in
practice therefore is to make the optimal decision on the
trade-off between practicality and aggregation bias, remember-
ing also that aggregation, especially where the proportions

of the components in the aggregate vary over time, may have
consequences for the variance properties of the disturbances
in the equations.

These import functions also exemplify several other
common econometric problems and much of the importance of
Orcutt's article is that he appreciated them as early as
1950. The first further problem is that of errors in variables,
which may, incidentally, become more serious with disaggregated
data.

Errors in the quantity variable merely result in a less
precise estimator (provided they are independently distributed
with a common variance), but errors in income and price are
shown by Orcutt to result in a bias towards zero of both
coefficients. He also argues that import prices are more likely
to be subject to error than import volumes. However, one of
his assumptions is that errors in the measurement of incomes
prices and quantities are uncorrelated. While this may be true
between incomes and prices and incomes and quantities it may
very well not be true for price and quantities. Import prices
are frequently measured in the form of unit values so that
for any given value, $V = QP$, if the quantity is under-estimated
then the price will be over-estimated and vice-versa.

The fourth of Orcutt's points is that the elasticities estimated are essentially short run in that only current values of income and price were used in the equations estimated before the time of his writing. Lags were clearly to be expected in the system and the long-run adjustment to a price change is likely to be larger than the short-run change. Clearly a further problem will also occur here, namely bias from the omission of variables and Orcutt mentions this in an appendix. If the true model should include prices lagged one period as well as current prices, the effect of the omission of lagged prices depends upon the correlation between P_t and P_{t-1}. If P_t and P_{t-1} are positively correlated the omission bias will reduce the bias towards zero caused by the use of current prices alone to estimate the long-run price elasticity (a negative correlation obviously increases the bias, while if P_t and P_{t-1} are uncorrelated there is no omission bias).

Finally Orcutt suggests that the elasticity may increase with the size of the price change. The argument is that for small changes people will only make marginal adjustments in their pattern of behaviour whereas for large changes they will have to make changes in the structure of their behaviour and thus may change by a larger relative proportion. Since the point of the analysis is to estimate the effect of a devaluation, which, in that period of fixed exchange rates, would involve a substantial step downwards rather than a

drift, this argument is clearly relevant. The data largely

reflect only small price changes whereas the estimate is

required for a large change.[2]

The only disappointing feature of this otherwise percep-

tive article is that Orcutt was very pessimistic about the

prospects for improvement, suggesting that disaggregation

seemed to be the only useful way forward - 'it is also believed

that it is unlikely that any greater success can be achieved

by an application of some of the newer statistical techniques

to these time series; for example, these designed to deal

with the problems arising from the existence of several

relations between the time series or with the presence of err-

ors of observations'. (p. 126).

7.1.2   A Time-series model of imports and exports

It is ironical that despite Orcutt's fears many modellers

are still employing the same sorts of equations 30 years later.

Certainly 20 years later Houthakker and Magee (1969) presented

import equations of the same form as (2) where M is measured

in 1958 dollars (merchandise imports only), Y is an index of

2

  Goldstein and Kahn (1976) test this hypothesis for several
countries.

Table 7.1   *Total Imports and Exports of Six Industrial Countries*
(Annual data 1951-1966)

Imports

Country	a_0	a_2	a_3	ρ	$\bar{R}^2$ (s.e.)	DW (d.f.)
United States (1)	4.98 (2.40)	1.51 (12.09)	−0.54 (−1.59)		0.976 (0.0421)	1.11 (13)
(3)	6.44 (2.70)	1.68 (10.66)	−1.03 (−2.43)	0.654	0.984 (0.0338)	2.00 (12)
United Kingdom (1)	1.14 (0.97)	1.66 (10.54)	0.22 (1.07)		0.975 (0.0314)	1.20 (13)
(2)	2.36 (8.07)	1.51 (23.93)			0.974 (0.0316)	1.29 (14)
(3)	3.57 (2.24)	1.45 (10.29)	−0.21 (−0.99)	0.128	0.986 (0.0230)	2.14 (12)
Japan (1)	4.12 (3.70)	1.23 (13.06)	−0.72 (−2.40)		0.985 (0.0777)	2.40 (13)
West Germany (1)	1.15 (1.07)	1.80 (17.25)	−0.24 (−0.91)		0.995 (0.0424)	1.17 (13)
(2)	0.18 (1.12)	1.89 (55.21)			0.995 (0.0422)	1.21 (14)
(3)	0.37 (1.27)	1.85 (30.19)		0.406	0.995 (0.0389)	1.85 (13)
France (1)	0.64 (0.28)	1.66 (9.31)	0.17 (0.26)		0.961 (0.0759)	1.42 (13)
(2)	1.22 (3.24)	1.62 (20.00)			0.964 (0.0734)	1.46 (14)
Italy (1)	−1.57 (−0.50)	2.19 (6.48)	−0.13 (−0.18)		0.979 (0.0808)	1.21 (13)
(2)	−2.15 (−5.65)	2.25 (27.48)			0.980 (0.0780)	1.17 (14)

Exports

Country	b_0	b_1	b_2	ρ	$\bar{R}^2$ (s.e.)	DW (d.f.)
United States (1)	12.18 (6.85)	0.99 (10.46)	−1.51 (−3.24)		0.933 (0.0480)	1.82 (13)
United Kingdom (1)	7.26 (7.17)	0.86 (9.38)	−0.44 (−1.45)		0.976 (0.0238)	1.29 (13)
Japan (3)	10.26 (4.96)	1.00 (8.25)	−1.24 (−2.37)	0.670	0.978 (0.222)	2.13 (12)
	−4.78 (−1.53)	3.55 (14.82)	−0.80 (−1.78)		0.984 (0.0925)	1.04 (13)
West Germany (1)	−8.45 (−2.66)	2.08 (9.56)	1.70 (1.97)		0.967 (0.0922)	0.55 (13)
(2)	−2.29 (−3.86)	2.44 (19.18)			0.961 (0.1013)	0.24 (14)
France (3)	11.32 (4.36)	0.91 (3.25)	−1.25 (−3.48)	0.887	0.997 (0.0263)	2.39 (12)
	11.98 (6.23)	1.53 (31.21)	−2.27 (−5.63)		0.987 (0.0394)	2.35 (13)
Italy (1)	−5.58 (−1.24)	2.95 (10.45)	−0.03 (−0.04)		0.988 (0.0703)	1.13 (13)
(2)	−5.74 (−15.47)	2.96 (37.10)			0.989 (0.0678)	1.13 (14)
(3)	0.67 (0.34)	2.68 (22.63)	−1.12 (−3.61)	0.105	0.998 (0.0278)	1.81 (12)

Source: Houthakker and Magee (1969).
The number in parenthesis below each coefficient is a *t*-ratio.
(1) unrestricted form; (2) price coefficient constrained equal zero; (3) Cochrane-Orcutt estimation of first order autoregressive form.

GNP and *PD* is the wholesale price index.[3] The interesting
features of the analysis were that not only did they present
comparable functions for some 29 countries and for United
States imports from 16 countries and 5 commodity classes,
but they also calculated similar export functions. It was
thus possible to consider both the effects of devaluation (in
a static framework) and the effects on the balance of trade
of various growth rates. These results have been widely
quoted as having important implications for economic policy,
particularly in the UK, and therefore merit critical scrutiny
here.

The export equations (whose estimates are shown with
the import equations for the six major countries in Table 7.1)
are of the same form as the import equation (2), but with
world activity as the 'income' variable and world export
prices as the 'relative price'.

$$\log X_{jt} = b_{0j} + b_{1j} \log WY_{jt} + b_{2j} \log (PX_{jt}/PWX_{jt}) \qquad (3)$$

where X_{jt} is the jth country's exports of goods to all other

---

[3] Magee (1975) in effect justified his earlier perseverance
with traditional import functions by producing a counter-list
of eight reasons why price elasticities might be *over*-estimated

countries during year t (in 1958 dollars), WY_{jt} is an index

of GNP for 26 importing countries *excluding* country j each

weighted by its 1958 share in the total exports of country j,

PX_{jt} is an index of country j's export prices in 1958 dollars

and PWX_{jt} is an index of the export prices of the other 26

exporting countries.[4]

Although the equations all fit the data quite closely -

the lowest value for $\overline{R}^2$ is 0.933 - there are clearly consider-

able problems with using this specification as it stands. Only

three out of the twelve price elasticities are clearly negative

as indicated by the t-values when the equation is estimated by

OLS, and all except one of the remaining nine equations have

values for the Durbin-Watson statistic in the uncertain range

or indicating positive autocorrelation. Upon re-estimation by

the Cochrane-Orcutt method four further 'significant' negative

price elasticities are obtained. Thus while all six countries

have price coefficients which are significantly less than zero

in their export equations only the United States and Japan do

for imports. Clearly Orcutt's problems have not been resolved.

---

[4]
   This index is constructed by first obtaining a price index for
the 25 other exporting countries in each of the 26 import markets (other than j) by weighting each price by the 1958 share in
that import market. Then these 26 weighted prices are combined
to form PWX_{jt} by weighting each by its 1958 share in j's exports.

The difficulties do not end here because Houthakker
and Magee do not quote the long-run elasticities implicit in
their autoregressive estimates. These are set out in Table
7.2 and show that behaviour is rather more dramatic than is
apparent from the argument in the original article (if the
specification is believed). The authors, not surprisingly,
concentrate on the income elasticities. They argue that the
discrepancy between the income elasticity of imports and the
income elasticity for a country's exports shows how fast that
country must grow relative to the rest of the world if it is
to avoid persistent surpluses or deficits on the balance of
trade (assuming a zero balance as the starting point). Thus
from Table 7.1 we see that the United States can only grow at
two-thirds of the world rate as can the United Kingdom; France
can grow slightly less than the world rate; Italy, slightly
more, and Japan nearly three times as fast. West Germany, however, presents a problem as soon as we consider equation (3) in
Table 7.1. On the basis of short-run elasticities Germany
can only grow half as fast as the rest of the world (clearly
false in practice) but from the long-run elasticities in Table
7.2. it can grow more than twice as fast. However, if we use
long-run elasticities we would obtain perverse results for the
United States with a permitted growth rate only one-fifth of
the rest of the world. There are obviously some specification
problems remaining especially with regard to the lag structure
of the model.

Table 7.2   Long run price and income elasticities implicit in Table 7.1

Imports			Exports	
Income	Price	Country	Income	Price
4.85	-2.98	United States		
1.66	-0.24	United Kingdom	3.03	-3.76
3.11	—	West Germany	8.05	-11.06
		Italy	2.99	-1.25

7.1.3   The role of supply

There is also a further problem. These equations are all demand functions and ignore the role of supply. Given the weakness of prices as an explanation, much of what these equations tell us is that Japan and Germany grew faster than the world average, Italy and France near it and the United States and United Kingdom rather slower. We may have some sort of reduced form result and not necessarily an explanation. Much of the complaint about the UK's export performance has revolved round specific non-price factors such as delivery, quality, marketing, etc., some of which reflected the inability of supply to meet rapid changes in demand. Such supply constraints would of course tend to entail that imports would also tend to rise rapidly on such occasions to help satisfy domestic demand.[5]

For this reason the first full OECD econometric model
(Adams *et al.*, 1969) incorporated supply factors into its
equations. They also used quarterly data - which makes the
careful specification of the lag-structure even more important.
Their import equation, (4), adds two sets of variables to the
simple form of (2), the first relate to trends and special
factors and the second to variations which occur because of the
business cycle.

$$M_t = a_1 + a_2\ IP_t + a_3\ (PM/PD)_{t-1} + a_4\ EC_t + a_5\ L_t$$
$$+ a_6\ D_t + a_7\ S_t + a_8\ C_t + a_9\ U_t + a_{10}\ UD_t \qquad (4)$$

In this equation the functional form is linear,[6] imports
are in index form based on 1960 as is the activity variable
which is industrial production in this case and relative
price is lagged one quarter. The trend and special factor var-

---

[5]
Morgan (1970) also mentions a number of further factors which
are ignored by Houthakker and Magee's simple specification, in
particular she draws attention to the problems of 'catching-up'
by some countries after the war and the general process of tar-
iff cutting that took place during the period whose omission
would distort not just the estimates of the parameters but
the inferences for policy drawn from them.

[6]
The 1970 version of the OECD model (Meyer-zu-Schlochtern and
Yajima, 1970) re-specifies the equations in log-linear form on
half yearly data over the period 1955(1)-1969(2).

Table 7.3   *Coefficients of Quarterly Import Functions*

Country	Constant	IP	EC	L	PM/PD	D_1	D_2	S	C	V	UD	$\bar{R}^2$	SEE	DW
France	364.92 (1.3)	1.32 (5.8)	-3.17 (1.2)		-0.81 (3.5)	-2.17 (0.6)			-0.93 (2.2)		0.11 (2.8)	0.976	4.74	1.09
Germany	332.75 (2.2)	1.34 (10.8)	-2.82 (2.0)		-0.85 (3.0)				-1.17 (3.7)			0.987	4.74	1.40
Italy	163.38 (0.4)	1.35 (5.1)	-2.00 (0.5)						-2.08 (2.2)			0.966	7.42	0.76
United Kingdom	495.54 (2.3)	1.07 (11.6)	-4.72 (2.3)	0.12 (1.4)		-5.65 (4.4)	-2.01 (1.0)	-0.42 (3.5)	-0.29 (2.2)	1.69[1] (1.6)		0.987	1.54	1.83
United States	140.06 (3.4)	0.76 (6.0)			-1.16 (4.1)				-0.28 (1.0)	8.30[1] (1.2)		0.956	3.90	1.19
Canada	71.49 (4.0)	0.90 (7.1)			-0.62 (2.1)				-0.24 (1.2)	39.41[1,3] (1.3)		0.923	3.71	0.98
Japan	5.91 (2.1)	0.93 (12.9)		0.11 (1.1)					0.63[2] (2.6)	1.64[2] (2.8)	0.95 (1.3)	0.991	4.16	1.08
Belgium	888.02 (2.1)	1.21 (6.4)	-8.49 (2.1)		-0.61 (5.1)				-0.28 (1.3)			0.981	3.90	1.15
Netherlands	159.40 (0.3)	1.35 (8.0)	-1.68 (0.3)		-0.24 (0.85)				-0.21[1] (1.4)	0.23[1] (3.8)	0.28 (3.6)	0.985	3.28	1.45

Sample period – 1955(4)–1965(4).
Figures in parentheses – *t*-ratio.
Source: Adams *et al.* (1969).

$\bar{R}^2$ – adjusted coefficient of determination
SEE – standard error of estimate
DW – Durbin-Watson statistic

(1) lagged one quarter
(2) without lag
(3) positive values only

iables are: EC, which is a dummy variable to take account of
the reduction in tariffs caused by the formation of the EEC
(EFTA in the case of the UK); L, which is a liberalization
variable reflecting the proportion of trade liberalized (in
terms of the share of 1953 imports); D, which is a dummy variable which allows for strikes, other policy shifts, etc., and S
which is the index of the import surcharge (imposed by the UK).
The remaining variables relate to the business cycle; C is the
value of deviations in stocks from the trend stock-output
relation (which is assumed to be linear) lagged two quarters,
U is the deviation in unfilled order/delivery ratio from its
linear trend relation to deliveries, and $UD_t = U_t - U_{t-1}$. Since
the function is linear it is not possible to calculate elasticities directly from Table 7.3 without knowing the absolute
values of the variables. The industrial production variable is
important in all cases as might be expected, but surprisingly t
EC variable only affects Germany, Belgium and the United Kingdc
Other evidence (as discussed in Section 7.2) would suggest that
the effect of joining the EEC for the other members must be reflected in the values of the other variables as there is clearl
an effect to be estimated. As in the case of Houthakker and Mag
it was not possible to obtain satisfactory price coefficients f
the United Kingdom or Italy, but surprisingly Adams *et al.* did
not obtain one for Japan. The cyclical variables have a clear
effect reflecting that these short-run dynamics are important

when using quarterly data. However, the use of stockbuilding

variations is a rather mixed benefit as these reflect more

than one influence (see Surrey (1971).   **In the first** place

if future expansions in output **are planned stocks**

will be increased prior to those expansions. Secondly if pro-

ducers miscalculate demand stocks will be built up or run

down according to whether the error is the result of an over-

estimate or underestimate. From a theoretical point of view the

unfilled orders/deliveries variables might have been expected

to be more appropriate indicators of pressure on domestic

industries.

Both import and export functions are estimated by ordinary

least squares, relying on the incorporation of domestic demand

variables to take account of any problems of simultaneity. The

export functions shown in Table 7.4 incorporate a similar pres-

sure of domestic demand variable to that in the versions of

(4) used for forecasting. This variable, *PD*, is the percentage

deviation of industrial production from its semilogarithmic

trend.[7] The form of *PD* and the 'relative competitiveness' var-

iable (i.e. export price, *PX*) used in the export equation (5) is

---

[7]

   Barker (1979) points out that there is an identification problem in the use of 'capacity utilization' variables of this form.

Table 7.4   Coefficients of Quarterly Export Functions

Country	Constant	PXX	PDX	PD	EC1	EC2	D_1	D_2	D_3	t	(R^2)	SD	DW
France	144.05 (7.7)	-1.06 (8.2)	-0.45 (4.3)		0.68 (5.3)	-0.47 (4.2)		7.98 (3.7)	-7.22 (3.9)		0.991	2.39	1.61
Germany	52.03 (1.9)	-0.65 (3.5)	-0.09 (0.5)		0.40 (2.6)	-0.14 (1.2)	8.09 (3.6)		1.19 (8.3)		0.994	2.12	1.76
Italy	188.81 (3.7)	-0.25 (1.0)	-1.19 (3.4)	-0.65 (1.7)	3.63 (6.5)	0.84 (2.4)	6.93 (1.5)				0.989	4.82	1.11
United Kingdom	87.31 (2.9)	-0.48 (1.4)	-0.33 (1.5)								0.915	2.81	1.20
United States	5.33 (0.1)	-0.60 (2.4)(a)	-0.33 (2.8)	0.86 (3.2)	-0.27 (1.6)		20.73 (7.5)	-0.82 (7.7) 14.86 (5.8)			0.973	2.68	1.85
Canada	-10.91 (0.3)	-0.23 (0.8)		0.41 (1.8)	-0.25 (1.0)		7.02 (1.4)	12.30 (2.3)	12.31 (4.4) 46.33 (11.4)		0.952	4.70	0.95
Japan	-45.79 (0.8)	-0.71 (1.5)	-0.15 (0.9)	0.99 (3.5)			-19.61 (3.3)			1.84 (7.8)	0.990	5.12	1.22
Belgium	-33.65 (0.7)		-0.77 (2.7)	1.07 (3.9)	1.26 (4.0)		13.44 (3.7)	-8.79 (4.7)		0.84 (5.8)	0.987	3.38	1.03
Netherlands	55.43 (1.1)	-0.59 (1.2)			0.17 (1.2)	-0.31 (2.0)	11.50 (3.1)				0.980	3.42	1.50
Other OECD	-0.69 (1.1)									0.09 (3.3)	0.992	1.98	1.38
Non-OECD	64.87 (8.5)			-0.56 (7.3)						-0.42 (25.8)	0.996	1.24	1.80

Source: Adams et al. (1969).
(a) Lagged 3 quarters
Figures in parentheses are t-ratios.

similar to that used to construct the export price index.

For each export market the ratio of PD (or PX) to the sum of

PD (PX) for all the other countries exporting to that market

weighted by their base year (1960) share, is calculated and

the sum of these weighted by the share of each market in the

exporting country's total exports, gives the variables PDX and

PXX actually included in (5):

$$X_i - XC_i = b_1 + b_2 \, PXX_i + b_3 \, PDX_i + b_4 \, PD_i + b_5 \, EC1$$
$$+ \; b_6 \, EC2 + \sum_{k}^{3} \, b_{k+6} \, D_k + b_{10}t \qquad\qquad (5)$$

where XC_i is the value of X_i which would be obtained if country

i kept a constant share of all markets to which it sold; $EC1$

and $EC2$ are time trends to take account of the first stage of

the formation of the EEC, 1959-61, and the second stage and the

formation of EFTA, 1962-5, respectively; the D_k are dummy var-

iables relating to strikes, the adjustment to exchange rate

changes (the Bretton Woods 'fixed' exchange rate regime pre-

vailed throughout the estimation period) and other identifiable

distortions to the patterns of trade flows.

This series of export functions, therefore, has an impor-

tant difference in specification over that of Houthakker and

Magee. The import functions (5) determine the aggregate flows

into each country and the export functions (6) allocate it

among all the export countries. Thus the model reconciles the trade flows by origin and by destination. This latter

approach reflects the overall consideration of most complete

trade flow models, including the most recent version of the

OECD model (OECD, 1979), the IMF model (Deppler and Ripley,

1978) and the Treasury model (Davies, 1979). This problem of

the allocation of predetermined import demands among exporting

countries is developed in a dynamic framework, using adaptive

expectations and explicit elasticities of substitution, by

Hickman and Lau (1973) for 25 countries and two areas to com-

plete a world model. The reconciliation of exports and imports

can, however, be approached differently by trying to model the

flows themselves and this is considered in the next sub-section.

7.1.4   Cross-section models

Thus far we have considered trade flows either from the

point of view of the importing country or the exporting country,

but not simultaneously from both. Clearly the problem of recon-

ciliation is much more simple if both factors are taken together

and the most straightforward approach to this lies in the

'gravity' models pioneered by Tinbergen (1962) and developed by

Linnemann (1966), Poyhönen (1963), Pulliainen (1963), Aitken

(1973) and Bluet and Systermanns (1968).[8] Here the flows

8

There are some more direct attempts at the reconciliation of
exports and imports such as Savage and Deutsch (1960), Waelbroec
(1964) and Mayes (1974).

themselves are determined by characteristics of the importing

and exporting countries and the barriers and encouragement to

trade between them, such as distance and preference agreements.

In its simplest form this can be expressed as

$$X_{ij} = f\ (Y_i,\ Y_j,\ N_i,\ N_j,\ B_{ij}) \qquad\qquad (6)$$

where X is the flow from country i to country j. The same

two factors determine the availability of export supply as the

level of import demand namely income, Y, and population, N.

The argument runs that the greater the income of a country

the greater its ability to produce and absorb products and

hence the greater its tendency both to export and import.

Population on the other hand has the opposite effect. It is

thought that for any given level of income the ability of a

country to produce for domestic consumption increases with

population. These two influences are confounded with the

effects of per capita income, with which imports and exports

are assumed to increase proportionately.

The income and population factors determine the levels

of total imports and exports of a country and if there were

no other factors affecting trade flows the bilateral flows

would be determined in proportion to the respective totals.

However, this proportionality is disturbed by the barriers

to the particular trade flow, B_{ij}, which is a combination of distance, D_{ij}, and dummy variables reflecting preference

areas, P_{ij}^k (where there are $k = 1, \ldots, K$ areas). Equation

(6) is usually expressed in multiplicative form and estimated

in logarithms, as is shown for Linnemann (1966) in Table 7.5

where the equation is

$$\log X_{ij} = c_0 + c_2 \log Y_i + c_3 \log Y_j + c_4 \log N_i$$

$$+ c_5 \log N_j + c_6 \log D_{ij} + \sum^K c_{k+6} \log P_{ij}^k$$

$$+ c_{K+7} C_{ij} + u_{ij} \tag{7}$$

and X is in US \$ million, Y in US \$ billion, N in millions and

D in thousand nautical miles. Linnemann uses data for flows

between 80 countries averaged over the years 1958–1960.

Observations were obtained for both exports and imports of

which 3,400 and 3,532 respectively were non-zero. The variable

C_{ij} reflects the commodity composition of the two countries'

trade.

The estimates of the basic form of (7) are given by

(8) and (11) in Table 7.5 using all the non-zero trade flows.

The values of the income elasticities are close to unity and

that for the exporting country exceeds that for the importing

country. The population coefficients are also similar and

well determined and distance clearly constitutes a very

important barrier to trade. The preference dummies, which are

Table 7.5 A gravity model of trade flows

	c_0	c_2	c_3	c_4	c_5	c_6	c_K	R
(a) Export data								
(8)	-0.31	1.11 (0.02)	0.96 (0.02)	-0.34 (0.03)	-0.28 (0.03)	-0.81 (0.03)		0.792
(9)	-0.91	1.79 (0.03)	1.46 (0.03)	-0.75 (0.03)	-0.58 (0.03)	-1.37 (0.03)		0.797
(10)	0.51	0.96 (0.02)	0.85 (0.02)	-0.27 (0.03)	-0.20 (0.03)	-0.87 (0.03)	0.83 (0.04)	0.821
(b) Import data								
(11)	0.12	0.98 (0.02)	0.86 (0.02)	-0.21 (0.03)	-0.14 (0.03)	-0.77 (0.03)		0.793
(12)	-0.08	1.42 (0.02)	1.27 (0.02)	-0.39 (0.03)	-0.46 (0.03)	-1.17 (0.03)		0.802
(13)	1.12	0.80 (0.02)	0.79 (0.02)	-0.13 (0.02)	-0.16 (0.03)	-0.81 (0.03)	0.86 (0.04)	0.818

Source: Linnemann (1966).
Income variable is real in the case of export data and nominal for import data. Numbers in parentheses are standard errors. Note the use of R instead of $\bar{R}^2$.

not shown in the table, have positive coefficients between
six and ten times as large as their standard errors. Given
the many other special factors involved which disturb the
trade pattern such as language differences, discrimination and
tastes, the degree of explanation is impressive. On the other
hand it should also be remembered that the clear determination
of the coefficients is aided by the extremely large number of
observations and the proportion of the total variance explained
is only just over 0.6. Hence the residual errors are often very
large. However, this cross-section model presents some interesting problems for estimation.

In the first place all flows which are less than $50,000
are excluded from the sample which will impart bias to the
estimates as at low values of X_{ij} only those observations with
large positive disturbances, U_{ij}, will be included. An idea of
the importance of the error can be obtained by calculating the
'explained' values of those flows whose observed value is less
than $50,000. A total of 1,532 of the export flows and 1,411 of
the import flows have an 'explained' value of greater than
$50,000. Linnemann, therefore, includes all the 'zero' flows
whose 'explained' values exceeded $150,000. If all zero flows
were included the opposite bias would tend to be introduced and
a large range of values of the exogenous variables would be associated with the same value of the endogenous variable. (Since

the equations are in logarithms, X_{ij} cannot be set equal to

zero. In any case the hypothesis is that it is not zero, so

Linnemann picks the arbitrary rule that all 'zero' values

using export data (i.e. measured f.o.b.) will be set at

$10,000, and $20,000 using import data (c.i.f.).)

These revised estimates for 4,831 observations are shown

as equations (9) and (12). The immediate effect is to make

all the coefficients differ more substantially from zero with-

out much change in their standard errors. However, a further

examination of the errors suggests that while in the first

case estimates of small flows tended to be too large, in this

second pair of equations it is the very large flows which are

over-estimated. The conclusions which might be drawn from this

are that either the shape of the function is misspecified or

that there are different determinants of trade depending upon

size (as largely reflected by level of economic development

(i.e. income per capita)). Linnemann approaches this by using

a commodity composition variable C_{ij} which is a measure of

complementarity. Thus the more similar the export composition

of i and the import composition of j the closer C_{ij} approaches

unity. The term C_{ij} is a very non-linear measure and this has

somewhat odd implications. However, it tends to mean that flows

between developed and less developed countries have larger

values of C_{ij} than flows between developed countries which in

turn are larger values than for flows between less developed
countries.

The inclusion of this variable as shown by equations (10)
and (13) is an improvement to the overall explanation, although
the equations should be compared with (8) and (11) rather than
(9) and (10) as all flows which are zero in either export or
import definitions are excluded leaving some 3,175 observations.

Although this type of unified model of trade flows has been
used to determine the effects of integration on trade, as we
shall see in Section 7.2, it has not been adopted in modern
models of trade flows. As we indicated at the end of the previous sub-section, they have developed from the approach of the
OECD and the theoretical work of Armington (1969) at the IMF,
allocating exports according to the determinants of import
demand.

7.1.5   World trade forecasting models

As we explained at the beginning of this chapter a
major problem in the explanation of trade flows is sheer size.
The listing of the Treasury World Economic Prospects Model
(Davies, 1979) for example, occupies some 44 pages. The IMF
and OECD models, (Deppler and Ripley, 1978 and OECD, 1979) are
summarized rather more simply.

The current IMF model (as reported by Deppler and Ripley) develops the approach of Adams *et al.* and the OECD into a complete world trade model by estimating import functions for 14 individual countries and four areas to cover the remaining countries. These imports are disaggregated by four commodity groups, food, raw materials, fuels and manufactures, which first enables the avoidance of the worst problems of the under-estimation of price elasticities of trade for manufactured products, but also allows incorporation of the different trade patterns and prices of the various categories of non-manu-factures. The major contribution of this model in addition to the disaggregation is that export and import prices are deter-mined endogenously in the model.

The process of determination in the model begins with export prices, which in the case of manufactured products are postulated to depend on domestic costs, and competitors' prices.

As the second stage import prices of manufactures are estimated as a simple function of the sum of exporters' prices weighted by their market share and multiplied by the appropriate exchange rates. (Determination is surprisingly mixed but the coefficients are almost all close to unity.) Price equations for the remaining three trade categories are largely related to component world price series and labour costs. Thirty-five spot market price series are used for 'world' prices.

The import demand equations follow the same general
form as before with three explanatory variables - relative
prices, activity and pressure on domestic supply. However,
the IMF model attempts to incorporate the important distinction
between intermediate and final demand and imports disaggregated
by four commodity groups.

The use of four commodity groups and the specification of
a complete model by having four groups for the countries in the
rest of the world represents a considerable step forward and
this brief discussion does less than justice to the model. However, these world trade models are still relatively rudimentary
compared with the other models of behaviour we have considered
up to this point. The further steps which have been taken all
involve very large models indeed, either specially developed
for the study of more than one country such as the COMET model
(see Barten *et al.*, 1976) or the Treasury World Economic Prospects Model (Davies, 1979) or the linking of models from
various countries such as Project Link (Ball and Moriguchi,
1972). As such it is not possible to discuss them in this book.
However, they do reflect very clearly the problem we set out
at the beginning of this chapter, that the sheer size of the
data to be considered tends to swamp the analysis. The results

of this swamping and the simplifications which are used is
exemplified by the use trade models have been put to in the
estimation of the effects of trading arrangements such as the
EEC and EFTA on trade flows.

7.2   The Effects of Trading Areas on Trade

The models which have been considered in the previous
sections all attempt to explain trade flows by a combination
of variables representing supply, demand, competitiveness and
specific barriers. The formation of a trading area such as
the EEC clearly has an effect on these variables and hence on
trade flows and thus should form a test of the forecasting
ability of these models.

The effect on a particular trade flow X_{ij} would be the
difference between the actual flow and the value of the flow
which is predicted by a given model when the determining variables hold the values they would have had, had the trading
area not been formed. It is thus necessary to create a
hypothetical world or 'anti-monde' as it is often called against
which to judge the likely effects of the area.[9] This, of course,

---

[9]
  This is analogous to comparing the results of policy
simulations with models as is examined in Chapter 9.

is no mean task. If we took the simplest case of the
gravitational model discussed in Section 7.1.4,

$$X_{ij} = a_0 \, Y_i^{a_1} \, Y_j^{a_2} \, N_i^{a_3} \, N_j^{a_4} \, D_{ij}^{a_5} \, B_{ij}^{a_6} \qquad (14)$$

it would be necessary to assess not just the effect of the
change in the barrier B_{ij} but also of the changes in Y_i and
Y_j, the incomes of the two countries (distance and population
being unaffected).

In general if we use the estimated equation to calculate
the anti-monde trade flow and denote the estimated difference
between the actual and anti-monde values as $\hat{\Delta}$,

$$\hat{\Delta}\log X_{ij} = \sum_i a_i \, \hat{\Delta}\log V_i \qquad (15)$$

where the V_i are the variables in the equation.

Determining the change in incomes to be used in (14) would
require the estimation of a substantial model reflecting the
feedback effects of trade on income and all the other effects
such as the exploitation of economies of scale which are expected to affect a country participating in a trading area (Lipsey,
1957). Partner countries will expect an increase in trade and
excluded countries will expect their exports to the member
countries to fall – these concepts are usually referred to as
'trade creation' and 'trade diversion'.

However, instead of utilizing the models of trade flows
we have discussed in the previous section most authors have
chosen to use much simpler models (see Mayes (1978) for a
survey and critique of these). They avoid the incorporation of
any feedback effects and tend to concentrate on shares in
trade.

The simplest approach, used by EFTA (1969, 1972) among
others, is to assume that, in the anti-monde, shares in the
apparent consumption[10] of a country continue to develop in the
same linear manner after the formation of the trading area
as they did over the previous few years. This approach suffers
not just from the drawback that apparent consumption is assumed
unaffected by the trading area, but that no cyclical factors
are taken into account in either the exporting or importing
countries, which, as the IMF models show, are very clearly
important. Furthermore, all competitiveness changes are
implicitly assigned to the effects of the trading area, as *all*
differences between actual trade and that in the anti-monde are
attributed to the trading area because trade in the anti-monde
is only determined by the trade share.

---

[10]

Output - exports + imports.

This use of the residual between the actual and the
hypothetical is an important point. In assessing the effect
of a change in an exogenous variable in a model on the endogenous variables, where there are no lagged endogenous
variables, there are two components in the comparison. In the
first place the model can be solved using the actual values of
the exogenous variables over the period to be considered (which
is not part of the period used in the estimation of the parameters of the model). This will give estimated values in year
$t + s$ for each endogenous variable of the form $\hat{X}_{ijt+s}$. This
will differ from the actual values of the variable, X_{ijt+s},
by some error $\hat{e}_{ijt+s} = X_{ijt+s} - \hat{X}_{ijt+s}$. If we then consider
the effects of changes in the exogenous variables and recompute
the values of the endogenous variable, from the model, let us
call this $\hat{X}^A_{ijt+s}$, where the superscript A denotes the anti-monde,
the effect of the change in the value of the exogenous variable
is, according to the model

$$\hat{X}_{ijt+s} - \hat{X}^A_{ijt+s} = \hat{E}_{ijt+s} \qquad (16)$$

i.e. the difference between the two estimates and not the
difference between *actual* values and the anti-monde

$$\hat{X}_{ijt+s} - \hat{X}^A_{ijt+s} = \hat{E}^*_{ijt+s}. \qquad (17)$$

The term $\hat{E}^*_{ijt+s}$ is a combination of the predicted effect of
the change in the exogenous variables in $t+s$ and the error of
the model in $t+s$, $\hat{e}_{ijt+s}$. Thus if there is a specification
error, as seems likely in the simple shares model, as well
as a random disturbance, the predicted effect will also include it.

The extent of this problem is shown by the work of
Aitken (1973) using a version of the gravitational model.
Column (1) of Table 7.6 shows the estimates of the total
increase in the trade of EFTA members as estimated by a dummy
variable in the equation for each year in turn. (Gross Trade
Creation is the sum of the changes in imports from all sources.)
In the second column the effect is calculated by estimating
(14) in 1958, the last year before either the EEC or EFTA began
to take effect, and then subtracting the actual value of the
trade flow from the value predicted by the equation given the
actual values of the exogenous variables in each year. Interest-
ingly enough Aitken uses neither (16) nor (17) but

$$\hat{X}_{ijt+s} - \hat{X}^A_{ijt+s} - \hat{e}_{ijt} \quad (t = 1958) \qquad (18)$$

as his measure of the effect, where $\hat{e}_{ijt} = X_{ijt} - \hat{X}_{ijt}$, because
'the cross-section residuals tended to be stable over time'
(p. 887) in an effort to approximate (16). The two columns in
Table 7.6 are very different after 1964 with the dummy variable

Table 7.6   *Net Effects of Integration on EFTA trade*^a

(US $ mn.)

	Dummy Variable Estimate	Projection Estimate
1959	0^b	-8
1960	0^b	140
1961	126	149
1962	222	243
1963	545	389
1964	1,151	573
1965	1,326	690
1966	1,773	919
1967	2,425	1,264

Source: Aitken (1973)

a   Gross Trade Creation.
b   Dummy variable has coefficient which is less than zero.

estimate being virtually double the estimate from (18).

The difference is easy to explain when we consider the estimates of (14) over each of the years 1958 to 1967. The parameters a_0 - a_6 change over time as is clear from the two end years shown below

	1958	1966
a_0	1.901	1.067
a_1	1.069	1.052
	(8.18)	(10.39)
a_2	0.740	0.911
	(5.66)	(9.00)
a_3	−0.481	−0.311
	(3.25)	(3.03)
a_4	−0.281	−0.369
	(1.90)	(3.38)
a_{5a}	−0.444	−0.349
	(2.55)	(2.74)
a_{5b}	0.758	0.892
	(2.94)	(4.41)
a_{6a}	−0.008	0.887
	(0.02)	(3.75)
a_{6b}	−0.159	0.572
	(0.66)	(3.21)
$\bar{R}^2$	0.770	0.874
SEE	0.291	0.217

(The distance variable has two components. The first, whose coefficient is a_{5a}, is defined as before but a_{5b} is the coefficient of a dummy variable, which has the value unity for countries with a common border.) The terms a_{6a} and a_{6b} are the coefficients of dummy variables for the EEC and EFTA members respectively. It is clear that trade flows are larger in 1967

relative to income and population of the importing country and
relative to the two distance variables. This is partly offset
by the population coefficient for the exporting country, but the
overall effect is that the estimates of trade flows from the
1967 equation will be larger than those from the 1958 equation.

A number of largely *ad hoc* adjustments to simple share
analysis have been proposed to circumvent these difficulties
(Williamson and Bottrill (1971) and Kreinin (1972) for example).
In the case of Williamson and Bottrill this is achieved by relating market shares in the anti-monde in the countries belonging to the EEC and EFTA to actual market shares in third countries
where members of the trading areas face exactly the same competitive conditions as non-members. The question of the determination of the actual level of trade is thus avoided and the
estimation of shares is akin to the second stage of the standard
trade models we have already examined. The greatest similarity
is probably with the current form of the OECD trade model (OECD,
1979) where a world trade matrix of coefficients is used to
allocate imports to the exporting countries. This avoidance of
levels can only be temporary as Williamson and Bottrill need to
present their estimates in levels and hence the results are
still subject to assumptions of independence of overall trade
from the formation of trading areas and improved general competitiveness on the part of members as a result of membership.

Feedback effects on income are also still excluded of course.

Kreinin (1972) and (1979) pursues a slightly different
approach by relating the overall performance of trade flows in
member countries to those in 'similar' excluded countries,
particularly the United States and Japan. He refers to this
process as 'normalization'. There are obvious complexities to
this procedure as it is very difficult to decide what constitutes
a 'similar' country. Nevertheless, this, combined with the
Williamson and Bottrill share approach provides an indication
of the level of the likely effect. In Mayes (1978) I set out a
chart showing the range of estimates which have made for trade
creation and trade diversion by the EEC. This chart is reproduced in Fig. 7.2 where Aitken's estimates are denotes by A for
the projection estimates using the 1958 equation with no EEC or
EFTA dummy variables and B for the dummy variable estimates.
Williamson and Bottrill's estimates are denoted by N and Kreinin's
by O in the non-normalized case and P when normalized by the
United States. The other letters denote estimates by other authors which are discussed individually in the Mayes (1978) article.
While these estimates may denote the likely range of outcomes
(for the static price effects of the trading areas alone) the
existence of annual estimates by Aitken dominates the chart and
could give a misleading impression of what may be the most
plausible results.

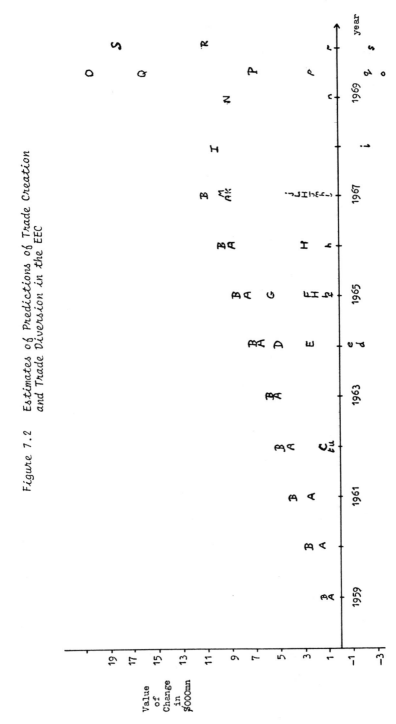

Figure 7.2   Estimates of Predictions of Trade Creation
and Trade Diversion in the EEC

Capital letters denote estimates of trade creation and small letters estimates of trade diversion.

The general impression of the section and of the earlier parts of the chapter is of a much slacker attention to econometric problems in the explanation of trade flows. Partly this is misleading because we have not considered the most complex models such as the Treasury World Economic Prospects model (Davies, 1979) nor the external sectors of major national macro-econometric models. However, it does reflect two prime considerations. The first is the sheer amount of data, but the second, and rather stranger, consideration is the very separate path that 'international economics' has tended to follow from the other macro- and micro-economic topics we have examined. International economics is not alone in this separation; 'development economics' is another example. It does, however, mean that estimates of international trade flows should in general be treated with even more care than the estimates we have considered in other fields. In particular the balance of trade and worse still the balance of capital flows should be treated with caution as they are the difference between two magnitudes which may be subject to wide and related errors.

References and Suggested Reading*

*ADAMS, F.G., EGUCHI, H. AND MEYER-ZU-SCHLOCHTERN, F.M. (1969)
*An econometric analysis of trade: an interrelated ex-
plantion of imports and exports of OECD countries*,   Paris,
OECD (January).

*AITKEN, N.D. (1973) 'The effect of the EEC and EFTA on
European trade: a temporal cross-section analysis'
American Economic Review (December).

ARMINGTON, P.S. (1969) 'A theory of demand for products
distinguished by place of production', *IMF Staff Papers*,
vol. 16 (March) pp. 159-176.

ARTUS, J.R. (1977) 'Measures of potential output in manufacturing
for eight industrial countries'. *IMF Staff Papers*.

BALL, R.J. AND MARWAH, K. (1962) 'The US demand for imports,
1948-58' *Review of Economics and Statistics* (November).

BALL, R.J. AND MORIGUCHI, C. (1972) eds. *International
Linkage of National Economic Models* Amsterdam:
North Holland.

*BARKER, T.S. (1970) 'Aggregation error and estimates of the UK
import demand function' ch. 5 in Hilton and Heathfield
(1970).

BARKER, T.S. (1979) 'Identification of activity effects, trends
and cycles in import demand' *Bulletin of the Oxford
University Institute of Economics and Statistics*.

BARKER, T.S. AND LECOMBER, J.R.C. (1967) *British imports, 1972*
    University of Cambridge Department of Applied Economics,
    Report to National Ports Council (August).

BARTEN, A.P. ed, d'ALCANTRA, G. AND CAIRN, G.J., (1976) 'COMET,
    a medium-term macroeconomic model for the European
    Economic Community' *European Economic Review*, vol. 7, no. 1
    (January).

BLUET, J.C. AND SYSTERMANNS, Y. (1968) 'Modele gravitationel
    d'echanges internationaux de products manufactures'
    Bulletin du CEPREMAP vol. 1 (new series) (January).

*DAVIES, S. (1979) 'The Treasury world economic prospects model',
    Treasury Working Paper No. 10 (May).

*DEPPLER, M.C. AND RIPLEY, D.M. (1978) 'The world trade model:
    merchandise trade', *IMF Staff Papers*, vol. 25, no. 1
    (March).

EFTA (1969) *'The Effects of EFTA on the Economies of Member
    States'* Geneva (January).

EFTA (1972) *'The Trade Effects of EFTA and the EEC, 1959-67.'*,
    Geneva (June).

GOLDSTEIN, M. AND KAHN, M.S. (1976) 'Large versus small price
    changes and the demand for imports' *IMF Staff Papers*.

HICKMAN, B.E. AND LAU, L.J. (1973) 'Elasticities of substitution
    and export demands in a world trade model', *European
    Economic Review*, vol. 4 no. 4 (December).

HILTON, K AND HEATHFIELD, D. (1970) (eds.) *The Econometric Study of the United Kingdom* London: Macmillan.

*HOUTHAKKER, H.S. AND MAGEE, S.P. (1969) 'Income and price elasticities in world trade', *Review of Economics and Statistics* (May).

JUNZ, H. AND RHOMBERG, R. (1973) 'Price competitiveness in export trade among industrial countries', *American Economic Review* (May).

KREININ, M.E. (1972) 'Effects of the EEC on imports of manufactures' *Economic Journal* (September).

KREININ, M.E. (1979) 'The impact of the Common Market on trade in manufactures', paper read at American-European Seminar on the impact of the EEC in theory and practice, Tilburg, June.

*LINNEMANN, H. (1966) *'An Econometric Study of International Trade Flows'*, Amsterdam: North Holland.

*LIPSEY, R.G. (1957) 'The theory of customs unions: trade diversion and welfare' *Economica*, vol. 24.

MAGEE, S.P. (1975) 'Prices, incomes and foreign trade' in P.B. Kenen (ed.)'International Trade and Finance'*, Cambridge University Press.

MAYES, D.G. (1971) 'The Effects of Alternative Trade Groupings on the United Kingdom', PhD thesis, University of Bristol.

MAYES, D.G. (1974) 'RASAT, a model for the estimation of commodity trade flows in EFTA', *European Economic Review*, vol. 5, pp. 207-221.

*MAYES, D.G. (1978) 'The effects of economic integration on trade'. *Journal of Common Market Studies* (September).

MEYER-ZU-SCHLOCHTERN, F.M. AND YAJIMA, A. (1970) 'OECD trade model: 1970 version', *OECD Economic Outlook*, (December).

MORGAN, A.D. (1970) 'Income and price elasticities in world trade: a comment' *Manchester School*.

*OECD (1979) 'The OECD international linkage model' *OECD Economic Outlook* (January).

*ORCUTT, G.H. (1950) 'Measurement of price elasticities in international trade', *Review of Economics and Statistics* (May).

POYHÖNEN, P. (1963) 'Towards a general theory of international trade' *Ekonomiska Samfundets Tidskrift*, no. 2.

PULLIAINEN, K. (1963) 'A world trade study: an econometric model of the pattern of the commodity flows in international trade, 1948-60' *Ekonomiska Samfundets Tidskrift*, no. 2.

SAVAGE, I.R. AND DEUTSCH, K.W. (1960) 'A statistical model of the gross analysis of transaction flows', *Econometrica* (July), pp. 551-572.

SURREY, M.J.C., (1971)'*The Analysis and Forecasting of the British Economy*, NIESR/CUP.

TINBERGEN, J. (1962) '*Shaping the World Economy*' New York: Twentieth Century Fund.

VERDOORN, P.J. AND SCHWARTZ, A.N.R. (1972) 'Two alternative
    estimates of the effects of EEC and EFTA on the pattern of
    trade', *European Economic Review*, pp. 291-335.

WAELBROECK, J. (1964) 'Une nouvelle methode d'analyse des matrices
    d'echanges internationaux', *Cahiers Economique de Bruxelles*,
    vol 21., no. 1.

WILLIAMSON, J AND BOTTRILL, A. (1971) 'The impact of customs
    unions on trade in manufactures' *Oxford Economic Papers*,
    vol. 23 (November).

Chapter 8

DEMAND ANALYSIS

The study of consumer demand and estimation of how families decide on the distribution of their purchases subject to the constraint of income is one of the most elemental in economics. In a thorough survey which is well worth reading, Brown and Deaton (1972) date the first numerical estimates as 1699 with a demand for wheat published by Davenant. However, following the precepts set out in Chapter 1 we shall make no attempt to provide a comprehensive survey but will instead concentrate on some points which are of econometric interest.

As was explained earlier the sequence of Chapters 6 to 9 tackles applications which involve the use of multi-equation models. This chapter is particularly concerned with an application where the system of equations can readily be taken together and described simultaneously so that one can see the properties of the system as a whole more clearly. While there is a discussion of some estimation problems with complete systems the major econometric interest centres on, first, the imposition and testing of restrictions required both by the economic theory of consumer demand and the need to limit the number of para-

meters for manageability, and secondly, on the testing and

comparison of competing explanations especially those which

cannot be 'nested' as different restrictions on a common form.

Because of the constraints of space and the desire to consider

the system as a whole, the discussion is couched in terms of

matrix algebra. We stressed the usefulness of matrix algebra in

Chapter 1 and it is exemplified here even if the reader's prior

knowledge is very limited. The meaning of the algebra is explain-

ed in the text.

In each time period each group of individuals with a common

expenditure - usually referred to as a household - have to

decide how to allocate their expenditures over the number of

commodities available. The total expenditure which each house-

hold can make is limited by its income augmented by borrowing

and diminished by saving. The result of this allocation problem

depends on the household's tastes and the prices of the various

commodities. This generates a system of interrelated equations,

one for each commodity. In the first section of this chapter we

shall therefore set out the form of these equations and the

constraints that the theory imposes upon them and then, in the

second, show how such a model can be estimated and the validity

of the restrictions on the data. This concentration on static

systems of demand functions for aggregate behaviour neglects some of the problems of the household behaviour on which it is

based; particularly those relating to functional form for

different commodities, the effects of family composition and

economies of scale in consumption. These issues together with

the development of a dynamic approach are discussed in the

final section of this chapter.

8.1   The Specification of Systems of Demand Equations

In this first section we set out very briefly the derivation

of systems of demand equations from their theoretical basis in

utility theory. Since the subject has been extensively examined

in textbooks and also in an applied context by Brown and Deaton

(1972) and Phlips (1974) the reader should look there for further

details.

In the first instance consumer preferences are usually

expressed in the form of a utility function $U = U (q)$ where q is

the vector of quantities of the n available commodities which

the consumer can purchase.[1] The consumer is thus posited to

---

[1]
 Following widespread convention, vectors and matrices are
denoted in the bolder script with capital letters for matrices
and lower case for vectors; a prime, ', is used to denote
transposition. There are other conventions but this conforms to
that in the *Economic Journal*.

derive utility from consumption of each of the elements in q
and the point at issue is to specify the basis on which these
elements are chosen. If for ease of exposition we treat the
problem in a static framework, then at any one time the consumer
is usually assumed to try to maximize utility, U, subject to
the budget constraint that the sum of total expenditures (the
quantities purchased multiplied by their respective prices) $p'q$,
where p is the vector of prices of the n commodities, is *equal*
to their income, Y.[2] In order to find the maximum we have to
consider the marginal utilities of consumption of the commodities
$\partial U/\partial q$, which we shall write as u, and then using a Lagrange
multiplier, l, the first order conditions for a maximum of U
can be expressed as

$$u - lp = 0. \qquad\qquad (1)$$

Using the budget constraint to eliminate the Lagrange multiplier

---

2
    This would of course be an inequality constraint $p'q \leqslant Y$ if
saving is identified separately, but for this analysis saving
is either deducted previously or liquid assets are treated as
some of the 'commodities' which can be purchased. We limit
ourselves to the easier problem of the complete allocation of Y
among purchases of commodities.

we can obtain the n demand functions where consumption is a function of income and prices

$$q = q \ (Y, \ p).\tag{2}$$

The form of these demand functions in (2) is general and must be subject to a number of constraints if the system as a whole is to maintain coherence as a rational set of preferences by consumers. In the first place the derivatives must be such that even if income or prices change the budget constraint must continue to be met. Thus in the case of the income derivatives, $\partial q_i/\partial y$ $(i = 1, \ldots, n)$ written as the vector q_y, the sum of the changes in expenditure in response to a change in income must be equal to the change in income,

$$p'q_y = 1.\tag{3}$$

The price derivatives, $\partial q_i/\partial p_j$ $(i, \ j = 1, \ldots, n)$ denoted by the matrix Q_p (where consumption of each commodity, row i, can be affected by each price, column j) however, can be decomposed into an 'income' effect and a 'substitution' effect. The substitution effect is the change when utility is held constant $Q_p\big|_U = S$, the remainder of the change being the result of the change in real incomes, $q_y q'$ thus

$$Q_p = S.- q_y q'.\tag{4}$$

The matrix of compensated price derivatives is usually denoted as S after Slutsky (1915) who set out this decomposition. The budget constraint applies to the S matrix as the uncompensated matrix Q_p includes changes in real incomes. Thus the compensate effects of price changes must be zero when summed over commodities (i.e. summed down the columns of S)

$$p'S = 0'. \qquad (5)$$

Constraints (3) and (5) are often referred to as the Engel and Cournot aggregation restrictions respectively.

The matrix S must bear further constraint if it is to provide a coherent representation of behaviour. In the first place if there is to be no money illusion a proportionate change in all prices (and no change in real income) should leav consumption unaffected. The row sum of compensated derivatives must therefore be zero for any set of price changes

$$Sp = 0. \qquad (6)$$

This constraint is one of *homogeneity*; in this case it is that (2), the demand functions, be homogeneous of degree zero in pri and income. (Anyone unfamiliar with homogeneity should consult Black and Bradley (1973) or a similar introductory textbook of mathematics for economists, however, its meaning in this contex is very straightforward.)

The third constraint on S is one of *symmetry*, namely that changes in relative price have the same effect however the two individual prices changed. Thus

$$S = S'. \tag{7}$$

We also need a sign constraint on S, in particular to ensure that own compensated price elasticities are negative and hence that compensated demand curves slope downwards. As Brown and Deaton (1972, p. 195) point out, the constraint, expressed as

$$a' Sa \leqslant 0, \tag{8}$$

and described as *negativity*, implies that the compensated demand curve for the whole bundle of goods slopes downwards when their proportions are held constant.

The number of constraints imposed by (3), (5), (6), (7) and (8) is large. There are n income derivatives and n^2 price derivatives. Equation (3) imposes only 1 constraint but (5) and (6) each impose n and (7) $\frac{n}{2}$ $(n - 1)$. The inequality constraints (8) are slightly more difficult to judge, for while constraints (3), (5), (6) and (7) will normally have to be *imposed* in estimation, (8) will normally be met by the data without the need for explicit restriction.

Further constraints are usually placed on the utility function in practice relating to *separability* or *additivity*. Separability implies that we can group commodities in such a manner that the marginal utilities of commodities in one group are independent[3] of the quantities consumed of commodities in other groups. Additivity is the harsher condition that marginal utility of each good is independent of the quantity consumed of all other goods.

The constraints we have set out in this section are suggested by economic theory. The next step is to specify particular demand systems from the general form of (2) to use in estimation. Some of those used in practice conform with some or all of the constraints; others cannot be related to any explicit utility function and are usually justified on grounds of manageability and consistency with the data. Lack of conformity with specific utility functions is particularly common in studies of demand for individual commodities and this is a major reason why we have devoted our limited space to estimates of complete syste?

We shall therefore examine in the next section how these constraints apply in practice with the most frequently used specifications of the demand functions, (2).

3

   The nature of the independence and hence the type of separabil ity has a number of different definitions in practice (Brown and Deaton, pp. 197-9).

8.2   The Estimation of Systems of Demand Equations

The restrictions on the specification derived in the
previous section do not imply a unique estimating equation and
while there are several systems of demand equations which have
received attention in recent years we shall only consider four
of them in any detail.   They are the Rotterdam system as set
out in Barten (1969), the Linear Expenditure System (LES),
Stone (1954), the addilog system, Houthakker (1960), and the
log-linear or constant elasticity of demand system, Houthakker
(1965). These have been picked for two main reasons, first
because the Rotterdam, LES and log-linear systems are widely used
in practice and secondly because Deaton (1974) and Goldberger and
Gamaletsos (1970) give comparisons of the different models on
the same data base. One of the most important features in considering the specification of systems of demand equations is to see
how well the constraints outlined in the previous section
actually relate to the data.

8.2.1   A Comparison of the Log-linear and LES system

Goldberger and Gamaletsos compare the log-linear and the
LES models using annual data for 13 OECD countries over the
years 1948-1959 for five commodity groups - food, clothing,
rent, durables and a residual category. The appeal of the log-
linear model LL, is its functional simplicity

$$\log q = a + \log (Y/P^*) \, b + \log (\hat{p}/P^*) \, c + e \qquad (9)$$

where P^* is the implicit deflator of total expenditure; $\hat{}$ denotes
a diagonal matrix; a, b and c are parameters; and e is a vector
of disturbances. The coefficients themselves are elasticities
(and hence constant) which although convenient tends to be
implausible over wide ranges of incomes. Rather than starting
from activity function and deriving the consequent demand
functions, (9) are specified directly as a set of demand
functions.

Equations (9) impose further considerable constraints on
the relative price term by aggregating over all the other prices.

The LES system also has functional simplicity

$$\hat{p} \, q = \hat{p} \, d + (Y - p'd) \, \xi + u \qquad (10)$$

where d and ξ are parameters and u a vector of residuals, and
moreover can be derived directly from an explicit utility
function

$$U(q) = \Pi (q_i - d_i)^{\beta i}. \qquad (11)$$

However, while (10) is linear in variables it is not linear in
parameters. The log-linear form is well known and widely used
(in the last chapter for example) but it does not satisfy the
aggregation constraint over incomes. As expressed in (9) the

price terms only approximate the correct price ratio by assuming
that all the off-diagonal elements in C log (p/P^*) are zero,
where C is the matrix of uncompensated price.elasticities. The
effects of these limitations and the applicability of the
specification are shown in Table 8.1[4] Ten of the 25 compensated
own price elasticities are negative (and six of them had
positive coefficients twice their standard error in the estimating equation).

The LES form may be non-linear in parameters, but the
variables have a clear meaning. The scalar $p'd$ can be described
as 'subsistence' or basic income as the consumer spends $p_i d_i$ on
each good plus a proportion f_i of the remaining or 'supernumerary'
income, $Y-p'd$. The utility function is *additive* in the sense set
out in the previous section and the 'Engel curves' (income-
consumption relations explained in the next section) are linear,
both of which might be thought unduly restrictive if anything
other than broad commodity groups or short income ranges are
used.

---

[4]
  Results are shown for only five of the thirteen countries
included in Goldberger and Gamaletsos' sample for ease of exposition and while this excerpt is not dissimilar from the full
sample, no detailed generalizations should be drawn from Table
8.1 alone.

The LL model can be estimated by OLS if (9) is set out as
a single equation, estimating all the parameters together,
thus treating the e as being drawn from a single distribution
and minimising the pooled residual sum of squares. The non-
linearity in parameters in (10) poses a rather greater problem.
Stone (1954) recommends the iterative use of OLS, again on the
criterion that it is the pooled residual sum of squares for all
time periods and commodities which is the minimand. Fortunately
the model is linear in d for given $\oint$ and linear in $\oint$ for
given d, so it is possible to solve the system by first choosing
starting values for say d and then solving for $\oint$ by OLS then
using those estimates to solve for d in turn by OLS. The convergence criterion was stability within 0.1 per cent between
iterations for all estimates, which Goldberger and Gamaletsos
admit required more than 150 iterations on some occasions. The
whole demand system is thus obtained by estimating only $2n$
parameters rather than the n $(n + 1)$ which would be required by
an unconstrained system of n income and n^2 price coefficients.

The estimation techniques used for both LES and LL ignore
the problem of the relation between equations (Goldberger and
Gamaletsos were fully aware of this but felt unable to incorporate the computational difficulties involved). In the first
place there is no reason to expect that the elements in the
vectors of disturbances in (9) and (10), e and u, will be

Table 8.1   Elasticities LES and log-linear Models*

(1948-59, annual data)

Country	Model	Income elasticity					Own price elasticity (uncompensated)					Own price elasticity (compensated)				
		F	C	R	D	O	F	C	R	D	O	F	C	R	D	O
Belgium	LES	0.63	0.99	0.21	2.45	1.17	-0.16	-0.06	0.02	-0.17	-0.43	0.02	0.04	0.01	0.07	0.03
	log-linear	0.87	0.87	0.11	1.91	1.00	-0.67	-1.36	0.21	-1.07	-0.34	-0.42	-1.27	0.22	-0.88	0.05
France	LES	0.68	1.09	0.69	2.55	1.02	-0.22	-0.11	-0.00	-0.09	-0.39	0.02	0.03	0.03	0.08	0.03
	log-linear	0.53	1.53	1.19	2.55	1.03	-0.52	0.35	-0.33	-0.29	-0.41	-0.33	0.56	-0.28	-0.12	0.01
Italy	LES	0.85	0.67	0.96	2.27	1.19	-0.49	-0.19	-0.21	-0.46	-0.53	-0.10	-0.11	-0.16	-0.38	-0.13
	log-linear	0.78	0.59	0.27	2.78	1.22	-0.71	-0.25	0.08	0.21	-0.33	-0.35	-0.18	0.09	0.31	0.07
U.K.	LES	0.57	1.28	0.60	3.33	0.88	-0.16	-0.10	-0.03	-0.20	-0.36	0.01	0.03	0.02	0.07	0.02
	log-linear	0.57	1.17	0.70	1.16	0.87	-0.08	-0.19	-0.13	-2.93	-0.25	0.09	-0.07	-0.07	-2.84	0.13
U.S.A.	LES	0.35	0.56	1.54	0.85	1.34	-0.13	-0.13	-0.37	-0.20	-0.66	-0.05	-0.07	-0.18	-0.10	-0.08
	log-linear	0.12	0.57	1.63	1.37	1.75	-0.48	-0.11	-0.41	0.56	1.45	-0.45	-0.05	-0.21	-0.71	-0.70

F, Food; C, Clothing; R, Rent; D, Durables; O, Other.

* Elasticities at the sample mean.
Source: Goldberger and Gamaletsos (1970)

homoscedastic. In the very simplest case we might reasonably

expect that the variances will be positively related to budget

shares. They may also be negatively related to the degree that

the particular commodity or commodity group can be classed as

a necessity rather than a luxury.[5] Furthermore, because of the

existence of the budget constraint (and the other cross-equation

constraints) the disturbances must be contemporaneously related

between equations.

   Goldberger and Gamaletsos assume first that the contempor-

aneous error variance covariance matrix between equations does

not change over time, and secondly that there are no relations

in the errors from the individual equations between time

periods. The first of these is the equivalent of the usual

assumption of homoscedasticity over time, although since this

is a system problem it is the variance covariance matrix of

the errors between equations which is assumed constant and not

the error variance. (Just because an assumption is common it

does not mean that it is necessarily correct in this instance.)

The inter-temporal independence of the errors is probably

reasonable for non-durables, but unlikely for durables, as was

---

[5]

   The distinction between 'necessary' and 'luxury' commodities
at any particular income usually depends upon whether their
income elasticity of demand is less or greater than unity.

mentioned in Chapter 2 and is discussed in the next section.[6]

There is a problem in assessing which of the log-linear
and LES models is the more appropriate specification of demand
behaviour because it is not readily possible to express them
as different constraints on a common model and hence assess the
validity of the various constraints.   Comparisons are easier
if it is possible to 'nest' hypotheses as Deaton (1974) does by
expressing the models in a common framework. Pesaran and Deaton
(1978) have also explained how to provide tests of 'non-nested'
hypotheses. While such a method is relevant to the present use
it is not possible to apply it without re-estimating the models.
Its general form is that one takes each model in turn as the
'null' hypothesis and tests the other against it. If the same
result is achieved under both tests then the conclusion is
clear, but in fact one may end up by either 'accepting' both
models or even 'rejecting' them both.

Goldberger and Gamaletsos adopt simpler criteria. We have
already noted that it is possible to discuss the plausibility of

---

[6]
   The imposition of the budget constraint in each period entails
that the errors across equations sum to zero and hence their
variance-covariance matrices are singular. This singularity can
be avoided in these systems by omitting one of the equations (the
constraints determine the values of the parameters in the omitted
equation) and using either the Zellner (1962) Seemingly Unrelated
Regression Equation (SURE) approach, (see Maddala (1977) for an
explanation), or maximum likelihood. This latter approach will be
discussed in the context of Deaton's (1974) comparison of the LES,
Rotterdam and direct addilog models.

the parameters in Table 8.1 and the goodness of determination of
the individual coefficients. We noted that while the estimated
income elasticities were relatively similar in many cases there
was considerable divergence in the own price elasticities.
However, it was not possible to draw any clear conclusions as
to which was the preferable model. Goldberger and Gamaletsos
therefore propose two further criteria related to goodness of
fit. Clearly there is not much point in a direct comparison as
the LES system estimates expenditures and the log-linear model,
logarithms of quantities. It is therefore necessary to reduce
them to a common base: Goldberger and Gamaletsos choose budget
shares as the base.

Calculating estimated budget shares from the two equations
it is possible to obtain either a Root Mean Square Error or an
estimate of a form of R^2. Denoting the errors in the estimated
budget shares as $\hat{V}_{LES}$ and $\hat{V}_{LL}$ respectively for each commodity
$R^{*2} = 1 - \Sigma V^2 / \Sigma (wd)^2$ where wd is the deviation of the budget share
from its mean. These are shown in Table 8.2. Although we can
count the number of occasions that R^{*2}_{LES} exceeds R^{*2}_{LL} this does no
give us an overall criterion for each country. Goldberger and
Gamaletsos suggest the measure

$$I = \sum_t^T \sum_i^n w_{it} \log (w_{it} / \hat{w}_{it}) / T \qquad (12$$

where w_{it} is the budget share of commodity i in year t and T is

the total number of years in the sample. These values are shown
in Table 8.3.

From Table 8.2 we can note that there are only 2 cases where
$R^{*2}_{LES} > R^{*2}_{LL}$ and from Table 8.3 that $I_{LES} > I_{LL}$ in all cases except Belgium. Since R^{*2} is only a measure of goodness of fit and
not the usual R^2 it can be negative (although it cannot exceed
unity) and I will be non-negative. The nearer I is to zero the
closer the overall fit. The two criteria therefore would appear
to argue in favour of the log-linear specification despite its
lack of theoretical merit compared with the constraints implied
by the LES. However, it may be that a system which estimates
expenditures is not properly tested by references to budget
shares but Goldberger and Gamaletsos conclude (p. 398) 'This
suggests that it may be appropriate to fit the models in terms
of average budget shares (or their first differences) ... the
estimation procedure is then more consistent with a natural
objective of the analysis'. This is exactly the context of the
Rotterdam model and Deaton's (1974) comparisons which we shall
now consider.

8.2.2 The Testing of Restrictions in the Rotterdam Model

Deaton sets out three models in the same framework. One of
these models is the LES system and the second another version of
the log-linear model by Houthakker (1960) known as the direct

Table 8.2   Goodness of fit of average budget shares

Country	Food		Clothing		Rent		Durables		Other	
	LES	LL	LES	LL	LES	LL	LES	LL	LES	LL
Belgium	0.944	0.953	-0.529	-0.156	0.975	0.986	0.788	0.783	0.835	0.861
France	0.950	0.979	0.947	0.986	0.935	0.971	0.934	0.977	0.951	0.964
Italy	0.928	0.970	0.916	0.922	0.990	0.999	0.765	0.886	0.789	0.842
United Kingdom	0.973	0.974	0.726	0.744	0.993	0.993	0.805	0.866	0.851	0.900
United States	0.934	0.948	0.960	0.941	0.826	0.852	0.202	0.240	0.828	0.884

Source: Goldberger and Gamaletsos (1970).

Table 8.3   Average inaccuracy
(Equation (12)) 1

Country	LES	LL
Belgium	102	151
France	155	62
Italy	191	116
United Kingdom	208	151
United States	376	333

Source: Goldberger and Gamaletsos
(1970)

addilog model which relates the logarithmic model to a particular

utility function. (There is an indirect version of the addilog,

Houthakker (1961), which we do not consider in this chapter.)

The model has not been widely used in practice because the

demand functions derived under it are defined only in terms of

relations between pairs of commodities. Most importantly Deaton

considers the validity of restrictions on the Rotterdam system

of demand equations. Thus he provides a testing procedure of

the validity of various restrictions suggested by the economic

theory derived in Section 8.1 on the data. As we mentioned

earlier much of the interest in this analysis is in the form-

ulation of the testing procedure.

The Rotterdam system is expressed in the form of elasticities weighted by budget shares. It thus combines the advantages of the easy interpretability of the elasticity form with the ability to satisfy the constraints imposed by the theory developed in Section 8.1. If we differentiate the original system of demand functions (2)

$$dq = q_y \, dY + Q_p \, dp \tag{13}$$

we can express this in the form of elasticities by dividing through by quantity (i.e. by premultiplying (13) by $\hat{q}^{-1}$)

$$\hat{q}^{-1} \, dq = \hat{q}^{-1} \, q_y \, dY + \hat{q}^{-1} \, Q_p \, d\,p$$

$$= \hat{q}^{-1} \, q_y \, YY^{-1} \, dY + \hat{q}^{-1} \, Q_p \, \hat{p}\hat{p}^{-1} \, dp \tag{14}$$

and this in turn can be expressed as first differences of logarithms

$$d \, \log q = g \, d \log Y + H \, d \log p \tag{15}$$

where g is the vector of income elasticities and H the matrix of uncompensated price elasticities. Finally we obtain the Rotterdam model by weighting (15) by budget shares,

$$\hat{w} \, d \log q = \hat{w} \, g \, d \log Y + \hat{w} \, H \, d \log p \tag{16}$$

and expressing the elasticities in their compensated form (see equation (4))

$$\hat{w} \; d \log q \; = \; j \; d \log Y^* \; + \; K \; d \log p \tag{17}$$

where $d \log Y^* \; \simeq \; d \log Y - w' d \log p$ (the change in real income) and $K = Y^{-1} \hat{p} \; S\hat{p}$ (S being the matrix of compensated price derivatives as in (4)).

As set out in (17) the Rotterdam model is general and Deaton expresses the six constraints on the demand equations we derived in Section 8.1 as (defining a vector of ones as i)

Engel aggregation	$j'i = 1$	(18)
Cournot aggregation	$K'i = 0$	(19)
Homogeneity	$K i = 0$	(20)
Symmetry	$K = K'$	(21)
Negativity[7]	$x'Kx < 0$ for all x	(22)
Additivity	$K = m \; (\hat{j} - jj')$	(23)

The purpose of his article is to test the validity of these six restrictions so he sets out a series of six models which impose successively more of the restrictions

(i)   unconstrained: j and K are parameters to be
         estimated subject to the constraints (18)
         and (19)

---

[7]
    Called "Convexity" in Deaton (1974) as opposed to "Negativity" as set out in Brown and Deaton (1972) quoted in Section 8.1.

(ii)   homogenous: as (i) with constraint (29) as
         well

(iii)   symmetric: as (i) with constraint (21) as
         well[8]

(iv)   'intermediate': j, j^* and m are parameters to
         be estimated with constraint (18) and additivity
         not linked to the income terms, thus K is
         constrained as $K = m^* (\hat{j}^* - j^* j'^*)$ (j^* indepen-
         dent of j).

(v)   additive: j and m are parameters to be estimated
         subject to constraints (18) and (23)

(vi)   No substitution: j are to be estimated subject to
         (18) and $K = 0$.

Nine expenditure categories (shown in Table 8.4) are distinguished for the UK and the constraints are tested using annual
data for the period 1900 to 1970 excluding the years affected by
war and rationing, 1914-21 and 1939-53, which leaves 45 observations as the model is in first differences. There are thus
nine parameters in j in the basic model (17) and 81 in K, a total
of 90, or 99 if intercept terms are included in each equation.
Even the basic model (i) is estimated subject to Engel and Cournot
aggregation constraints so the maximum number of 'free' parameters in (17) is 80 (88 with intercepts). Homegeneity (model
(ii)) imposes eight more constraints; symmetry, model (iii), 36

---

[8] This automatically entails (19) homogeneity as well.

constraints (compared with (i)); additivity without relations between income and price parameters of 73 constraints; full additivity adds a further eight constraints; and lastly, the no substitution model, (vi), has only eight free parameters.

Although all the models are estimated by maximum likelihood they do in fact present four different models. Models (i), (ii), (iii) and (vi) are all linear models, but models (i) and (vi) require an adding up restriction which is automatically imposed by OLS.   OLS also provides the maximum likelihood estimates of model (ii) when it is estimated subject to the identical within equation constraint of homogeneity (this is sometimes known as restricted least squares, RLS).   The remaining linear model, model (iii), requires cross-equation constraints, which will, as we noted in the Goldberger and Gamaletsos example, require consideration of the variance covariance matrix of the errors. In all these models Deaton assumes that there are no inter-temporal correlations between the errors, $E[e_t\, e_s'] = 0$, in the same manner as Goldberger and Gamaletsos, and also that the contemporaneous error variance covariance matrix $E[e\, e']_t$ is the same for all t. If the error variance covariance matrix were known Restricted Generalized Least Squares would be the maximum likelihood estimator, but since it is not it is necessary to iterate with estimates of both the parameters and the variance covariance matrix $T^{-1}e\, e' = V$, where T is the number of observations, until the maximum likelihood estimator is found.[9]

The remaining models, (iv) and (v) are non-linear and subject to linear constraint. Again this entails iteration with estimates of both the parameters and the error variance covariance, but this time linearization of the model with respect to the parameters is required at each iteration as well (Deaton (1974) pp. 349-353).

In order to avoid confusing the analysis, results are shown for model (i), the unconstrained form, and model (iii), the form with symmetry imposed. The results as presented in Tables 8.4 and 8.5 show the values of the coefficients j and K rather than the elasticities g and H although these can readily be calculated by dividing through by the budget shares as from (15) and (17), $g = \hat{w}^{-1} j$ and $H = \hat{w}^{-1} K$. It is clear from Table 8.4 that while all the own price coefficients are of the expected sign in the unconstrained case and six of them have values more than twice as large as their standard errors, the cross-price terms are more random and insignificant. Twenty-nine of the 72 cross price coefficients are negative. The constant terms which

---

[9]
    As we pointed out on p. 319 V is singular and following Barten (1969) the maximum likelihood estimator is found when the determinant $|V + i^* i^{*\prime}|$ is a minimum (subject to $e' i = 0$ for all t) where $i^* = T^{-\frac{1}{2}} i$.

Table 8.4   Rotterdam Model Unrestricted with Intercepts (Equation (17))

i	j_i	K_{i1}	K_{i2}	K_{i3}	K_{i4}	K_{i5}	K_{i6}	K_{i7}	K_{i8}	K_{i9}
1. Food	0.135072 (0.04418)	-0.103773 (0.03548)	-0.009268 (0.03129)	0.016353 (0.03448)	0.001008 (0.01168)	-0.001308 (0.02792)	-0.034550 (0.04447)	0.014085 (0.03033)	-0.006625 (0.01472)	0.078700 (0.04868)
2. Footwear and clothing	0.177639 (0.03335)	0.018906 (0.02684)	-0.030411 (0.02366)	-0.016823 (0.02608)	-0.004209 (0.00883)	0.023468 (0.02112)	-0.023264 (0.03363)	-0.004787 (0.02294)	0.012913 (0.01113)	0.025128 (0.03681)
3. Housing	0.084590 (0.01788)	0.025374 (0.01439)	-0.029457 (0.01268)	-0.016667 (0.01398)	-0.000010 (0.00473)	-0.012011 (0.01132)	0.037734 (0.01803)	0.010112 (0.01230)	-0.000796 (0.00597)	-0.028316 (0.01973)
4. Fuel	0.089326 (0.03003)	0.006438 (0.02416)	-0.003114 (0.02131)	-0.004935 (0.02348)	-0.022042 (0.00795)	0.001125 (0.01901)	0.050402 (0.03028)	-0.009050 (0.02066)	-0.014028 (0.01002)	0.003279 (0.03315)
5. Drink and tobacco	0.229275 (0.02549)	0.009825 (0.02051)	0.040699 (0.01808)	-0.007015 (0.01993)	0.009880 (0.00675)	-0.042878 (0.01614)	-0.005588 (0.02570)	-0.003446 (0.01753)	0.008205 (0.00851)	0.012928 (0.02813)
6. Travel and communication	0.103688 (0.01489)	0.041007 (0.01198)	-0.000546 (0.01056)	0.025342 (0.01164)	-0.003091 (0.00394)	0.019203 (0.00943)	-0.058615 (0.01501)	0.016429 (0.01024)	0.007308 (0.00497)	-0.013219 (0.01643)
7. Entertainment	0.023798 (0.00920)	-0.011800 (0.00740)	0.016214 (0.00653)	0.000476 (0.00719)	0.003617 (0.00244)	0.007844 (0.00582)	0.003895 (0.00928)	-0.018019 (0.00633)	0.001462 (0.00307)	-0.002538 (0.01016)
8. Other goods	0.069496 (0.01556)	0.003932 (0.01252)	-0.006816 (0.01104)	0.014819 (0.01216)	0.001975 (0.00412)	-0.005145 (0.00985)	0.012303 (0.01569)	-0.023728 (0.01070)	-0.005415 (0.00519)	0.009458 (0.01717)
9. Other services	0.087225 (0.01913)	0.010089 (0.01539)	0.003164 (0.01357)	0.021156 (0.01495)	0.012872 (0.00506)	0.009702 (0.01211)	0.017683 (0.01929)	0.018405 (0.01316)	-0.003024 (0.00638)	-0.085420 (0.02111)
Intercepts		0.000477 (0.00081)	-0.000955 (0.00061)	0.001525 (0.00033)	-0.000445 (0.00055)	-0.002424 (0.00047)	0.000648 (0.00027)	0.000132 (0.00017)	0.000096 (0.00029)	0.000946 (0.00035)

Standard errors in parentheses

Source: Deaton (1974)

Table 8.5   Rotterdam Model Symmetric With Intercepts (Equation (17))

i	j	K_{i1}	K_{i2}	K_{i3}	K_{i4}	K_{i5}	K_{i6}	K_{i7}	K_{i8}	K_{i9}
1. Food	0.151593 (0.04085)	-0.072760 (0.02559)	0.021231 (0.01548)	0.010511 (0.00993)	0.002436 (0.00921)	0.010733 (0.01128)	0.042088 (0.00960)	-0.013969 (0.00570)	-0.001375 (0.00770)	0.001104 (0.01117)
2. Footwear and clothing	0.191381 (0.02588)	0.021231 (0.01548)	-0.016513 (0.01529)	-0.027013 (0.00829)	-0.003534 (0.00630)	0.031628 (0.00870)	-0.025480 (0.00749)	0.014013 (0.00434)	0.010209 (0.00608)	-0.004541 (0.00826)
3. Housing	0.074695 (0.01659)	0.010511 (0.00993)	-0.027013 (0.00829)	-0.016036 (0.01019)	0.000133 (0.00403)	-0.004457 (0.00741)	0.019958 (0.00765)	0.002228 (0.00431)	-0.001190 (0.00449)	0.015867 (0.00834)
4. Fuel	0.099717 (0.02360)	0.002436 (0.00921)	-0.003534 (0.00630)	0.000133 (0.00403)	-0.022519 (0.00671)	0.010799 (0.00499)	-0.005137 (0.00390)	0.003282 (0.00192)	0.001571 (0.00347)	0.012969 (0.00422)
5. Drink and tobacco	0.214030 (0.02172)	0.010733 (0.01128)	0.031628 (0.00870)	-0.004457 (0.00741)	0.010799 (0.00499)	-0.062191 (0.00992)	-0.000752 (0.00693)	0.005481 (0.00377)	-0.001934 (0.00481)	0.010692 (0.00750)
6. Travel and communication	0.092968 (0.01608)	0.042088 (0.00960)	-0.025480 (0.00749)	0.019958 (0.00765)	-0.005137 (0.00390)	-0.000752 (0.00693)	-0.046522 (0.01011)	0.000775 (0.00457)	0.005448 (0.00416)	0.009621 (0.00826)
7. Entertainment	0.019279 (0.00763)	-0.013969 (0.00504)	0.014013 (0.00434)	0.002228 (0.00431)	0.003282 (0.00192)	0.005481 (0.00377)	0.000775 (0.00457)	-0.019404 (0.00419)	0.001275 (0.00221)	0.006318 (0.00567)
8. Other goods	0.076850 (0.01366)	-0.001375 (0.00770)	0.010209 (0.00608)	-0.001190 (0.00449)	0.001571 (0.00347)	-0.001934 (0.00481)	0.005448 (0.00416)	0.001275 (0.00221)	-0.008633 (0.00470)	-0.005370 (0.00462)
9. Other services	0.079567 (0.01685)	0.001104 (0.01117)	-0.004541 (0.00826)	0.015867 (0.00834)	0.012969 (0.00422)	0.010692 (0.00750)	0.009621 (0.00826)	0.006318 (0.00567)	-0.005370 (0.00462)	-0.046659 (0.01274)
Intercepts		0.000371 (0.00068)	-0.000806 (0.00041)	0.001113 (0.00025)	-0.000721 (0.00040)	-0.002073 (0.00034)	0.000977 (0.00027)	0.000102 (0.00012)	0.000244 (0.00021)	0.000793 (0.00026)

Standard errors in parentheses

Source: Deaton (1974)

should be zero according to the theoretical specification (17)
are included to take some account of omitted variables. In
four out of the nine cases they exceed twice their standard
error, but the validity of their incorporation is better considered by testing the joint hypothesis.

In Table 8.6 the likelihood values are shown for each of
the models estimated both including and excluding the constant
terms. The likelihood function is of the form

$$L = ae^b \tag{24}$$

so for ease of maximization the log-likelihood function is
usually derived,

$$\log L = \log a + b. \tag{25}$$

This function is then maximized with respect to the variance
covariance matrix of the errors (here $V + i^*i^{*\prime}$) and the calculated values of that matrix substituted into (25) to give the
concentrated likelihood function, $\log L^C$. This can then be solved
for the parameters of the model j and K. The values shown in
table 8.6 are $2 \log L^C$ because the test of the validity of the
constraints on the model used here is the *likelihood ratio*, LR

$$LR = \frac{L^C \text{ (model with constraint)}}{L^C \text{ (model without constraint)}} = \frac{L^C(1)}{L^C(2)} \tag{26}$$

where $-2 \log LR$ is distributed as $\chi^2 \, (nc)$, nc denoting the

number of constraints. Hence subtracting $2 \log L^C$ for model (i)

with no intercepts from $2 \log L^C$ for model (i) with the inter-

cepts included, $4353.75 - 4306.50 = 47.25$, gives a $\chi^2 \, (8)$

variate under the null hypothesis that the intercepts are zero,

in other words that the constraint is not rejected by the data.

$\chi^2 \, (8)_{0.05} = 15.51$ so the constraint that intercepts be zero in

model (i) is clearly rejected. In fact the constraint is

rejected for all eight models.

Reading down Table 8.6 for the models without the inter-

cepts constrained to zero, the homogeneity constraint is rejec-

ted, $\chi^2(8) = 31.05$, as is the symmetry constraint $\chi^2(36) = 74.25$

$(\chi^2(36)_{0.05} = 51.00)$. However, it is the homogeneity element

of symmetry which contributes most to the rejection as comparing

models (ii) and (iii) $\chi^2 \, (28) = 43.20$ $(\chi^2 \, (28)_{0.05} = 41.34$ and

$\chi^2 \, (28)_{0.01} = 48.28)$.

It is clear that additivity is rejected whether or not the

income and price coefficients are related. But additivity is to

be preferred to there being no substitution at all (model (vi)).

Deaton stresses, however, that these tests alone do not

determine the most suitable model, but give us an idea of the

costs of imposing various restrictions which are implied by the theory. For consistency it may be thought essential to impose symmetry as in models (iii)-(v). It may also be the case that we only have partial information in forming our model, say only income and own price elasticities. The indications from Table 8.6 might therefore be that under these circumstances model (iv) is to be preferred to model (v). Even so, discussion of likelihood values alone is not sufficient; the parameter estimates themselves must be examined. The imposition of symmetry for example does reduce the number of negative cross price coefficients compared with unconstrained model (Table 8.5 compared with Table 8.4).

These comparisons of complete, aggregate demand systems cover up a number of important facets of demand analysis which affect the plausibility of the final form selected. In particular there are problems over the specification of the elasticity of demand with respect to income and the aggregation of demand over households, commodities and individuals. Therefore to set the complete systems in their context this chapter is concluded by a short section on Engel curves, household composition and aggregation.

Table 8.6   Twice concentrated log-likelihood values

Model	With intercepts		Without intercepts	
	2Log L^c	NF[a]	2Log L^c	NF[a]
(i) Rotterdam unconstrained	4353.75	88	4306.50	80
(ii) Rotterdam homogenous	4322.70	80	4267.35	72
(iii) Rotterdam symmetric	4279.50	52	4222.80	44
(iv) Rotterdam 'intermediate'	4209.30	25	4161.60	17
(v) Rotterdam additive	4173.75	17	4119.75	9
(vi) No substitution	4137.75	16	4054.95	8

(a) Number of 'free' parameters in model.

Source: Deaton (1974).

8.3   Further Problems in Demand Analysis

8.3.1   The form of Engel curves

Engel curves are the relation between a consumer's demand
for a particular commodity and his income when prices are held
constant. We have already noted that in the models considered
in section 8.2 that total expenditure is used as a measure of
income. It is also clear at the level of the individual consumer
that 'income' will have important inter-temporal properties
and will be affected by wealth particularly in the demand for
durables. Even without this difficult of specification of the
variable it is clear that there are problems of the specificatio
of the functional form of the relation. The use of constant
elasticities of demand as in the log-linear model we discussed

at the beginning of the previous section entails that consumption rises increasingly rapidly with income in the case of luxury goods (income elasticity greater than unity) or rises increasingly slowly but without limit for necessities.

There are clearly limits to people's willingness to consume products whatever their income and hence a model which incorporates extremes must permit the consumer to reach saturation or in many cases allow the product to move from being a normal good (income elasticity greater than zero) to being an inferior good (income elasticity less than zero). Functional forms must also, of course, not permit negative consumption. The merits of various functional forms are discussed in detail by Prais and Houthakker (1955, 1971) in the analysis of family budget data for 1937-8 and 1938-9 in the UK. They investigate in particular, in addition to linear and log-linear functions, the semi-logarithmic,

$$\log p_i q_i = a_i + b_i \, Y \tag{27}$$

the inverse or hyperbolic

$$p_i q_i = a_i - b_i/Y \tag{28}$$

and the log-inverse

$$\log p_i q_i = a_i - b_i/Y. \tag{29}$$

As a result of comparing both estimated parameter values and
goodness of fit (subject to the difficulty of comparing dependent variables in both linear and logarithmic form) they
analyse all food items in semi-logarithmic form and all non-food
in logarithmic form.

The problems are more acute because of the range of incomes
confronted by the use of cross-section data rather than the
aggregate time series we considered in the previous section.
Their analysis does not cover all possible forms for the Engel
curve, nor do they claim it does. One interesting development
is the PIGL and PIGLOG functions of Muellbauer (1975, 1977)
where PIGL stands for 'price independent generalized linearity'
These functions are developed primarily to solve the problem of
aggregation across consumers.

We noted in the first section that we could tackle the
problem of aggregation across commodities by assumptions of
separability in the utility function. The second problem of
aggregation over consumers we ignored and it was the purpose
of Muellbauer's (1975) article to derive demand functions which
enable *consistent* aggregation across consumers. He shows 'that
aggregate market demand equations are consistent with the micro
demand equations corresponding to some level of income so that

this level does not vary as relative prices vary if and only
if PIGL (or PIGLOG) holds' (p. 526).

8.3.2   Household composition and problems of aggregation

A further more important aggregation difficulty concerns
the nature of household composition. Even if it is possible to
formulate a function which is additive across consumers if they
behave in a similar manner, it is clearly unreasonable to suggest
that all consumers are similar irrelevent of their age or the
size of the household. In the first instance it is clear that
a child's consumption bundle of products will be different
from that of adults for a given expenditure per head. Furthermore,
there are economies of scale in consumption. Clothes can be
passed on from child to child, one car, washing machine,
television etc. will receive fairly similar use as extra members
are added to the household (although not without limit). Thus if
we are using cross-section data we must take these considerations
into account.

In a study of the demand for food, Thomas (1972), tests
hypotheses of equality of consumption patterns not just between
different family compositions but also between different social
classes and areas of the country. As is common with cross-
section studies, the budget constraint is not applied and single-
equation techniques are used in estimation. The equation, (30),

is semi-logarithmic and the social class, family composition

and regional variables are

N_1 number of persons in household more than 14 years of

   age

N_2 number of persons in household aged between 5 and

   14 years

N_3 number of persons less than 5 years of age

S_1 professional[10]

S_2 white collar – non professional

S_3 manual

		Number of households in sample
R_0	Wales[11]	263
R_1	Scotland	673
R_2	Northern	933
R_3	North West	739
R_4	North Midlands	721
R_5	Midlands	419
R_6	South West	378
R_7	London Conurbation	850
R_8	South and South East	479
	TOTAL	5,455

---

[10]
   See Thomas (1972) pp. 73-74 for exact definitions of social
class.
[11]
   National Food Survey regions.

$$P_F Q_F = a_1 + a_2 \log Y + a_3 N_1 + a_4 N_2 + a_5 N_3 + a_6 S_1 +$$
$$a_7 S_2 + a_3 \log Y.S_1 + a_9 \log Y.S_2. \tag{30}$$

The results for the unrestricted estimates of (30) are shown
in Table 8.7 using data from the National Food Survey in
Great Britain for 1965.

It is immediately clear from the table that in all cases
bar one the family composition effects are as expected with
declining levels of consumption age. (Equation (30) assumes
that there are no economies of scale.) Since the constraint
of equality of N_1, N_2 and N_3 is a strictly nested hypothesis
in an OLS model a simple F-test of the validity of the constraint
can be used. An F-value of 182.18 is obtained with regions 2
and 5,450 degrees of freedom (compared with a 1 per cent value
of 4.60) thus rejecting the hypothesis of equality very clearly.
(It should be noted that the authors test the constraints one
at a time without using the totally unrestricted model as the
null hypothesis thus weakening the validity of the tests to the
extent that the three constraints of composition, social class
and region are interrelated.)

It is possible to construct adult-equivalent scales for
children from the coefficients of the three variables, N_1, N_2 and
N_3, giving values of 0.59 and 0.44 for the N_2 and N_3 categories

Table 8.7   Family expenditure on food

Regions	Intercept	$\log Y$	N_1	N_2	N_3	S_1	S_2	$\log Y.S_1$	$\log Y.S_2$	$\bar{R}^2$
0	-1.106 (0.509)	1.635 (0.246)	0.811 (0.120)	0.618 (0.088)	0.470 (0.163)	-3.022 (4.108)	0.469 (3.255)	0.955 (1.380)	-0.226 (1.122)	0.61
1	-0.753 (0.292)	1.081 (0.136)	1.203 (0.075)	0.786 (0.049)	0.492 (0.074)	-0.476 (1.049)	0.318 (0.957)	0.291 (0.452)	-0.124 (0.324)	0.67
2	-1.491 (0.221)	1.456 (0.108)	1.119 (0.066)	0.601 (0.048)	0.532 (0.073)	-0.889 (1.219)	1.119 (0.987)	0.284 (0.379)	-0.449 (0.332)	0.68
3	-1.355 (0.346)	1.337 (0.159)	1.092 (0.092)	0.706 (0.067)	0.512 (0.089)	1.705 (1.424)	-0.031 (1.069)	-0.500 (0.448)	-0.024 (0.371)	0.55
4	-1.076 (0.260)	1.103 (0.117)	1.255 (0.073)	0.628 (0.053)	0.525 (0.076)	-2.165 (1.259)	0.532 (1.091)	0.740 (0.382)	-0.217 (0.364)	0.66
5	-1.609 (0.364)	1.453 (0.164)	1.100 (0.098)	0.669 (0.067)	0.365 (0.110)	0.782 (1.85)	-1.683 (1.223)	-0.343 (0.569)	0.422 (0.416)	0.66
6	-1.301 (0.429)	1.266 (0.203)	1.139 (0.113)	0.550 (0.083)	0.616 (0.144)	-0.076 (1.649)	1.493 (1.891)	0.055 (0.528)	-0.526 (0.633)	0.58
7	-1.027 (0.263)	1.177 (0.113)	1.154 (0.065)	0.742 (0.056)	0.498 (0.074)	0.236 (0.966)	-0.175 (0.784)	-0.032 (0.289)	0.002 (0.253)	0.67
8	-1.174 (0.388)	1.069 (0.172)	1.208 (0.090)	0.739 (0.063)	0.568 (0.095)	-3.113 (1.437)	0.846 (1.190)	0.987 (0.444)	-0.303 (0.400)	0.63
Country as a whole	-1.160 (0.104)	1.238 (0.048)	1.154 (0.027)	0.684 (0.020)	0.512 (0.030)	-0.391 (0.456)	0.212 (0.366)	0.139 (0.141)	-0.130 (0.123)	0.64

Numbers in parentheses are standard errors

Source: Thomas (1972).

for the country as a whole. Muellbauer (1977) extends this
analysis to his PIGL and PIGLOG and shows results for a much
wider range of ten commodity groups, shown in Table 8.8. It
is particularly interesting to note that there is variation in
the effect of children not just according to economies of scale
but that these effects and the economies of scale vary with the
size of reference budget. The first older child imposes a bigger
cost on the budget than the first younger child and economies
of scale are greater for children of the same age group.

The tests of the effects of social class are more interesting because (30) assumes that they take two forms, affecting
not just the constant term but also the slope of the income
parameter. The values and standard errors of the individual
coefficients a_6-a_9 might lead us to reject all the social
class effects; however, they should be taken together. Again
using the F-test procedure a value of 4.10 is obtained for the
test of the income coefficients alone (2 and 5,440 degrees of
freedom - 5 per cent value is 2.99). Further tests are shown
under the hypothesis that all coefficients including the
family composition effects vary with social class and this is
also borne out at the 5 per cent level.

Lastly the authors also test the hypothesis that region
has no influence on family consumption of food. As is clear from

Table 8.8   General Equivalence Scales with Age Differences at 1975 Prices and Different 1975 Weekly Expenditure Levels (for the Reference Household)

N_4 = no. of children aged 0-5, N_5 = no. of children aged 5-16

Reference Household Expenditure	$N_4 = 0,$ $N_5 = 0$	$N_4 = 1,$ $N_5 = 0$	$N_4 = 0,$ $N_5 = 1$	$N_4 = 1,$ $N_5 = 1$	$N_4 = 2,$ $N_5 = 0$	$N_4 = 0,$ $N_5 = 2$
£20	1	1.156	1.297	1.424	1.271	1.567
£30	1	1.115	1.253	1.337	1.185	1.477
£40	1	1.087	1.223	1.278	1.127	1.416
£50	1	1.066	1.200	1.235	1.085	1.371
£70	1	1.035	1.167	1.171	1.023	1.305
£100	1	1.004	1.132	1.108	0.962	1.338

Source: Muellbauer (1977).

Table 8.7 regressions were estimated for each region separately thus not only allowing all the parameters to change between regions but also allowing the residual variance to be different. Again the F-statistic of 1.69 exceeds the 1 per cent value (1.41 with 72 and 5,374 degrees of freedom).

8.3.3   Dynamic models

While in cross-section studies the analysis of family budgets is necessarily static, the treatment of demand as static in time series models runs completely against the findings of the aggregate consumption models of Chapter 2. Furthermore these models were concerned with consumers' expenditure on non-durables. Studies of expenditure on durables must inevitably consider the existence of stocks as durability entails that items bought in one time period are not totally used up in that period and can be used in subsequent periods. Since stocks of durables are very difficult to estimate, models of expenditure on durables tend to incorporate either a stock or expenditure adjustment mechanism which involves only lags in expenditures and prices which are readily observable. Houthakker and Taylor (1970) argue that this adjustment process should be incorporated in all demand functions.

They derive their model from a quadratic utility function and derive a discrete approximation for estimation as

$$q_t^* = g + \hat{h} q_{t-1}^* + \hat{j}\ l p_t^* + \hat{k}\ l_{t-1}\ p_{t-1}^* \qquad (31)$$

where quantities, q^*, are per capita, prices, p^*, are expressed
relative to the general price level and the g, $\hat{h}$, $\hat{j}$, $\hat{k}$ and l are
parameters. It is however possible to solve back from (31) to
obtain the structural parameters of the model.

Estimates are given for the United States, Canada, the
Netherlands and Sweden. The elasticities for Sweden are shown
in Table 8.9.

While the inclusion of lags gives well determined coefficients in most cases there is no opportunity to test this
specification against alternative lag-structures, and with the
presence of a lagged dependent variable the Durbin-Watson
tatistic quoted is somewhat uninformative about the presence
of autocorrelation. Cross-equation error correlations are neglected. The total expenditure elasticities appear plausible, iden-
tifying luxuries and necessities as one might expect with the
exception of miscellaneous services which appears to be an
inferior good. However, two of the long-run price elasticities
are positive, that for housing, fuel and light being greater
than two.

This approach has been developed further by Phlips (1974)
and other work on dynamic demand systems has been undertaken.

Table 8.9 *Elasticities from the Dynamic Demand System - Sweden*

| | | Total expenditure | Price | |
| | | | Compensated | Uncompensated |
		Elasticity	Elasticity	Elasticity
Food and beverages	SR	1.00	-0.20	-0.59
	LR	0.97	-0.29	-0.67
Housing, fuel, and light	SR	0.45	0.14	-0.20
	LR	2.65	1.75	2.13
Clothing	SR	1.59	-0.40	-0.63
	LR	1.99	-0.69	-0.97
Household goods	SR	1.56	-0.46	-0.55
	LR	1.91	-0.81	-0.93
Miscellaneous services	SR	0.11	-0.04	-0.04
	LR	-0.46	0.22	0.24
Travel	SR	1.83	-0.51	-0.65
	LR	4.99	-1.50	-1.88
Recreation	SR	0.78	-0.24	-0.28
	LR	2.11	-0.91	-1.01
Medical and personal care	SR	0.82	-0.26	-0.29
	LR	2.67	-1.12	-1.24

Source: Houthakker and Taylor (1970)

SR, short run; LR, long run.

The difficulties in determining family expenditure on a
cross-section basis suggest that the constraints imposed by
utility theory on the complete system of demand equations are
likely to be found harsh. The results of Deaton (1974) show
the limits of the constraints in practice, and the lack of
inter-temporal relations in a context which clearly has dynamic
properties shows the analysis requires even further constraint.
It is interesting to note that other models of highly constrained
behaviour such as portfolio models tend to find that their
constraints are often rejected by the data and that the models
of the whole economy considered in the next chapter are
characterized by their flexibility despite their high degree of
interrelation.

References and Suggested Reading*

BARTEN, A.P. (1969) 'Maximum likelihood estimation of a complete system of demand equations', *European Economic Review*, vol. 1, pp. 7-73.

BLACK, J. AND BRADLEY, J.F. (1973) *'Essential Mathematics for Economists'* London: Wiley.

*BROWN, J.A.C. AND DEATON, A.S. (1972) 'Surveys in applied economics: models of consumer behaviour', *Economic Journal*, vol. 82, pp. 1145-1236.

DAVENANT, C. (1699) *'An Essay upon the Probable Methods of Making a People Gainers in the Balance of Trade'*, London.

*DEATON, A.S. (1974) 'The analysis of consumer demand in the U.K. 1900-1970' *Econometrica*, vol. 42, pp. 341-368.

*GOLDBERGER, A.S. AND GAMALETSOS, T. (1970) 'A cross country comparison of consumer expenditure patterns', *European Economic Review*, pp. 357-400.

HOUTHAKKER, H.S. (1960) 'Additive Preferences' *Econometrica*, vol. 28.

HOUTHAKKER, H.S. (1961) 'The present state of consumption theory' *Econometrica* vol. 29.

HOUTHAKKER, H.S. (1965) 'New evidence on demand elasticities' *Econometrica* vol. 33.

*HOUTHAKKER, H.S. AND TAYLOR, L.D. (1970) *'Consumer Demand in the United States'* 2nd edn. Cambridge, Mass: Harvard

University Press.

MADDALA, G.S. (1977) *'Econometrics'*, New York: McGraw-Hill.

MUELLBAUER, J. (1975) 'Aggregation, income distribution and consumer demand', *Review of Economic Studies*, vol. 42, pp. 525-543.

MUELLBAUER, J. (1977) 'Testing the Barten model of household composition effects and the cost of children', *Economic Journal*, vol. 87 (September) pp. 460-487.

PESARAN, M. AND DEATON, A.S. (1978) 'Testing non-nested non-linear regression models' *Econometrica*, vol. 46 pp. 677-694.

*PHLIPS, L. (1974) *'Applied Consumption Analysis'* Amsterdam: North Holland.

PRAIS, S.J. AND HOUTHAKKER, H.S. (1955) 2nd edn. (1971) *'The Analysis of Family Budgets'* Cambridge: Cambridge University Press.

SLUTSKY, E. (1915) 'On the theory of the budget of the consumer'. *Giornale Degli Economisti.*

STONE, J.R.N. (1954) *'The Measurement of Consumers' Expenditure and Behaviour in the U.K. 1920-1938'* vol. 1, Cambridge: Cambridge University Press.

*THOMAS, W.J. (1972) ed. *'The Demand for Food'* Manchester: Manchester University Press.

ZELLNER, A. (1962) 'An efficient method for estimating Seemingly Unrelated Regressions and tests for aggreation bias', *Journal of the American Statistical Association* (June) pp. 348-368.

Chapter 9

MODELS OF THE ECONOMY

In chapter 1 we set out four main steps in econometric

analysis. In early chapters we have directed most of our att-

ention only at three of these: specification, estimation and

hypothesis testing. Therefore, in this chapter we concentrate on

the remaining step, which was forecasting, and examine the use

of a forecasting model for the whole economy. Such a model has

to take account of all the difficulties we have considered up

until now, lag-structures, non-linearities, errors in variables,

simultaneity, restrictions in and between equations, etc. It

is, therefore, impossible to consider the specification and

estimation of one model in detail let alone make comparisons

between models. We shall therefore consider the problems assoc-

iated with forecasting in the context of a single model – the

National Institute model of the UK (NIESR, 1979).

The chapter is divided into four sections, the first of

which sets out the form of the National Institute model. The

second section discusses the methods and purposes of forecasting

and explains in particular how forecasts are produced in practice

a process which is very different from that described in
theoretical textbooks. The third section considers how the
accuracy of forecasts can be assessed and the chapter is
completed by a section on the use of the models in simulation
mode.

9.1   The Structure of the National Institute Model of the Economy

There are several models of the UK economy (see Ormerod
(1980)), many models of the US economy and a number of well
respected models of other economies, so it is legitimate to
question why the National Institute model has been chosen in
particular. Other than the obvious characteristic of familiarity, the National Institute model has four appealing characteristics. In the first instance the model is readily available and
its properties are frequently discussed, and forecasts have been
produced on a detailed basis for many years in the quarterly
issues of the National Institute Economic Review. Of the major
alternative models of the UK only very limited forecasts are
published by the Treasury[1] (twice each year, under the terms
of the Industry Act) and the Bank of England[2] do not publish

---

[1] Treasury (1980) see also Hilton and Heathfield (1970) and Rentor
(1975) for earlier discussions of the major UK econometric model
and the problems of modelling.

[2] Bank of England (1979).

forecasts as such from their model. The remaining contender is
the London Business School model[3] for which a little less
detailed information is available on the forecasting techniques
and performances.

Secondly the National Institute model although having
approximately 180 equations is relatively manageable and can be
conveniently summarized. The LBS and Treasury models are more
than twice as large. In the third place the National Institute
model deliberately has a clear economic basis. It is frequently
thought of as being primarily Keynesian in character because
of the way its main structure is built up through the components
of income and expenditure, but it also has a full monetary
sector and enables the user to study the impact of the full range
of policy variables available to a government as well as the
influence on the system from exogenous factors. Changes in money
supply do not however act directly on activity and prices and the
modelling of the transmission mechanism largely through interest
rates and the cost determination of prices also contributes to
the 'Keynesian' reputation. The LBS model tends to be given a
more monetarist label and is usually described as 'international

---

[3] LBS (1979). There is also of course the model used by the
Cambridge Economic Policy Group, but it is on an annual basis and
not so well documented.

monetarist' (although Beenstock and Burns in Major (1979)

suggested that they would also be happy to have their ideas

described as 'international Keynesian'). The method of model

building is also rather different in the LBS case because they

have an overall vision of the economic system and build up

their model to yield long-run results consistent with their

a priori expectations. The NI model is more eclectic seeking

satisfactory explanations on a sectoral and even equation by

equation basis.

Taken together these characteristics provide all the

necessary requirements for a considered study of the issues in-

volved in forecasting the UK macro-economy, although it is clear

that other models might have been used.

The NI model as is usual with macro-econometric models which

are in frequent use, is an evolving process and we can only

consider the model at a particular vintage, here August, 1979.

It is the fourth econometric model (in terms of the Institute's

own nomenclature) in twenty years of forecasting. The first was

described in Surrey (1971) and had less than 20 equations. The

second, developed by George Fane and others, is described in the

series of National Institute Discussion Papers (Nos. 10A-D).

It was largely overtaken by model III which is similar to the

model described here. The major difference is that Model IV uses

the newer CSO data series based on 1975.

The actual listing of the model, NIESR (1979), is some 44 pages long so no attempt is made to reproduce it here; however, it can be simplified for purposes of general exposition.

GDP is built up initially from the expenditure definition and is expressed at factor cost

$$GDP = TFS + DS - M - AFC \tag{1}$$

where

$$TFS = CE + DK + EX + PAC^*. \tag{2}$$

All variables are in 1975 prices and * denotes an exogenous item. TFS is total final sales, DS is stockbuilding, M is imports of goods and services, AFC is adjustment to factor cost, CE is consumers' expenditure, DK is gross fixed investment, EX is exports of goods and services, and PAC^* is general government expenditure on current goods and services.

There are thus five categories of expenditure to be endogenously determined, DS, M, CE, DK and EX.[4] Of these five categories, consumers' expenditure is explained in the framework discussed in Chapter 2.

---

[4] The pedigree of the model is very clear at this level of aggregation and its structure can readily be traced back to Model I described in Surrey (1971). A companion version is planned for Model IV.

$$CE = 1206 + 0.2033 \ (DY - CG^*) + 0.1944 \ CR + 0.2748 \ CG^*$$
$$\quad (3.3) \quad (3.6) \qquad\qquad\qquad (2.9) \qquad\quad (3.1)$$

$$+ \ 0.6879 \ CE_{-1} - 11.97 \ CPID$$
$$(10.0) \qquad\qquad (2.2)$$

$$\overline{R}^2 = 0.99 \quad DW = 1.96 \quad h = 0.18 \quad SEE = 120$$

$$1963II - 1978II \hspace{8cm} (3)$$

where DY is real personal disposable income, CG^* is current

grants to persons, and CR is a credit variable equal to the sum

of the change in bank loans and hire-purchase credit advanced

to the personal sector.

All three variables are deflated by the consumer price

index CPI and $CPID$ is the rate of consumer price inflation over

a year earlier.[5]

As consumers' expenditure is not disaggregated into its

durable and non-durable components, the CR term is included to

take account of the availability of new borrowed funds to con-

sumers. The personal sector is also assumed to have a higher

marginal propensity to consume out of transfer incomes as these

tend to be paid to those on low incomes, hence the separate CG^*

---

[5] This equation and the model are estimated by OLS which may result in some simultaneity bias. The model has been re-estimated
using 2SLS on the principal components of the exogenous variable
by the author and in general the character of the model is not
altered (see Mayes and Savage (1980) for the example of the mone
tary sector).

term. (It is likely that by the time of publication consumers'
expenditure will be disaggregated and the effects of inflation
explained in a more behavioural manner by a variable representing personal sector holdings of liquid assets.)

Gross fixed investment is determined in a much more complex
manner with nine individual components, six of which are exogenous. Again this can fortunately be simplified. Investment in
the public sector is treated as exogenous as is investment in
other areas subject to large measures of government influence or
discontinuities where a small number of decisions affect the
outcome. These industries include iron and steel, petroleum and
natural gas and shipping. The three endogenous categories are
private dwellings, manufacturing and the remaining parts of the
private sector. The last of these, which consists primarily of
investment by service industries, is determined by the pre-
existing capital stock, a distributed lag on consumers' expenditure and a dummy variable, but the other two equations are
much more interesting. Investment in private dwellings is
determined through demand for new housing using real personal
disposable income, the relative price of houses to other goods,
taking mortgage costs into account, and the rate of inflation in
house prices relative to the rate of interest thus incorporating
both consumption and investment influences. However, demand is

also constrained through the availability of building society
finance represented here by the increase in deposits deflated
by house prices. (This inflow is itself endogenously determined
in the model.) This relation, shown as equation (4), is thus an
important source of influence from monetary variables on real
output in the model.

$$IPD = -204.2 + 0.0212 \; DY + 0.679 \; IPD_{-1}$$
$$\quad\quad (2.17) \quad (2.32) \quad\quad\quad (7.29)$$

$$-16.39 \; \frac{PNH}{CPI} \; [RM \, (1-0.01SRT^*)]_{-1}$$
$$(2.47)$$

$$+ \; 90.87 \left[\frac{1+(PNH-PNH_{-4})/PNH_{-4}}{1+0.01RLA} \right] + 0.1538 \left(\frac{BSD+GL^*}{PNH} \right)$$
$$(1.64) \quad\quad\quad\quad\quad\quad\quad\quad\quad\quad (0.8)$$

$$R^2 = 0.84 \quad h = 0.63 \quad DW = 1.9$$

1963I - 1977III

$$(4)$$

where IPD is investment in private dwellings, PNH is the price o
new homes, RM is the building society mortgage rate, SRT^* is the
standard rate of income tax, RLA is the rate of interest on loca
authority temporary debt, BSD is the net increase in building
society deposits, and GL^* is a government loan which was temporarily made to attempt to keep down RM.

The remaining investment equation for manufacturing is
an augmented flexible accelerator (see Chapter 4) and thus
provides an important element in the cyclical behaviour of the
economy.

$$IMF = 1172 - 0.0073 \underset{(13.63)}{KMF}_{-2} + \underset{(5.62)}{759.2} CF + \underset{(4.74)}{139.9} DG^*$$
$$\underset{(25.29)}{}$$

$$+\underset{(12.91)}{\Sigma w_i} \Delta(UT \times OMF)_{-i}$$

$$\overline{R}^2 = 0.93 \quad DW = 1.2 \quad SEE = 27$$

1967I – 1977III $\hspace{5cm}$ (5)

where IMF is investment in manufacturing industry (excluding the exogenous categories already mentioned); KMF is the capital stock of manufacturing industry; CF is a cash flow measure defined as trading profits after allowing for taxation and stock appreciation, deflated (by the fixed investment price index) after the removal of a linear time trend; DG^* is a dummy variable to take account of the change in the rate of investment grants in 1968IV; UT is a measure of capacity utilization; OMF **is** output **of manufacturing**; and the w_i are

i	w_i
1	0.67
2	1.71
3	2.87
4	3.94
5	4.77
6	5.23
7	5.27
8	4.86
9	4.04
10	2.86
11	1.46

obtained as Almon lags giving a smooth profile and a mean lag of 5.4 quarters.

The third of the five endogenous components of the expenditure GDP identity, stockbuilding, is divided into three; manufacturing, distributive trades and a residual. Stockbuilding in manufacturing, DSM, is also determined by a flexible accelerator.

$$DSM = 0.1736 + 0.535 \; DSM_{-1} - 0.281 \; DSA + \Sigma w_i \; (OMF-OMF_{-1})_{-i}$$
$$ (0.01) \quad (5.13) \quad\quad (2.6) \quad\quad (5.11)$$

$$\overline{R}^2 = 0.62 \quad DW = 1.8 \quad h = 1.24$$

$$1961III - 1977III \tag{6}$$

where $DSA = SA-SA_{-1}$ is the change in stock appreciation in the company sector and the w_i are

i	w_i
0	46.70
1	18.53
2	7.73
3	8.25
4	14.07

Stockbuilding by the distributive trades is related to consumers expenditure and the residual category moves in relation to the other two categories.

The equations in the external sector are log-linear and are determined by a combination of activity and relative price variables in the common form we discussed in Chapter 7. Exports

of goods are divided into four categories of which oil and a
residual are determined exogenously. The equations for the
remaining two categories, manufactures and food and basic goods
are particularly notable for the small size of both the 'income'
and price elasticities.

$$\ln XMF = 5.712 + 0.572 \ln WTM^* + \Sigma w_i \ln RPXMF$$
$$(25.44) \quad (11.63) \qquad\qquad (2.5)$$ (7)

i	w_i
0	-0.0765
1	-0.1081
2	-0.1243
3	-0.1259
4	-0.1137
5	-0.0881
6	-0.0500
Σ	-0.6867

$\overline{R}^2 = 0.96$ DW = 1.5   SEE = 0.496

1964I - 1977III

$$\ln XFB = 3.871 + 0.576 \ln WTT^* - 0.12 \ln RPXFB_{-1}$$
$$(40.78) \quad (25.60) \qquad\qquad (1.34)$$

+ dummy variables

$\overline{R}^2 = 0.94$ DW = 1.7   SEE = 0.50

1962II - 1977III (8)

where XMF and XFB are exports of manufactures and food and basic
materials; WTM^* and WTT^* are world trade in manufactures and in

total; and *RPXMF* and *RPXFB* are the relative price of *XMF* and *XFB*
to the world price. (While world prices and world trade are
exogenous from the point of view of this econometric model they
do of course have to be forecast by the Institute.)

In both cases the income elasticities are of the order of
one half and as might be expected relative price is not important for *XFB*; however, the distributed lag on *RPXMF* shows that
the effects of a change in relative price will be very small
initially and still relatively small in the long run. Thus one
would expect a perverse movement in the *value* of exports for a
change in relative price. In fact if we look at the import
equation (9) for goods (excluding oil and natural gas) we can
see that the Marshall-Lerner condition is not quite met on these
coefficients alone.

$$\ln MG = -5.151 + 0.9577 \ln TFE + 0.8437 \, \Delta\ln TFE$$
$$\quad\quad (2.72) \quad (3.63) \quad\quad\quad (1.99)$$

$$\quad\quad -0.1213 \ln RPMG_{-2} \; -0.3368 \, \Delta\ln RPMG +0.4987 \ln MG_{-1}$$
$$\quad\quad (1.12) \quad\quad\quad\quad (2.06) \quad\quad\quad\quad (3.73)$$

$$\overline{R}^2 = 0.97 \quad DW = 2.15 \quad h = -1.64 \quad SEE = 0.036$$

1963III - 1977III   (9)

where *MG* is imports of goods excluding oil and natural gas, and
RPMG is their price relative to the domestic price level.

There are of course equations to determine trade in services and the other items of the current balance, so a concentration on (7), (8) and (9) alone could be misplaced. Certainly
the initial effect of a depreciation of the rate of exchange is
to worsen the balance of payments on current account, but as
the lagged effects come into play the balance improves. This
path is usually known as the $'j'$ curve (time being on the
horizontal axis and the current balance on the vertical one).
The full effect of a fall in the rate of exchange in the model
also includes an expansion in GDP due to increased demand for
exports and decreased demand for imports and an increase in the
rate of inflation.

This leaves only the adjustment to factor cost, AFC, to be
determined from equations (1) and (2). It is a technical
function of indirect taxes rates and their base. However equations
(3)-(9) have introduced further endogenous variables which now
need explanation. These relate to incomes ((3), (4) and (5)),
monetary aggregates and interest rates ((3) and (4)), prices (all
equations), output and capacity utilization (5), and the rate of
exchange ((7), (8) and (9)). In other words we have to fill in
the whole of the rest of the real, nominal and monetary sectors
of the economy. The ordering of this completion is largely
arbitrary, so for ease of reference we shall follow that in
NIESR (1979).

In the first place, having built up GDP from expenditures
it is necessary to see what the implications are for output
of the various sectors of the economy and hence, after determining productivity and capacity utilization, to work out the
implications for employment and unemployment. Sectoral output
is determined primarily by a stylized form of input-output
matrix and exogenous information. Productivity and capacity
utilization are dealt with in the form of ratio to trend and
employment is largely a distributed lag on output. This is most
clearly seen in manufacturing

$$
\Delta \ln EMF = \begin{array}{c} -0.002 \\ (3.7) \end{array} + \begin{array}{c} 0.561 \\ (6.61) \end{array} \Delta \ln EMF_{-1} + \begin{array}{c} 0.111 \\ (5.47) \end{array} \Delta \ln OMF_{-1}
$$

$$
+ \begin{array}{c} 0.061 \\ (2.69) \end{array} \Delta \ln OMF_{-2} + \begin{array}{c} 0.034 \\ (1.45) \end{array} \Delta \ln OMF_{-3}
$$

$$
\overline{R}^2 = 0.7 \quad DW = 2.18 \quad h = -1.047 \quad SEE = 0.0035
$$

1961II - 1978II   *(10)*

where *EMF* is employment in manufacturing. Unemployment is then
determined by changes in the labour force relative to employment,
where the labour force is exogenously determined from Department
of Employment forecasts and thus the expost equation is an
identity after allowing for the proportion of those without a
job who actually register as unemployed and is not estimated.

The remaining real variables to be determined are then
incomes. Income from employment is estimated by a two-stage

process whereby the wage rate is determined and then earnings

by multiplication by average hours and employment, both of

which are determined elsewhere in the model. The wage rate

equation is of course extremely important in that it acts as a

major determinant of the price level. It is the more unfort-

unate therefore that this equation was not directly used in fore-

casting (according to Allsopp and Joshi (1980)) when the

determination of inflation in the UK is such an important issue.

The National Institute places great emphasis on the very specific

factors which affect bargaining in the wage 'round' each year

and hence augment their econometric relation with such extra

information as is available on each occasion. The estimated

function is a simple augmented Phillips curve (see Chapter 6)

$$\frac{\Delta_4 WR}{WR_{-4}} = \underset{(4.19)}{0.1007} + \underset{(1.38)}{0.1806} \frac{\Delta_4 CPI_{-1}}{CPI_{-5}} + \underset{(8.44)}{0.7362} \frac{\Delta_4 WR_{-1}}{WR_{-5}}$$

$$\underset{(4.08)}{-2.076} \; U/(U+E) \; \underset{(3.25)}{-0.0014}t$$

$$\overline{R}^2 = 0.86 \quad DW = 1.97 \quad h = 0.02$$

1963I – 1978IV   (11)

where WR is the wage rate, U is unemployment, and E is employment.

(It should be noted that the wage equation has been revised twice

since (11) but these newer versions had not been incorporated in

the published listing at the time of writing.)

The remaining categories of income are straightforward: rents are related to the previous quarter's GDP at market prices; income from self-employment (after stock appreciation) is related to average earnings of employees and gross trading profits of companies after tax and stock appreciation property incomes are related to interest rates, and each sector's holdings of financial assets and profits are determined residually, as the difference between incomes and expenditures. A thirteen-equation direct tax model determines income after tax and hence, after incorporation of current grants, we can obtain disposable incomes which are the variable used in equations (3) and (4).

As we mentioned, wages are an important determinant of prices and this is clear from the CPI equation

$$\frac{\Delta_4 CPI}{CPI_{-4}} = \underset{(4.08)}{0.1538} \ PMA + \underset{(14.29)}{0.4516} \ WCA + \underset{(4.31)}{0.2783} \ \frac{\Delta_4 PWMF}{PWMF_{-4}}$$

$$\underset{(3.68)}{-0.1934} \ \frac{\Delta_4 PRO_{-2}}{PRO_{-6}} + \underset{(3.37)}{0.0012} \ \Delta_4 OMF_{-3} + 0.9 \ CET$$

$$\overline{R}^2 = 0.98 \quad DW = 1.4 \quad SEE = 0.1$$

1966I - 1977III   (12)

where $PMA = \frac{1}{4}[\overset{4}{\underset{1}{\Sigma}} \ (PM_{-i}/PM_{-i-4})] \ -1$ (PM is import prices); $WCA = \frac{1}{4} \ [\overset{4}{\underset{1}{\Sigma}} \ (WC_{-i}/WC_{-i-4})] \ -1$; WC is the wage cost per man including employers' National Insurance contributions; PWMF is the wholesal price index for manufacturing (excluding food, drink and tobacco); *PRO* is output per head (GDP/E); and *CET* is a variable reflecting the change in the tax rate on consumers' expenditure, whose coefficient is imposed.

PWMF is itself determined by wage costs, import prices and productivity as is the price of investment goods. This leaves the price of public authorities current expenditure and exports to be determined. Export prices are formed by a combination of domestic and world prices and *PAC* prices from public sector wage costs and domestic prices.

The exchange rate plays an important role in price determination and is determined by relative prices, the covered interest differential on the US dollar and the visible trade balance of trade. The cost of cover, the forward premium on the dollar, is also endogenous, depending on the rate of change of the dollar exchange rate and the visible balance.

$$\frac{RE-RP}{RE} = \underset{(2.2)}{-13.43} + \underset{(2.27)}{0.5378} \; [(RE-RP)/RE]_{-1} + \underset{(0.48)}{0.3436} \; \Delta CID$$

$$+ \underset{(0.24)}{0.1556} \; \Delta CID_{-1} + \underset{(0.72)}{0.4948} \; \Delta CID_{-2} + \underset{(2.45)}{0.9366} \; VB/PWMF$$

$$- \underset{(0.87)}{0.495} \; (VB/PWMF)_{-1} - \underset{(0.61)}{0.2352} \; (VB/PWMF)_{-2}$$

$\overline{R}^2 = 0.61$ DW = 1.95   SEE = 4.17

1972I – 1977I   *(13)*

where *RE* is the effective rate of exchange; *RP* is ratio of world
to domestic *PWMF*; *CID* is covered interest differential on the US
dollar; and *VB* is the visible balance.

This approach, explained originally by Batchelor (1977),
assumes that the exchange rate adjusts to achieve a
combination of 'purchasing power parity' and 'interest rate
parity' (with the US dollar). This explanation was largely
satisfactory for the period of floating exchange rates up to 1977
but has gone seriously astray in the explanation of the appreciation of the pound in 1978-80 (see Cuthbertson *et al.* (1980)).

This leaves the financial sector to complete the model.
It is composed of seven behavioural equations which determine the
demands for financial assets and five behavioural equations to
determine interest rates. Net acquisitions of financial assets
by sector are already determined as residuals from the net
transactions in the rest of the model: taking the company
sector, for example,

$$NAFAC = GTPC + RC + NPIC + KTC - TC - TXC - GDKC \qquad (14)$$

where *NAFAC* is net acquisition of financial assets by companies;
GTPC is gross trading profits of companies; *RC* is rent of the
company sector; *NPIC* is net property income of the company sector
KTC is capital transfers to the company sector; *TC* is capital

transfers to charities by companies; TXC is company taxation;
and $GDKC$ is gross domestic capital formation by companies. This
structure enables the model to incorporate all the variables,
such as the money supply, which are of interest, particularly
$\Delta\pounds M3$, the change in sterling $M3$.

$$\Delta\pounds M3 = \Delta BLPUB + \Delta BLPRIV - \Delta BNL - \Delta FC + \Delta CUR \qquad (15)$$

where $BLPUB$ and $BLPRIV$ are bank loans to the public and private
sectors; BNL is banks' non-deposit liabilities; FC is foreign
currency finance;[6] and CUR is currency.

The first of the terms in (15), bank lending to the public
sector, is solved from the identity with the $PSBR$ less sales of
public debt to the private sector, the change in currency and
foreign sector financing of the public sector. Bank loans to the
private sector are demand determined in the form of stock
adjustment equations. They are distinguished into loans for
house purchase to the personal sector, loans to industrial and
commercial companies and the residual of all other loans to the
personal sector. This last equation is typical of the general

---

[6]
  See $NIER$ no. 92, p. 31 for an exact definition. (The model
listing in NIESR (1979) shows $M3$ rather than $\pounds M3$.)

form

$$\Delta BLO = -721.139 - 25.58 \; RBL - 0.3721 \; NAFAPER - 91.08 \; LPER*$$
$$\quad\quad\quad (1.37) \quad (1.47) \quad\quad\quad (5.12) \quad\quad\quad\quad (2.12)$$

$$\quad\quad + 486.2 \; CCC + 0.0989 \; DY - 0.0767 \; BLO_{-1}$$
$$\quad\quad\quad (3.58) \quad\quad (2.62) \quad\quad\quad (2.45)$$

$\overline{R}^2 = 0.65 \quad DW = 2.4 \quad SEE = 158$

1963I - 1977III   (16)

where the interest rate variable RBL is that on bank loans, $NAFAPER$ is the personal sector net acquisition of financial assets and $LPER*$ is a dummy variable to take account of the Bank of England's requests for restraint in bank lending. (DY is real personal disposable income as in equation (3) and CCC is a dummy variable to allow for a change in behaviour after the introduction of Competition and Credit Control in 1971.)

The demand for currency by the non-bank private sector is a simple function of consumers' expenditure with a small trend. Sales of public sector debt to the non-bank private sector are divided into National Savings and a major cateogry (GDS) composed of government securities, local authority debt, public corporation stocks and Treasury bills (there is a small unexplained residual.) Although these equations are built up on the basis of a 'portfolio' approach to asset holding by the sector only limited substitution is explicitly included in common with a number of other studies (Treasury (1980) for example).

$$GDS = 36.78 + 0.6739 \; NAFAPRI + 0.0100 \; \Delta YRC_{-1} + 0.0022 \; \Delta YRC_{-2}$$
$$(0.44) \; (6.3) \qquad\qquad (3.52) \qquad\qquad (0.74)$$

$$+ \; 0.0006 \; \Delta YRTB_{-1} + 0.0066 \; \Delta YRTB_{-2} - 0.0038 \; \Delta YRBD_{-1}$$
$$(0.2) \qquad\quad (2.36) \qquad\qquad (1.27)$$

$$- \; 0.0033 \; \Delta YRBD_{-2}$$
$$(1.15)$$

$$\bar{R}^2 = 0.58 \quad DW = 1.6 \quad SEE = 406$$

$$1965I - 1977III \hspace{6cm} (17)$$

where *NAFAPRI* is net acquisition of financial assets by the private sector and *YRC, YRTB* and *YRBD* are the yield on $2\frac{1}{2}$ per cent consols, Treasury Bills and bank deposit accounts each multiplied by *NAFAPRI* as a scaling factor. (This ensures that the demand for government debt is homogeneous of degree one with respect to financial wealth.)

Interest rates are set by an explanation of the differential between the US and UK Treasury Bills rates and then through the term structure of interest rates and market spreads.

$$RTB - RTBUS^* = 2.715 - 0.0023 \; (CCC \times VB/P) - 0.0005 \; RES^*$$
$$(6.3) \quad (8.1) \qquad\qquad\qquad (3.22)$$

$$+ \; 1.291 \; MT^*$$
$$(4.98)$$

$$\bar{R}^2 = 0.67 \quad DW = 1.0 \quad SEE = 1.1$$

$$1963I - 1977III$$

where *RTBUS* is the US Treasury Bill rate, P is the GDP deflator, *RES* is foreign exchange reserves (deflated by P) and *MT* is a dummy variable to take account of monetary targets.

This completes the model. Such a brief description in only
18 equations of a model with 50 behavioural equations and over
120 identities and internal definitions is bound to leave much
out, but the nature of most of the crucial relations and parameters is clear. GDP is built up through the determination of
expenditures. These expenditures are dependent upon and
influence incomes and output, both through total final expenditure and the balance of imports and exports. The levels of
output interact through productivity and labour force projections
to determine employment and unemployment. Nominal levels of the
real variables are determined by the relationship between costs
and prices, central to which is the expectations augmented
Phillips curve. Despite the generally Keynesian label given to
the NIESR model financial variables have an important role to
play through interest rates, credit, bank loans and the
exchange rate. Given the net acquisition of financial assets by
sectors determined by incomes and expenditures their portfolio
is determined by relative yields. These yields themselves relate
to foreign interest rates, the domestic interest rate structure
and the stance of monetary policy.

The major exogenous influences on the economy come through
world trade and prices, US interest rates and governmental fiscal

and monetary policy. Reaction functions for government policy
are deliberately not used so that simulations and forecasts
with the model are on the basis of pre-specified policies. There
are other facets of the model which may be thought to be substantial disadvantages, say the treatment (or lack of treatment)
of expectations, but we do not have the opportunity to discuss
possible improvements here; it is of more value to consider forecasting and simulation with the model.

9.2   Forecasting in Theory and Practice

In the last section we have summarized the form of the NIESR
econometric model. Given the estimated values of the parameters,
'optimal' forecasts can be obtained by substituting the values
for the exogenous variables in the forecast periods into the
equations and solving for the endogenous variables iteratively
until they meet some criterion of convergence. In practice the
macro-economic forecaster is faced by a much more complicated
problem. In the first place he has to forecast the values of the
exogenous variables because they lie in the future. Secondly,
he has several further sources of information on behaviour other
than the parameter estimates of the model. In the recent past
equations may appear to have shown consistent forecasting errors.
Specific stochastic events such as strikes, droughts and even
revolutions may have occurred or be thought likely to occur
which might influence behaviour in addition to the variables

specified in the model.

In the light of these difficulties this section considers
two issues: first the purposes of forecasting and secondly
the way in which macro-econometric forecasting is undertaken
in practice using the National Institute forecast as an example.

In the context posed in this section, the purpose of macro-
econometric forecasting is to provide the 'best' understanding
of what is likely to happen in the UK economy over the next two
years or so, and why. That is thus a highly qualified statement.
In the first instance the forecast is for a relatively short
period. Secondly, it is not merely the intention to produce
the most accurate forecast in the sense of minimum discrepancy
from the actual outcome (which in any case can only be judged
after the event). This is not of course to deny that accuracy
is a criterion. However, ex post accuracy can occur for two
reasons; on the one hand because of the validity of the model
and the accuracy of the forecasts of the exogenous variables, but
on the other because of the fortuitous combination of errors.
In the next section we shall discuss an interesting analysis by
Teal and Osborn (1979) where they show that with correct
information the NIESR forecast for GDP in 1975 made in February
1975 would have been almost completely correct, whereas the forecast for 1976 made in February 1976 was virtually correct *but*

if the full information had been available at the time of forecasting it would have been more inaccurate.[7]

To some considerable extent the purpose of forecasting
varies with the time period over which it is made. Short-run
forecasts where the forecast period is measured in months
rather than years are dominated by considerations of accuracy
and modelling for this purpose tends to be primarily in terms
of the time series characteristics of the data. Here a close
statistical (rather than economic) explanation of the past movements in the variables can be used for forecasting because most
new influences on the variables during the forecast period do
not have time to cause any substantial deviations from the predetermined path of the series. (Pindyck and Rubinfeld (1976) give
a good exposition of these considerations.) When the forecast is
extended to eighteen months to three years or so the characteristics of the economic structure and relations between variables
become much more important. Events during the forecast period
can have substantial effects on the economy although lagged
values of variables continue to play an important role. In such
a short-run period the dynamics of behaviour are very important
as this is forecasting within the business cycle. Longer-run

---

[7]
  Further revisions of the published official statistics since
the assessment was written may alter the ex post conclusions
of accuracy.

forecasts over more than seven or ten years can on the other hand afford to neglect short-run dynamics and can concentrate on trends and characteristics of the underlying structure of the economy.

The remaining category, usually referred to as the medium term lies between three and seven years ahead. In this period short-run dynamics cannot be neglected, but on the other hand forecasts are becoming increasingly inaccurate. To take a simple example, in a linear model of the form $y = Xb + e$ where the variables in X are exogenous, e is distributed $N(0, \sigma^2 I)$ and the best linear unbiased predictor for period p, $\hat{y}_p | X_p$,[8] is given by $X_p \hat{b}$, where $\hat{b}$ is the OLS estimator of b, the variance of $E(X_p \hat{b})$ is $\sigma^2 [X_p (X'X)^{-1} X_p']$. If X_p is the vector of means of the original sample of values, X, then $\sigma^2 [X_p (X'X)^{-1} X_p'] = \sigma^2 / N$, where N is the sample size. As X_p diverges from that value, then the variance increases quadratically. Thus any variable whose values tend to increase over time, due for example either to inflation or real expansion in the economy, will be subject to a rapidly increasing forecasting variance.

---

[8]

X_p here is merely a row vector comprising values for all the variables which make up the columns of X for the single time period p.

On top of this X_p itself has to be forecast and errors
may increase over the forecast period for this reason as well.
Thirdly, in practice models are rarely as simple as was suggested in this example and include lagged values of the endogenous
variable. Thus forecast errors in one time period may have a
cumulative effect in subsequent time periods because of the
dynamic structure of the model. In simultaneous equation models,
of course errors may creep in from poor forecasts of other
endogenous variables in the model. (This topic will be dealt
with in more detail in the next section on the assessment of
forecasts.) Medium-term forecasts thus suffer from increasingly
inaccurate short-run dynamics while being unable to concentrate
on the underlying paths of the variables alone.

Fortunately the two-year forecasts we are considering here
are not subject to such extreme problems. The quarterly forecasting cycle, culminating in publication in February, May, August
and November (as explained in the case of an earlier exposition
of analysis and forecasting of the UK economy at the National
Institute by Surrey (1971)),[9] consists of five main steps. In
the first instance it is necessary to update the data base for
all the new information and revisions to the past which have been
published in order to base the forecast on the most recent actual

---

[9]
    Also summarized in Teal and Osborn (1979).

information available. Forecasting dates are actually related
to data availability. Thus the February forecast incorporates
information up to the end of the last quarter of the previous
year and so on. Typically some variables are either unknown or
data for only one or two of the three months in the quarter have
been published. It is therefore necessary to estimate them
consistently with the rest of the published information.

The second step is to determine the values of the exogenous
variables during the forecast period. These variables relate
primarily to the external sector and to items directly determined by government policy. The external sector, principally
world trade and prices, is determined from forecasts of the
levels of activity and other major variables in the main
countries of the world (comprising 98 per cent of OECD GDP) and
the likely paths of a large number of commodity prices, among
which oil plays an important role. These forecasts form a
separate chapter in each *Review*.

The variables affected by government policy - tax rates,
public expenditure, etc. are forecast on the basis of 'constant
policies'. Tax rate changes as the result of discretionary
Budgets in the future are not, therefore, forecast although
indexation of direct tax allowances and indirect tax duties is
incorporated.

Once the data base has been updated the model is run over the recent past to check how the various equations have been performing. While in an ideal world there would be no systematic errors remaining this is not normally the case in practice. It may be possible to detect a coherent path in the calculated residuals. (In this case we are referring to the residuals from an individual equation estimated using actual values of other endogenous variables and actual lagged values of the endogenous variable in that equation itself – Single Equation Static Residuals – neither dynamics from mis-estimated lagged values, nor system effects from other equations are included.) Values for these errors are then projected into the forecast period so that the forecast in the simple case becomes $X_p \hat{b} + \hat{e}^*_p$ where $\hat{e}^*_p$ is the projected value of the error. The term $\hat{e}^*_p$ may be determined judgementally or by some simple rule such as the average recorded error over the previous year or two in the past. Other specific effects may also be incorporated in this way, if for example some effects are expected for a strike, or a pre-Budget spending spree is expected to be offset in the next two quarters (see Surrey and Ormerod, 1977).

Having got these residual adjustments and the forecasts for the exogenous variables it is possible to make an initial run of the model. In a purely theoretical world one might argue that this should constitute the forecast, but in practice the

results are carefully checked for plausibility and consistency.
Consequently, some of the future values of the exogenous variables may be changed or new adjustments to the residuals
inserted. There will thus be several runs until the forecast
team are satisfied with their product. All macro-economic forecasts of this type thus contain a measure of judgement and are
not merely the uncritical product of an econometric model.

9.3   The Accuracy of Forecasts

When the accuracy of forecasts of the future is assessed
after the forecast events have taken place the error which is
observed between the forecast and the actual outcome is a
complex variable. As we noted in the last section the forecast
is not just the product of the econometric model, but the model
plus judgemental and statistical additions. This final error
can therefore be decomposed into four parts (Teal and Osborn,
1979): errors in the forecast of exogenous variables, errors
because the published data used in making the forecast were subsequently revised, errors of judgement (in imposing residual
adjustments), and lastly, model error. In table 9.1 we have
shown a decomposition of the sources of errors in the National
Institute forecasts for the UK economy in 1975 and 1976 as
published in the February *National Institute Economic Review* of
each year.

The first line of each part of the table shows the actual
value which occurred and the second line the error of the
forecast. (These 'actual' values are those reported in the May
Review following each year in question - May 1976 and May 1977.)
If these 'actual' values of the exogenous, lagged endogenous
and policy variables had been used in making the forecast then
the error made would have been as in line 3. Of the nine categories shown, the forecast would have been more accurate in six
cases and less accurate in three. The increase in accuracy is
striking in the case of GDP with only a £4 million error. In
some cases, particularly the rate of consumer price inflation,
the results using the revised data are substantially different
- 5.3 percentage points for the CPI. The picture for 1976,
however, is very different; in six out of the nine cases the
forecast is *worse* using the revised data. Ironically exactly the
opposite picture for GDP is observed in 1976 compared with 1975.
In 1976 the original forecast was almost exactly correct but
the revised forecast was 3.2 percentage points too large (predicting that GDP would not change would have given only a 2.2
percentage point error).

The effect on the forecasts of differences in the values
of each of the three categories of exogenous and predetermined
variables from their 'actual' values is shown in lines 5, 6 and 7
of each part of the table. The effect of 'tax changes'is the

Table 9.1 NIESR Forecasting errors 1975 and 1976

(change over previous year)

	GDP	Consumers' expenditure	Gross fixed investment	Stock-building	Imports of goods and services	Adjustment to factor cost	Total employment	Real personal disposable income	Consumer price index
			£ million, 1970 prices					Percentages	
1975									
Actual	-340	-188	-138	-350	-106	-111	-1.3	-3.3	23.4
Ex ante error	-548	-356	-142	-301	-246	-149	-0.1	-2.3	4.5
Error after revision	4	-258	-45	-131	-320	-118	2.1	3.9	-1.8
Changes in forecast	-552	-98	-97	-170	-74	-31	-2.2	-6.2	6.3
Effect of change in exogenous variables	-106	249	69	18	230	69	1.8	3.4	4.0
Tax changes	-119	-91	-10	-12	14	-7	-0.6	-1.5	1.0
Lagged endogenous variables	-321	-263	-141	-174	-167	-91	-3.3	-7.7	0.8
1976									
Actual	259	236	-127	110	244	123	-0.6	-0.3	12.6
Ex ante error	-23	263	-112	-163	147	116	-	1.5	2.3
Error after revision	-412	115	-200	-138	201	132	-0.5	-0.7	-6.4
Changes in forecast	389	-148	-88	-25	-54	-16	0.5	2.2	8.7
Effect of change in exogenous variables	434	127	288	66	8	61	3.0	3.4	-0.1
Tax changes	44	65	6	9	22	14	0.2	1.1	0.2
Lagged endogenous variables	-155	-95	-108	-105	-66	-87	-2.6	-3.0	-1.4

Source: Teal and Osborn (1979).

difference between taxes calculated by the model to be raised

under the 'unchanged' policies assumption of the NI forecast

(as defined on page 377) and those estimated to have been

actually paid after the event thus including any policy change.[10]

These are relatively small in both years. Secondly the line

labelled 'lagged values of endogenous variables' shows the

effect of inserting the values up to the last quarter before

the forecast period. Thus this change ensures that the periods

before the forecast are correct, but the 'forecasts' themselves

are still dynamic and not just one step ahead as actual values

of lagged endogenous variables are not inserted in the forecast

period. The remaining line shows the effects of inserting the

true values of the exogenous variable in the forecast period.

While the effects of changes in exogenous variables and lagged

endogenous variables are likely to be offsetting because of the

economic relations of which they form part, nevertheless many

of the changes are sufficiently large that they totally alter

the character of the forecast. The relative importance of data

revisions and errors in forecasting the exogenous variables is

different in the two years. In 1975 the data revisions are far

---

[10]
  Official estimates of the effects of the tax changes are used
rather than putting the new rates into the NIESR model's tax
functions and calculating the difference.

more important while in 1976 the two are of roughly the same
order.

The effects of judgement error are more difficult to disentangle. Perfect judgement would of course exactly offset
model error - one might even argue that it should go some way to
offsetting data revision error (errors in forecasting the exogenous variables are in a sense judgement errors already). Teal
and Osborn make use of residual adjustment rules for deciding
what changes should be made to the forecasts of variables in the
light of recent systematic single equation static residuals, $\hat{e}_p^*$
(stage 3 of the forecasting process described on pp. 375-380)
and it is only the remaining discrepancy from the actual values
which they describe as judgement errors. Since these adjustment
rules are not applied uniformly in practice at the Institute or
by the other major UK macro-econometric forecasters these calculations are not reproduced.

Forecasting performance of the model, rather than the forecasting team is usually assessed by taking a period in the past
which is subsequent to the estimation period and then calculating
the dynamic system errors from the model using the actual values
of the exogenous variables and the correct values of the endogenous variables up to the period before the forecast starts. This
is the same as we have just described for the forecasts after

data revisions for 1975 and 1976. However, from any base period, b, it is possible to calculate forecast errors k periods ahead provided $b+k$ is still in the known data period. Thus for example if we set $k = 8$ and we have 5 years of post estimation data available (ie 20 quarters) we can make 13 forecasts 8 periods ahead. If the twenty quarters are defined as $i = 1, \ldots, 20$, b can be set equal to $0, \ldots, 12$. We can also make 14 forecasts 7 periods ahead, 15 forecasts 6 periods ahead, and so on. Let us denote the forecast errors generated from this as $\hat{e}_{b+k}$. We can then get measures of forecast accuracy of a number of forms: (i) average absolute error $\frac{1}{n} \sum_{}^{n} |\hat{e}_{b+k}|$ where n is the number of forecasts k periods ahead; (ii) average error $\frac{1}{n} \sum_{}^{n} \hat{e}_{b+k}$ (iii) Root **Mean Square** Error $\sqrt{(\frac{1}{n} \sum \hat{e}_{b+k}^2)}$; (iv) Theil's $U \sqrt{[(\sum_{b=1}^{n} \hat{e}_{b+k}^2)/\sum_{b=1}^{n} (y_{b+k} - y_b)^2]}$, where y_i is the actual value of the forecast variable in period i (see Osborn (1979) for an example of this with the NIESR model).

These measures of the errors are all different: (i) is a measure of the average inaccuracy of the forecasts, whereas (ii) treats the forecast period as a whole and indicates whether the errors lie above or below the true values; (iii) is a measure of the standard error of the forecast while (iv) compares this with the errors which would be obtained if the variable were assumed unchanged during the forecast period. If the model used is a worse explanation than the naive, no change, model then

$U > 1$, the closer U is to zero the more accurate the forecasts. This point of comparison with naive or simple time series models is extremely important. It is the raison d'être of the economist that the specification of an economy behavioural explanation for human activity should be more informative than pure time series representations of individual variables. Moreover their emphasis on the economic rationale should be supremely important in forecasting where interest lies in responses to changes in the economic conditions of activity. This characteristic forms the centre point of the next section on the simulation of macro-econometric models.

Measures of average error alone are insufficient in forming judgements about the validity of forecasts. The actual path of errors over time is important, both whether forecasts show systematic discrepancies - initial over-prediction and subsequent under-prediction, for example, implying a misspecification of the dynamic structure - and whether turning points in the series are forecast. A forecast of whether the rate of price inflation is going to fall or rise under 'unchanged' policies may be more important in the determination of those policies than the average level of inflation. A fall followed by a rise would imply totally different economic circumstances from a rise followed by a fall even though measures (i) to (iv) may have the same values. Forecasters therefore examine why they have 'missed' turning points very closely.

Unfortunately Osborn's (1979) results refer to the period
1970-5 when the NIESR model was rather more simple than that
described in Section 1 of this chapter. Nevertheless those
results, summarized in Table 9.2, illustrate the characteristics
of forecasting very clearly. The forecasts evaluated are those
made between August 1970 and May 1975 for the period 1970III-
1975II. As was explained in the previous section, NIESR forecasts
are normally quarterly for 6 to 8 quarters ahead, however, in
some cases the full six quarters were not forecast. Thus while
there are 20 forecasts one quarter ahead, 19 forecasts two
quarters ahead, etc. there are only 11 six quarters ahead instead
of the 15 that might otherwise have been expected.

As one might anticipate errors are smallest for a single
quarter forecast but there is a striking absence of a rising
trend in the errors 9 to 18 months ahead. It is immediately
clear from the average error that the NIESR tended to overestimate the level of real GDP but that this error did not worsen
in absolute terms between forecasts two and six quarters ahead.
Mean quarterly GDP during the forecast period was approximately
£20 billion in 1970 prices so, as percentages, errors of
£200 million and £250 million are of the order of 1 per cent and
$1\frac{1}{4}$ per cent respectively. However, this gives a misleading im-

pression of accuracy as the average quarterly increase in GDP
was only about £100 million. The relative importance of the
errors is shown by the Theil U (iv) which indicates that
although the forecasts are better than the assumption of no
change they are not strikingly so.

Table 9.2 Error measures for National Institute real GDP forecasts
(Forecasts made between August 1970 and May 1975 for the period
1970III - 1975II)

£ million, 1970 prices

Error measure		Forecast horizon (quarters)					
		1	2	3	4	5	6
Average absolute error	(i)	163	193	240	210	234	271
Average error	(ii)	60	104	109	111	109	102
RMSE	(iii)	204	255	310	286	320	357
Theil U	(iv)	0.95	0.87	0.90	0.73	0.73	0.72

Source: Osborn (1979).

Real GDP is of course only one out of many variables forecast by the National Institute and a full assessment would
require consideration of other variables and a comparison with
other forecasts as well as with the data. Osborn makes a comparison with US forecasts during the same period because of the
lack of alternative UK forecasts. However, this comparison has
many difficulties and it is perhaps rather more meaningful to
consider the relative performance of the various US forecasters
(McNees, 1975, 1977) alone. The relative forecasting performance
of UK models since 1975 has received rather variable coverage
and so their properties are compared here in terms of simulation
rather than merely forecasting. This is the subject of the next
section.

9.4   The Simulation of Macroeconometric Models

In the previous sections we emphasized that macro-econometric
forecasts were in practice made not *by* an econometric model, but
with one. Varying amounts of judgement are applied by forecasters
to produce the published conclusions. Thus if one wants to know
properties of the model alone the model must be used under arti-
ficial conditions unmodified by judgement. The simplest solution
is to run the model in simulation mode. Using data for all the
exogenous and lagged endogenous variables it is possible to run
the model dynamically over a number of time periods – these may
or may not form part of the data period used to estimate the
original equations. Such a run will generate paths for the

endogenous variables in the model which form a basis for the
discussion of the properties of the model.

Although we may know the sizes of coefficients in individual
equations in the model, it is not usually possible to know what
effects changes in the values of the exogenous variables will
have on the system as a whole. While the reduced form (if
calculable) may tell us the impact of a change in the first
quarter it is introduced, the solution of the time path is much
more complex given the existence of an elaborate lag-structure.
The only real possibility is thus to change the values of the
exogenous variables and rerun the model. These changes can take
the form of a single change in one variable in one time period
(a 'pulse' effect) or a change maintained throughout the period
(a 'step' effect) or of course variable changes or changes in
more than one variable to represent quite complex changes in circumstances.

In assessing the properties of models one usually takes very
simple changes in the form of pulse or step shifts in single
variables such as taxes, public expenditure, exports, etc. In
National Institute Economic Review No. 91 (February, 1980) for
example the effects of different budget strategies in the 1980
budget are shown for the main few variables in the National

Institute forecast, see Table 9.3.[11] From this it is clear

that a cut in either indirect or direct taxation is expansionary

in both the first and second years. However, a direct tax cut

has a slightly larger effect than an indirect tax cut of the

same size. On the other hand an indirect tax cut is followed

quickly by a fall in the rate of price inflation. In Table 9.3

the results are expressed in terms of the new paths of the

endogenous variables, but it is more common when considering

the properties of the model to use changes or 'multipliers'.

Multipliers are expressed as the effects of a unit change in an

exogenous variable on the endogenous variables. Thus if a

decrease in public expenditure of £1 billion reduces GDP in the

same period by £700 million the impact multiplier is 0.7. As

time passes the effect may change and hence the dynamic multi-

plier showing the effect of the initial shock some number of

periods hence, may be higher or lower than the impact multiplier.

Laury *et al.* (1978) consider the effects of seven sim-

ulations on three econometric models of the UK, the National

Institute model,[12] the Treasury model and the London Business

---

[11]
    Actually reproduced from Henry, Mayes and Savage (1980).

[12]
    Model III (estimated from 1970 based data) not Interim Model IV
described in Section 9.1. The structure of Model III was similar
although of course the parameter estimates were different.

Table 9.3   Summary of effects of Budgetary simulations

Simulation	Real GDP (per cent change year/year) 1975 prices	Real personal disposable income (per cent change year/year)	Real fixed investment (per cent change year/year)	Unemployment (fourth quarter, million)	Consumer price index (per cent change year/year)	Real consumers' expenditure (per cent change year/year)	Imports of goods and services (1975 prices, per cent change year/year)	Exports of goods and services (1975 prices, per cent change year/year)	Current account year (£ billion)	PSBR (fiscal year, £ billion)	Effective exchange rate (May 1970 = 100) fourth quarter
(i)											
1980	-0.4	3.8	-3.7	1.57	15.8	3.0	2.7	2.5	-2.1	10.9	71.9
1981	2.2	1.2	-0.6	1.82	13.1	3.2	4.4	4.0	-2.0	8.3	71.8
(ii)											
1980	-0.4	3.4	-3.7	1.57	15.1	3.0	2.6	2.6	-2.1	10.8	71.9
1981	2.1	1.4	-0.8	1.82	13.3	3.0	4.3	4.0	-1.8	8.3	72.0
(iii)											
1980	-0.8	2.6	-4.0	1.62	15.8	2.6	1.9	2.5	-1.5	8.4	72.2
1981	2.2	1.7	-1.1	1.86	12.8	2.9	4.2	3.9	-1.4	8.6	72.1
(iv)											
1980	-0.7	3.3	-3.9	1.62	16.1	2.8	2.1	2.5	-1.6	9.3	72.1
1981	2.3	1.3	-0.8	1.84	12.7	3.1	4.5	4.0	-1.7	8.5	71.9
Forecast											
1980	*-0.5*	*2.8*	*-3.9*	*1.58*	*15.8*	*2.7*	*2.3*	*2.5*	*-1.8*	*9.1*	*72.0*
1981	*2.0*	*1.7*	*-1.0*	*1.84*	*13.0*	*3.0*	*4.2*	*4.0*	*-1.7*	*8.5*	*72.0*

Note: For our direct tax changes we have merely assumed changes in personal income tax revenues without regard to the distributional effects of different changes and for indirect taxes changes in duties other than VAT. Public expenditure changes are assumed to fall on current goods and services. All changes are assumed to take effect from the second quarter and to be spread even/over the fiscal year and not be lagged by several months as was the case with the direct tax changes in 1979. The changes are imposed for the year 1980/1 only and the forecast levels are kept for 1981/2. Thus we are measuring the effect of a pulse on economic activity not a permanent change. The changes in 1981/2 therefore show the carry over of the 1980/1 changes and do not complicate the picture by incorporating the effects of a futher set of alterations in policy from the forecast path (NIER, No. 91, February 1980). The changes considered are, in current prices, (i) a direct tax cut of £2 billion; (ii) an indirect tax cut of £2 billion; (iii) a public expenditure cut of £1 billion and (iv) a direct tax cut of £1 billion and a public expenditure cut of £1 billion.

Source: Henry et al.

School model over a period of 24 quarters starting in 1972 I.
In Table 9.4 we have shown the path of the effects of Laury *et
al.'s* second simulation, an increase in public authorities current expenditure on goods and services by £100 million in 1970
prices in each quarter relative to their level in the base run.
(Interest rates are assumed to be held constant thus entailing
that the money supply must accommodate the increased expenditure.)

While the impact multiplier on GDP is 0.66 the dynamic
multiplier reaches a maximum at eight quarters and actually
falls thereafter. There is thus an offsetting effect which takes
effect only with a lag. The offsetting effect occurs largely
through the progressivity of the tax system (Laury *et al.* p. 58)
which causes real incomes to decline, with consequent effects on
consumption and GDP. The current balance worsens as the initial
impact increases imports and decreases exports slightly. The
fall in the exchange rate, however, stimulates exports with a
lag of nearly two years returning the balance towards its base
level. (It should be noted that multipliers will be dependent
upon the base chosen, and in particular will vary with the stage
in the economic cycle.)

Once these dynamic properties of the model are known it is
possible to discuss the effects of different policies on the
economy. However, because of the inter-dependencies in the model

Table 9.4 Effects of the simulation of a change in consumption in NI model
(Change is final consumption +£100m, 1970 prices: with interest rates
fixed, earnings endogenous, floating exchange rate)

| | £m (1970 prices) | | | | | | | (000s) | % change | | | | £m | |
Quarter	RPDI	C	I	S	X	M	GDP	E	EARN	CED	ER	MS	GDP	CB
													Differences from base run	
1	21	7	1	-16	-1	14	66	35	0.1	–	-0.1	0.1	87	-17
2	36	16	3	–	-2	22	81	80	0.1	–	-0.3	0.1	106	-30
3	45	23	6	8	-3	27	91	116	0.1	0.1	-0.6	0.4	123	-42
4	53	30	9	6	-3	29	96	143	0.2	0.1	-0.9	0.7	131	-52
5	52	32	11	4	-1	31	96	161	0.2	0.2	-1.0	1.1	145	-59
6	56	35	13	2	–	32	98	174	0.3	0.2	-1.1	1.4	159	-65
7	58	37	15	–	2	32	103	185	0.5	0.3	-1.4	1.4	176	-76
8	57	37	16	-1	3	32	106	193	0.6	0.4	-1.6	1.5	195	-89
16	25	13	3	-2	18	33	80	176	1.8	1.5	-2.9	3.4	539	-11
24	-30	-28	2	-7	12	22	47	121	3.0	2.5	-3.1	4.0	953	-10

Key to tables:
RPDI = real personal disposable income
C = consumers' expenditure
I = total fixed investment
S = total stockbuilding
X = total exports of goods and services
M = total imports of goods and services
GDP = gross domestic product at factor cost
1970 prices and at current prices

E = total UK employment
EARN = average gross earnings per head
CED = consumers' expenditure deflator
ER = effective exchange rate
MS = money stock (sterling M3 definition)
CB = balance of payments on current
account (£m)

Note: Δ nominal GDP = Δ price × level of GDP in base + ΔGDP × price level in simulation (ignoring
second-order terms).

Source: Laury et al. (1978).

it is not possible to add together the effects of changes in
several variables taken singly and obtain the result of their
joint movement. This is clear from the last illustration (iv) in
Table 9.3, where a reduction in public expenditure which is
'balanced' by shifts in taxation has a deflationary result and
actually increases the Public Sector Borrowing Requirement
because the lower level of activity increases the benefits which
have to be paid out and lowers the yield from taxation.

In practice very considerable use is made of macro-econometric models in their simulation mode. According to a recent
internal survey the Treasury model is on average run several times
each day to help users in the various Civil Service departments
to decide what the effects of various policies and potential
events are. As was made very clear in Surrey (1971) the purpose
of the NIESR model is for the forecasting *and analysis* of the UK
economy. The existence of clear routes of economic influence is
therefore essential and models have to meet very strong
specification criteria and not just be able to produce accurate
forecasts in the short run.

References and Suggested Reading*

ALLSOPP, C AND JOSHI, V. (1980) 'Alternative strategies for the
    UK' *National Institute Economic Review,* no. 91 (February)
    pp. 86-103.

BANK OF ENGLAND (1979) 'Bank of England model of the UK
    economy', Discussion paper No. 5 (September).

BATCHELOR, R.A. (1977) 'Sterling exchange rates 1951-76: a
    Casselian analysis' *National Institute Economic Review,*
    (August).

CUTHBERTSON, K.C., HENRY, S.G.B., MAYES, D.G., AND SAVAGE, D.
    (1980) 'Modelling and Forecasting the Rate of Exchange',
    paper presented at the International Economics Study Group
    annual conference at the University of Sussex, September
    1980 and forthcoming in proceedingsed. J.H. Dunning,
    Macmillan.

HENRY, S.G.B., MAYES, D.G., SAVAGE, D. (1980) 'Memorandum on
    Monetary Policy' House of Commons Treasury and Civil Service
    Committee, 17 July HMSO, pp. 147-159.

*HILTON, K. AND HEATHFIELD, D.F. (eds.) (1970) *The Econometric
    Study of the United Kingdom,* Macmillan.

*LAURY, J.S.E., LEWIS, G.R. ANDORMEROD, P.A. (1978) 'Properties
    of macro-economic models of the UK economy: a comparative
    study' *National Institute Economic Review,* no. 82
    (February).

LBS (1979) 'The London Business School Quarterly Econometric

model of the United Kingdom economy - relationships in the

basic model as at February 1979'.

MAJOR, R.L. (1979) *Britain's trade and exchange rate policy*

Heinemann for the National Institute of Economic and Social

Research.

MAYES, D.G. AND SAVAGE, D. (1980) 'The Structure, tracking and

simulation performance of the monetary sector of the

National Institute Macroeconometric model', NIESR Discussion

Paper, No. 36.

MCNEES, S.K. (1975) 'An evaluation of economic forecasts' *New*

England Economic Review, (November/December).

MCNEES, S.K. (1977) 'The forecasting performance of economic

forecasts', Research Department Federal Reserve Bank of

Boston.

NIESR (1979) 'Listing of the interim NIESR model IV' Discussion

Paper No. 28.

ORMEROD, P.A. (ed.) (1980) *Economic Modelling*, Heinemann.

*OSBORN, D.R. (1979) 'National Institute gross output forecasts:

a comparison with US performance', *National Institute Eco-*

nomic Review, no. 88, (May).

*PINDYCK, R.S. AND RUBINFELD, D.L. (1976) *Econometric models and*

economic forecasts, McGraw-Hill.

RENTON, G.A. (ed.) (1975) *Modelling the Economy*, Heinemann for

the SSRC.

*SURREY, M.J.C. (1971) *The analysis and forecasting of the British economy*, Cambridge University Press.

SURREY, M.J.C. AND ORMEROD, P.A. (1977) 'Formal and informal aspects of forecasting with an econometric model', *National Institute Economic Review*, no. 81 (August).

*TEAL, F. AND OSBORN, D.R. (1979) 'An assessment and comparison of two NIESR econometric model forecasts' *National Institute Economic Review*, no. 88, (May).

TREASURY (1980) Treasury Model - Technical Manual.

Chapter 10

COMPUTER PACKAGES

The purpose of this brief chapter is to give a resumé of
e of the main computer packages which are widely available for

analysis of the applications which have been discussed in

foregoing chapters. On this basis it would be possible to

ertake the re-estimation of the models discussed and to con-

r the effects of alternative specifications. Perhaps the

r deficiency of most courses in econometrics is that they do

involve substantial practical experience in the whole process

pecification, estimation, hypothesis testing and forecasting.

s one thing to appreciate why it is that a particular person

decided to draw his conclusions, but it is quite another to

rtake a complete problem oneself and follow it through in a

er which other people find convincing. In many cases it is the

mpt at such practical work which really reveals whether one

rstands the principles which have been put forward.

We shall only consider five packages which between them are

rehensive but are certainly not exhaustive. Most of them are available to all users either through university networks or

through computer bureaux. The packages are TSP/ESP, SPSS, DEMOS

(HASH), GENSTAT and GIVE.[1] Of these two, SPSS and GENSTAT, are

general statistical packages which can handle a wide variety

of problems such as simple data analysis, analysis of variance

and a range of multi-variate methods and not just specifically

econometric problems. Two others, TSP/ESP and DEMOS (HASH) are

---

[1]
   These packages evolve steadily over time and the current
versions are likely to differ from those described here. However,
the differences can be expected to take the form of additional
facilities or improvements to the routines already available. The
general character of the programmes will probably not change. (HASH
and GIVE have undergone major changes in the late 1970s. ESP is an
expanded version of TSP and other expanded versions exist, some
of which are still called TSP, distinguished by a more recent date
of implementation and a qualification such as Version 2 or Version
3.) The versions described are: TSP as implemented at United
Computing Services Ltd., UCS, (on CDC 6600 series machines); ESP
at the South Western Universities Regional Computing Centre,
SWURCC, on an ICL 2980; SPSS, version 8 also on the 2980 at SWURCC
(a more limited version, as implemented on the GEC 4070 small
computer, Mayes (1980), is very similar); DEMOS as implemented by
SIA Ltd on a CDC CYBER 720 and a CDC CYBER 175; GENSTAT, release
4.02 as implemented in the South Western Universities Regional
Computer Network (on the ICL 4-70 at Cardiff), at UCS and on the
Burroughs B6700 at the University of Otago and other sites in New
Zealand; GIVE as on the CDC 7600 at the University of London
Computing Centre (and a slightly more limited version at UCS).
The date of consideration was June, 1980. This somewhat hetero-
geneous choice reflects machines directly available to the author
at the time of writing and does not rely on reported performance
of other machines and systems. No attempt to set out a comprehensive list for other regions or countries could be comprehensive
or accurate because of the speed at which changes are taking
place.

general econometric packages which will enable the user to

undertake a wide range of analyses, and the remaining package,

GIVE, is particularly useful for the study of the dynamic proper-

ties of time series relationships as discussed particularly by

Davidson *et al.* (1978), (Chapter 2) Bean (1979) (Chapter 4),

Hendry and Mizon (1978) (Chapter 5) and Sargan (1980 *a,b*) in

Chapter 6.

The packages require different degrees of sophistication,

but with the exception of GIVE can be readily mastered in a

fairly short period of time by someone with no computing ex-

perience and only the limited econometric background assumed in

this book. This chapter therefore begins by a brief description

of the nature and means of using computer packages and then

proceeds with a brief examination of the individual packages.

10.1   The Use of Computer Packages

The main purpose of computer packages is to try to protect

the user from the need to know how computer systems work and to

learn a general programming language such as FORTRAN, COBOL,

ALGOL, PL1,BASIC or APL and yet enable him to undertake all the

commonly required tasks of analysis. The packages are largely

invariant between machines so that once having learnt how to use

a particular package the user can access it on different

machines, when either he moves his job or the site changes its

computer, without having to learn anything else. He merely
requires the computing centre to provide him with a set of job
control commands which enable him to access the package. This
access may take the form of interactive work through a terminal
whereby the user can manipulate the working of the program step
by step as the computer undertakes the commands or remotely by
submitting a card deck for running with a batch of other jobs by
the computer operators.[2]

With the exception of GIVE the package programs expect
instructions in a simple language of their own which involves
the use of a number of keywords that either use or abbreviate
the English words which describe the task in hand. Thus for
example TSP/ESP uses SMPL to define a sample period and OLSQ to
run an ordinary least squares regression. GIVE on the other hand
requires instructions to take the form of a sequence of numerical
codes which have assigned columns on various cards. While this
is simple to use once one has some experience, the translation
process required is greater and the care in checking the cards
has to be considerable.

---

[2]

Many variations of this distinction exist in practice; one can
initiate batch jobs from a terminal and use magnetically stored
files on a disc or tape instead of cards for example.

The disadvantage of the big packages is that they usually

require large computers to run them and that they take up

sufficient portions of machines that the turn around time from

submitting the job to obtaining the output may be very consider-

able.[3] The costs of the computation will also tend to be high

with a substantial fixed cost to setting up a run however trivial

the particular task. For this reason students with simple jobs

involving the use of say ordinary least squares on untransformed

data are often directed to simple programmes, which, although they

require numerical coded instructions like those in GIVE, they use

only small amounts of space and computer time and are hence fast

and cheap to run.

Although it might be profitable to use only one package

because of the need to learn how to use all the various keywords

and instructions it is unfortunately often the case that a com-

bination of programs is required. However, it is important to

check before embarking on a particular piece of computation that

the package chosen is the most appropriate one for the whole

analysis and not just the first stage, because the data may other-

wise have to be repunched, which can easily introduce errors, and

considerable time and effort used up in adapting to a second or

subsequent package.

---

[3] It is overnight for SPSS and ESP in the South Western Universities Computer Network and approximately a day for GIVE. On the
other hand GIVE is run almost immediately at UCS as is DEMOS at SIA.

10.2   The Features of the Computer Packages

In Table 10.1 the major capabilities of the packages are

shown, but becuase of variations between implementations and

particular definitions the user should check with the computer

centre advisory service, if one is available, and with the

manuals.[4] The purposes of the packages are clearly different but

in general terms their particuar advantages are described below.

10.2.1   TSP/ESP

TSP is one of the most widely used package programs for

simple estimation of linear models in economics. It is very

---

[4]
Manuals referred to are:

TSP   Time Series Processor, User's Manual R.E. Hall,
           J. Brode, F.C. Ripley and S. Robinson, 1973.

ESP   Econometric Software Package, User's Manual,
           J.P. Cooper, May 1973 (University of Chicago).

SPSS   Statistical Package for the Social Sciences (2nd ed-
           ition) N.H. Nie, C.H. Hull, J.G. Jenkins, K. Stein-
           brenner and D.H. Bent, McGraw-Hill, 1975.

DEMOS   Interactive Econometric Modelling System, User Guide,
           SIA Computer Services, February 1980.

GENSTAT   A General Statistical Program, N.G. Alvey and 15 others
           Rothamsted Experimental Station, October, 1977.

GIVE   'General Instrumental Variables Estimation of Linear
           Equations with Lagged Dependent Variables and First
           Order Autoregressive Errors, Technical Manual', D.F.
           Hendry and F. Srba, London School of Economics,
           October 1978.

flexible in that it allows all instructions and data to be

input in free format. Thus alterations and additions can be

made to files without having to repunch whole sequences of

cards. It has its own set of error messages which are reasonably

informative although it is possible to obtain FORTRAN error

messages under some circumstances.[5] The TSP language is very

simple with only a few keywords all of which have obvious

meaning: PRINT, GRAPH, etc. Variables are referred to by names

which the user chooses, so they can be mnemonic, and all the

usual sorts of transformations of series; addition, subtraction,

exponentiation, creating leads and lags, etc. can be used to

generate new variables. The symbols used are very similar to

those in the normal writing of algebra.

The running of regression equations merely requires the

listing of the names of the variables in the order in which they

occur in the equation. Data periods can be varied at will with

observations omitted at any points within the series as well as

at either end. The statistical information printed out contains

most usually required – R^2, standard error of estimate, calculated

residuals, etc. but it is not quite as comprehensive as GIVE.

Similar information is given by SPSS, DEMOS and GENSTAT. Like

---

[5]
  The source program is written in FORTRAN and is relatively easy
to implement, provided that the program does not have to be over-
layed, with the exception of a single routine for character handling which is specific to each machine. Therefore there should be
little difficulty for a computer centre to obtain and offer TSP
if it does not currently do so.

Table 10.1 Major Features available on Package Programs

	TSP	ESP	SPSS	DEMOS	GENSTAT	GIVE
Interactive	–	–	ltd.	yes	–	–
Free format input	yes	yes	yes	yes	yes	(a)
Data transformations	yes	yes	yes	yes	yes	some
Cross-tabulation of data	–	–	yes	–	yes	–
Elementary statistics of data series	–	yes	yes	yes	yes	–
Plot of data	yes	yes	yes	yes	yes	yes
Multiple plots	–	yes	yes	yes	yes	two
Correlation matrix	yes	yes	yes	yes	yes	yes
Covariance matrix	–	yes	yes	yes	yes	–
Ordinary least squares	yes	yes	yes	yes	yes	yes
Instrumental variables (2SLS)	yes	yes	–	yes	–	yes
Autoregressive models	–	some	–	yes	–	yes
3SLS	–	yes	–	–	–	–
Non-linear least squares	–	yes	–	–	yes	–
Logit, probit	–	–	–	–	yes	logit
ANOVA	–	–	yes	–	yes	–
Principal components	–	yes	yes	–	yes	–
Factor analysis	–	–	yes	–	yes	–
Discriminant analysis	–	–	yes	–	yes	–
Canonical correlation	–	–	yes	–	yes	–
Cluster analysis	–	–	–	–	yes	–
Time series analysis	–	yes	–	–	–	–
Distributed lags	yes	yes	–	yes	–	yes
Single equation forecasts	yes	yes	–	yes	yes	some
Model solution	–	–	–	yes	–	–
Simulation, multiplier calculation	–	–	–	yes	–	–
Links with other packages	–	–	one	yes	yes	–
Matrix routines	–	most	–	–	yes	–

(a)   User determined fixed format using FORTRAN instructions.

DEMOS and GIVE, TSP also has the advantage that instrumental
variables estimation can be used (including two stage least
squares by appropriate choice of instruments) but with TSP
instrument selection has to be made by the user and the appro-
priateness of the instruments is not indicated. Thus under many
circumstances GIVE (or often DEMOS) may be preferable for
instrumental variable estimation, especially if one wants to
examine the dynamic structure of the equation. TSP allows the
user to fit Almon lag distributions to variables in the regression with or without constraints on the values at the end
points.[6] Thus in the light of the discussion in Chapter 4 it
is possible to obtain various shapes of lag distribution. The
equations quoted for the National Institute model in the last
chapter were all estimated using TSP (although GIVE was also
used in the estimation process).

It is also possible to use the coefficients, estimated
values and residuals obtained from running one equation, in
subsequent calculations, say for forecasting outside the
estimation period. Further routines are available in ESP which

---

[6]
   There is a question of the validity of the way in which the
end point restrictions are imposed in some versions of TSP.

is an expanded version of TSP (all TSP jobs *should* run on ESP,

but may not in particular instances if the implementations of

the two packages on a given computer are not the same).[7] The

extra features, listed in Table 10.1, are considerable and

permit the estimation of equations with first order serially

correlated errors by the Cochrane-Orcutt method or maximum-

likelihood (instrumental variables or distributed lags can also

be incorporated). The estimation techniques available for

simultaneous equation systems are extended to include three-

stage least squares although not surprisingly the size of

equation systems that can be accommodated is fairly small.

A second important area of expansion of estimation methods

is in a group of subroutines to use the Box-Jenkins framework of

univariate time series analysis. It is also possible to calculate

principal components and use them as variables in subsequent

regressions. A random number generator is included in the package

so it is possible to do stochastic simulations and checks for

robustness of estimates to random shocks. These and other faci-

lities such as matrix handling, evaluation of forecast errors,

multiple variable plots and the ability to incorporate sub-routines

---

[7]

Another similar expanded version of TSP, TSPSX, is also available at ULCC as is a more limited interactive version.

of one's own make ESP a package which will cope with a large
portion of econometric computational research work.

10.2.2   SPSS

SPSS is intended as a package for social science users in
general, and for most ordinary econometric purposes it is not
particularly helpful. It is best suited to the analysis of
cross-section or survey data and has good facilities for cross-
tabulation, analysis of variance and a number of forms of
multi-variate analysis such as factor analysis, discriminant
analysis and canonical correlation. There is, however, a much
greater fixed cost to learning how to use the package - the
manual is 675 pages long. There is a large number of keywords
and many options. It is therefore very important to be clear
that SPSS is the right medium for undertaking the analysis before
starting to try to use it. However, the same complexity does allow
the user to undertake a wide range of computations on the data.
(An interactive version is available at some sites called SCSS and
some versions of SPSS allow a preliminary checking of the validity
of each instruction without actually having to have a full run of
the job; thus saving considerable time over small errors if turn
around is slow.)

10.2.3   DEMOS

DEMOS has a number of characteristics which make it very

useful to the econometric modeller. In the first place it is

conversational as well as batch so it is possible to undertake

the analysis step by step.[8] Although interactive computing may

cost more per unit of time used because people quite naturally

often prefer to work during the prime time of the day it fre-

quently saves money because with a slow batch turn around, users

tend to consider far more hypotheses on each occasion. Also a

small error early in a job may not cause the job to stop, but

result in all the remaining calculations being rubbish.

Secondly, DEMOS is structured in terms of models rather than just

variables so it is well attuned to the estimation, simulation and

forecasting of complete systems of equations and not just un-

related equations.

Input, output and transformation facilities are fairly

similar to ESP. Estimation procedures available include instru-

mental variables, autoregressive error structures and distributed

lags on particular variables. The main gain comes in simulation

and forecasting with models. DEMOS will order the model for

solution by finding the simultaneous blocks and recursive

---

[8]
An earlier version of DEMOS called HASH which is not inter-
active is available at some sites. The author of both of them is
T. Harrison.

structures to enable the most efficient solution. The solution

algorithm is a modified form of Gauss-Seidel iteration. In

simulation it is possible to 'exogenize' variables, i.e. to fix

the values of some endogenous variables and not use the model

to solve for them. Secondly, it is possible to make adjustments

to the residuals of equations in the manner described in

Chapter 9, so that specific amounts can be added to or subtract-

ed from the values predicted by a particular equation.

The manual is deliberately simple and short and the user

can obtain further information from the package itself by using a

HELP command. Furthermore the use of a command, EXPLAIN, gives

information on why any error has occurred to help the user find

and correct it. The implementation at SIA has the added ad-

vantage that the CSO databank of 2,000 UK macro-economic series

is available with DEMOS as a source of data as are databanks

of the OECD 'Main Economic Indicators' and the IMF 'International

Financial Statistics'.

10.2.4   GENSTAT

Of all the packages described here GENSTAT is the most

sophisticated. It has a very wide range of options and permits

very extensive matrix and variable manipulations. It is not

aimed specifically at economists but statisticians in all

subjects and hence some of its facilities may be of little

relevance. However, it proved extremely efficient in calcu-

lating the principal components, regression equations and canon-

ical correlations used in the description of the US, UK and New

Zealand economies in Matatko and Mayes (1979) and Mayes (1979)

and even produced the graphs which were printed together with

their headings and labelled axes. The drawback of the sophisti-

cation is that the package is relatively difficult to use and

like SPSS requires a fair amount of time for familiarization.

One can only admire the shorthand which is used to facilitate

many tedious or repetitive operations which would require many

more instructions in say SPSS.

10.2.5 GIVE

GIVE is very different from the previous packages we have

considered as it has no keywords and uses numerical codes on a

series of 19 types of control cards. The program 'is designed

to estimate the coefficients of linear equations having both

current and lagged endogenous variables as regressors, when the

error term on the equation is a first order autoregressive

process' (Technical Manual, p.1). The advantage of the package

is not just the availability of the estimation methods but the

very comprehensive test statistics that are provided to enable

the user to decide on the most appropriate dynamic specification

of the model. Some 16 sets of statistics can be obtained for

ordinary least squares alone. Unfortunately the meaning of the

statistics is not explained in the manual and the user is
directed to the original sources for explanation although many
of the references are not complete. As some of these statistics
are not described in most textbooks, this can make them a
little hard to follow. GIVE, therefore, will tend only to be
appropriate for a user who both has some experience of computing
and is well versed in econometric methods. This is rather unfortunate as the program will in many cases be the one which
ought to be used. Perseverance and consultation with other users
is probably the best recommendation that can be made.

10.2.6   Other packages

There are many other excellent packages, some for the
purposes described here and others for specific areas of
econometric method such as FIML, optimal control and spectral
analysis which we have not discussed. Their omission does not
in any way imply a reflection on their quality merely on their
availability, the amount of usage they receive and how central
they are to the range of applications of econometrics discussed
in this book. It is now fortunately the case that there are
relatively few econometric problems for which one has to write
specific computer programs oneself. Applying econometrics does
however entail an inescapable familiarity with computers and
the understanding of the practicalities of econometrics will be
greatly eased by the obtaining of that familiarity right at the

beginning of study of the subject.

References and Suggested Reading

BEAN, C (1979) 'An econometric model of manufacturing investment
in the UK'. Government Economic Service (Treasury) working
paper no. 29.

DAVIDSON, J.E.H., HENDRY, D.F., SRBA, F. AND YEO, S. (1978)
'Econometric modelling of the aggregate time series relat-
ionship between consumers' expenditure and income in the
United Kingdom' *Economic Journal* (December).

HENDRY, D.F. AND MIZON, G.E. (1978) 'Serial correlation as a
convenient simplification and not a nuisance: a comment
on a study of the demand for money by the Bank of England'
Economic Journal (September).

MATATKO, J.M. AND MAYES, D.G. (1979) 'Preliminary analysis of
economic data sets: a multivariate approach' forthcoming
in the proceedings of the AUTE annual conference at Exeter,
D. Currie and W. Peters eds.

MAYES, D.G. (1979) 'The analysis of the New Zealand macroeconomy'
forthcoming in New Zealand Economic Papers.

MAYES, D.G. (1980) 'The Implementation of SPSS on a small dedi-
cated computer - the SSRC - GEC 4070 project' in M.M. Barrit
and D. Wishart eds. *COMPSTAT 1980: Proceedings in computational statistics* Physica-Verlag.

SARGAN, J.D. (1980a) 'A model of wage-price inflation', *Review of Economic Studies*, vol. 47, pp. 97-112.

SARGAN, J.D. (1980b) 'The consumer price equation in the post-war British economy: an exercise in equation specification testing' *Review of Economic Studies*, vol. 47, pp. 113-135.

The list of computer package manuals is on p. 402.

INDEX